Praise for
Devoted To Dogs

For years, Sarah Ferrell's award winning newspaper column has extolled the virtues and rewards of dog-friendly dog training. Her first book, Devoted to Dogs, is long overdue. She teaches us to respect dogs as dogs, to give them an education, yet to revel in the nuances of their individuality, their undying loyalty, and their inimitable camaraderie. Devoted to Dogs positively shines with Sarah's esteem for the canine spirit. Her message will no doubt enhance countless people-dog relationships and improve the lives of dogs and their human companions.

**Dr. Ian Dunbar, Founder,
The Association of Pet Dog Trainers**

Sarah has crafted a motivating, humane and highly informative book for everyone who shares life with dogs, or is considering it. It's a great portal for insight about the relationships between them.

**William E. Campbell,
"Behavior Problems in Dogs"**

In this book Sarah Ferrell shows us that the human-dog relationship has two sides. She explores the deep inter-dependence that exists between the canine and human partners and helps us to better understand why things go right and wrong. With humor, compassion and understanding Ms. Ferrell's writing shows that she really "gets it". What most of us call training she shows us is just good communication skills. When you make your desires known in the appropriate way you will get positive results. As a practitioner of Holistic Medicine I appreciate her "Holistic" approach to everything she writes about from commentary on available medical services to letting our old friends go when the time is right. I highly recommend this book to everyone and recommend that you give a copy to everyone you know, especially those that thought they weren't dog lovers.

Jordan Kocen, DVM, MS, Certified Veterinary Acupuncturist, Department of Holistic Medicine, SouthPaws Veterinary Specialists

Sarah Ferrell's delightful columns draw on her knowledge, expertise, and off-kilter sense of humor to instruct and amuse us. Reading her work is like talking with a good friend who knows a lot about dogs, and loves them as much as you do.

Bronwyn Taggart, AKC GAZETTE Magazine

Sarah Ferrell's words of wisdom provide a warm welcome to new fanciers and owners. They also bring warm memories to long-time dog owners. Make no mistake, this book will help you avoid mistakes!

Chris Walkowicz, "Choosing a Dog for Dummies", AKC judge, DWAA President Emeritus

For a fun, frolicking, free-wheeling visit into the mind of a dog, you can't do better than these essays by Sarah Ferrell. At turns hilarious and heartfelt, Ferrell is always insightful about not just our beloved companions, but also about those of us who are lucky enough - and sometimes crazy enough - to have dogs in our lives. If you love dogs, own a dog, or even just admire them from a distance, you are guaranteed to enjoy Ferrell's wit and wisdom in Devoted to Dogs.

Elaine Fox, author USA Today best-seller, "Guys & Dogs"

Sarah Ferrell takes us into the heart and soul of the dog. Her understanding of this beloved companion is uncanny. We will never again look at our canine friend in the same way after reading this remarkable book. "Devoted To Dogs" takes us on an intimate journey into the hearts and minds of our most beloved companions with humor and compassion. Be prepared though; she takes a few jabs at our own behavior with regards to these gentle souls. This book is as much about human behavior as it is about dog behavior. The reader will be entertained, enlightened, and humbled.

Dr. Terri Horton, Veterinarian

Although I live 3000 miles away from the newspaper where Sarah Ferrell's work is published, I have enjoyed reading her work each year in the Dog Writers of America writing contest; a contest she has won more than once. "Devoted to Dogs" is a 'must read' for all dog owners. You will appreciate Ferrell's knowledge, devotion and empathy for dogs and their owners.

Liz Palika, "The Ultimate Dog Treat Cookbook"

For over twenty years Sarah Ferrell has used her wit and wisdom to counsel my clients to be better dog owners. Now in "Devoted To Dogs" she shares her insights with everyone who has or ever will have a dog in their life. Often humorous, always insightful and honest, her approach to training dogs is to train their owners. She provides a window into the heart and soul of our beloved companions. This book will captivate and motivate all dog lovers.

Dr. Sheri Bakerian, Veterinarian

Sarah must have been a dog in another life because she has such extraordinary insight into the canine mind. Her sensitivity, respect and joyous love for dogs shines through in every word she writes. Her longtime "Devoted to Dogs" column in The Free Lance-Star, filled with dog psychology, training tips and gentle humor, is a howling success with readers.

Gwen Woolf, The Free Lance-Star Newspaper

DEVOTED
TO
DOGS:
HOW TO BE YOUR
DOG'S BEST OWNER

Sarah A. Ferrell

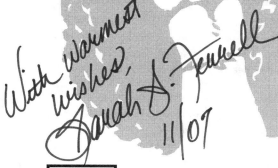

With warmest
wishes,
Sarah A. Ferrell
11/07

Abroham Neal Publishing
Locust Grove, VA 22508

 Abroham Neal Publishing
P.O. Box 1111
Locust Grove, VA 22508
www.abrohamneal.com

Production design by Neal P. Campbell
Graphic designs by Andrew McAfee

Grateful acknowledgement is expressed for permission to re-print portions of this book that originally appeared in The Free Lance-Star newspaper's "Town & County" magazine, Fredericksburg, VA.

In order to protect the privacy of interviewees and their lovely dogs, some names have been changed and identities disguised.

Library of Congress Cataloging-In Publication Data
Ferrell, Sarah A., 1954–
    Devoted To Dogs: How To Be Your Dog's Best Owner
    1. Dogs–Training Essays
    2. Dog–Training Humor

First Printing, January, 2007
1st Abroham Neal Publishing trade pbk.ed.
ISBN # 0-9788062-0-4

CONTENTS

Acknowledgements

I am blessed to hear a voice in my head, encouraging and reining in, keeping me company as life unfolds. That voice belongs to my most dear friend, Margot McBrayer Wagner. Thank you, Margot, for your steadfast friendship, wise counsel, and your valuable contributions to this book.

Thank you, Gwen Woof, editor of the "Town and County" section of The Free Lance-Star newspaper, In Fredericksburg. VA. for making this book possible. Thank you for your keen editorial eye and encouraging guidance for every 'Devoted To Dogs' column. Thank you for your dogged devotion to offer The Free Lance-Star readers' entertainment and education that gently enhances the well-being and protection of dogs, cats and other four-footed friends.

I owe a great debt of gratitude to Josiah P. Rowe III, publisher, and Edward W. Jones, editor of The Free Lance-Star newspaper, for allowing me to use previously published 'Devoted To Dogs' columns in this book. I am very grateful for

The Free Lance-Star's professional and always supportive staff; with special thanks going to Carol Lee, Clint Schemmer and to all the paper's fine copy editors and administrative staff .

With sincere appreciation I thank the writers, mentors and veterinarians who unfailingly answered writing, dog behavior, dog breeding and dog health questions for this book. Their endorsements for this book are great treasures to me because they come from writers and dog professionals whose work has enabled dogs to live better trained, happier lives with their humans.

Thank you, Dr. Ian Dunbar for revolutionizing dog training by teaching positive, dog-friendly "lure and reward" behavior shaping. Thank you for showing dog trainers and dog owners that time-worn punitive training techniques do not enhance the learning capacity of dogs, nor build a bond of partnership between dogs and owners. For your courage to speak your own truth, with humor, conscience and clarity, thank you.

I thank William Campbell for teaching students of dog behavior that solving a dog behavior problem requires careful "why" analysis rather than reactionary punishment. Campbell's text, "Behavior Problems in Dogs" is a beacon of enlightenment to dog lovers who learn to train their dogs, rather than blame their dogs.

Thank you to author and AKC judge, Chris Walkowicz, for always gracious and wise counsel. As President Emeritus of the Dog Writers Association of America, Ms. Walkowicz' support and advocacy for fledgling dog writers is selfless and motivational. Than you, too, for thoughtful interview input from how to breed healthy pups to how to best love your elderly Beardie.

Thank you, Elaine Fox, for fiction that dog lover's who love to read can take to heart. Thank you for writing love scenes that remind us there is no finer fun than curling up in a big bed with a fine human and a warm dog.

Thank you, Liz Palika, for your generous heart that embraces the writing dreams of other dog writers. Thank you for your always knowledgeable quotes for writers serving the dog fancy.

Thank you, Bronwyn Taggart, for your editorial insights, and encouragement. Your editing makes me proud and delighted. Thank you for your inimitable wit, your magnificent vocabulary, and for sharing your joie de vivre with your writers.

Thank you Dr. G. Frank Wagner for innumerable acts of kindness sharing your professional skills. Thank you for your patience and generosity answering twenty years of medical questions, and for caring for all our canine family members.

Thank you, Dr. Terri Horton, for your brilliant mind, your calmly considered voice of reason on veterinary health questions, and for having a heart that understands how deeply a human can love a dog. Thank you for allowing your patients to marvel at your compassion, medical proficiency, and your deep bond with your own dogs, and for conveying reassurance that you care for your patients just as if they were your own.

Thank you, Dr.Jordan Kocen, for showing me that gentle, considered, individualized treatment is the basis for optimal medical care. Thank you for the many medical and behavioral facts and insights you have contributed to this book.

Thank you, Dr. Sheri Bakerian for treating pets with exceptional veterinary medical expertise coupled with equal care for their emotional well-being. For your outpouring of medical knowledge and your unfailing caring to educate pet owners I express my deepest appreciation.

Thank you Mary Susan Billingsley and Charlotte Mills for sharing, living and teaching dog joy, dog training and for your unwavering friendship. Thank you both for being the two very finest examples of dog mothers and human friends. This book would not have been written without your sharing of canine experience. Thank you for your lovely photographs and canine behavior insights printed throughout this book.

For unfailingly answering hundreds of dog behavior, breeding and dog show questions, I thank Don and Carol Callahan of Donahan Springers. Thank you, Carol, for being my touchstone as the ultimate steward of responsible breeding and living your life surrounded by a steadfast dog family.

Pam Bullock, editor of "SoulMates", thank you for suggesting that my first dog article written many years ago, be shared with another publication. Your encouragement changed my life forever.

Thank you, dear friend, artist, and dog mother, Maureen Greenwood, for your brilliant company traveling thousands of miles across Belgium, France and Virginia, sharing dog stories and dog love.

Phyllis Broderick, thank you for tirelessly explaining competition rules and dog training techniques from both your AKC judge's point of view and as mother of big-hearted, devoted working dogs like Ringo, Cassie, Belle and Boeing. You shared volumes about obedience training and competition, but even more about lovely manners under pressure, gentle dog love, and always putting the needs of your dogs first.

Andrew McAfee, artist and graphic designer, created the spaniel face art in this book. Thank you, Andrew, for capturing the gentle, watchful spirit of the dogs who have shared their stories in "Devoted to Dogs".

Thank you to everyone at the Fredericksburg Parks and Recreation Department for making teaching Dog Manners Obedience classes possible, with special thanks to Jane Shellhorse, Bob Antozzi, Patty Sparks, Pam Jewett-Bullock, Kim Graves, Sonya Wise, Anne Hamm, and Michelle Simpson.

If not for the breeders who brought the dogs I have loved into the world, and then trusted them to our family's care, I would have had nothing to write about. Thank you Mark Gunn, Mike Whitcraft, Wayne and Phyllis MaGill (Phylwayne Springers), Julie Hogan and Donna Thompson (Pride 'n Joy Springers), Amber Carpenter (Connemara Bearded Collies), Lynn Zagarella (Ragtyme Beardies), Henriette Schmidt (Hillcrest Springers), Carol and Don Callahan (Donahan Springers) for dogs we have loved from the moment you placed them in our hands.

I am fortunate to know an abundance of people, both dog professionals and warm and gentle dog mothers and fathers who have shared their dogs with me in my obedience classes, who have devoted their lives to understanding, and living great lives with dogs. Many of these people have contributed hours of interview questions, and have unfailingly shared their gifts of canine expertise with me. I thank everyone that has ever told me about their lovely dogs.

Thank you, especially, to Dr. Liz Ubelhor, Dr. Pam Fandrich, Dr. Filip de Troij, Dr. Carol Getty, Cathi Allison, Sue Lough, Meg Raymond, Marge Brandel, Sue Peetoom, Yvonne Stickleman, Debra Kidwell, Kim Bolster, Maureen Redmond, Cindy Setliff, Wendy Schwartz, Susan Rodenski, Tracy Johnson, Melissa Felts, Deborah Jacob, Teresa Patton, Ruth Dehmel, Sandy McDonald, Howard Gallas, Kim Loveless, Elena Prokos, Ann Reamy, Diane Smart and Scottee Meade.

At the heart of dog writing is getting to know and developing personal friendships with dogs. What could be better? One thing: being loved and spending time with an old dog. Above all else, I thank the fine, lovely, exceptional old dogs that I have been blessed to love. My best thank yous go to Michael Horton, Ellen Wagner, Miss Bean Raymond, Marley Coble, Millie Billingsley–Mills, Benny Redmond, Favor Hogan, Connie Stickleman, T. Topsy Wagner, Peyton McShulskis, Moses Campbell, Ringo Broderick, Buster Patton, Colours Schmidt, Zack Bakerian, MaggieMoo Lay, Saffie Fischer, Bailey Carpenter, Bubby Zagarella, Danny DeMatteo, Dundi Steinberg, Cassie Lough, Atlee Elmont Strobel, Pumpkin Allison, and John Uther Pendragon Greenwood.

Thank you all.

Dedication

These Three Men

This book is dedicated with gratitude and the greatest admiration for three men who have shaped my life, supported my writing, and who are shining examples of kindness, gentleness, integrity and keen insight into human and canine behavior.

For my husband, Neal Pearson Campbell.
For my father, Thomas Hawtoi Ferrell.
For my business partner, forever friend,
English Springer Spaniel,
Donahan's Phylwayne Abroham, CD.

These selections are dedicated to these three loves of my life.

Let Cupid Choose with Canine Clues

"He cannot be a gentleman which loveth not a dog."
John Northbrooke

He scooped her up into his arms. She brushed his cheek with soft breathy kisses.

Around him, people were watching, his cell phone was ringing. Life and responsibility called to him. And yet, time stood still while returned her velvet kisses. His eyes drank in her unconditional, relentless esteem for him. Her eyes locked onto his.

Warm in his lap was the place she most wanted to be. His fine, gentle hands were her reward at the end of a day. There was nothing on this Earth, in this lifetime, that thrilled her so.

She was his puppy. He was a big, strong dad to chew on, romp with and love. Who would not love a man like that?

3

Search For A Partner

Finding the perfect partner, who deserves your best affection, requires perception into the secret recesses of a human's heart. As with all great decisions and best rewards on life's journey, your dog may be your secret discerning tool to help you decide, "Is this one the one for me?"

Find Your Love Partner The Dog's Way

In support of Cupid's efforts to bring love to all, I offer my "Finding Your Love Partner" self test.

Do not actually quiz the would-be loved one with these questions. Decide by his actions if he is qualified to love you and to be a part of your fine dog's life. (In the interest of easy reading, I am using the male pronoun for the love candidate. Please read in your own gender of love choice.)

Love Test One: Critique Greeting Behavior

Meet with the would-be loved one. Your lovely dog is with you. After the would be loved one acknowledges you, does he notice your dog? Does he speak to your dog? He gets high points if he drops to his knees and pets the dog. Points are subtracted if he lunges over the dog and rubs the dog roughly without waiting for the dog to offer to be rubbed.

A loved one who rushes headlong in physical, unprepared for attention may do the same with you. Bad sign. First impressions speak aptly to a person's love style. High marks are given for a soft voice, knowing when to make eye

4

contact and when not to make eye contact, and for knowing how to match the dog's response for acceptance of affection.

Love Test Two: Is he more interested in your needs, or will his own needs always come first?

Assume you have developed a relationship with this person. You have been out to dinner, the movies, played scrabble at his house, worked on your fence together at your house.

You decide to go away on a day long trip. If he is not a dog owner himself, we will give him a wee bit of leeway on how quickly it occurs to him that your dog has needs (wee wee, dinner served on time, etc.) while you are away. It is not reasonable for you, the dog lover, to think your  dog must be sitting between the two of you participating in adult human conversation and adult human physical activities. Your dog should know that if a door is closed he can go and lie on his dog bed. The dog is required to be well adjusted and well trained to quietly allow his humans a dog-less interlude. If your dog is so accustomed to your constant presence that he whines, carries on and demands to be a part of all you do, there, gentle dog lover, is a dog behavior problem that you have created and that must be retrained.

You and your human companion could take the dog to obedience class as a weekly date. At

5

class, all of you would learn many telling things about each other.

Is your man understanding that your dog needs to go out every six hours? Will a side trip to a kennel or doggy day care facility be seen as an inconvenience? If needed dog care is not available, will the prospective loved one understand and suggest a long, lazy weekend at home? Along with giving you clues to his true concern for another creature that you love, his reaction to these concerns will tell you a great deal about this partner's ability to respond to the needs of others

Love Test Three: Does he have neatness, orderliness, cleanliness needs that are compatible with your own?

Years ago, in college, I attended a human sexuality psychology class. During a discussion of compatibility between partners, our professor

told a riveting and hilarious story about waking up in bed with his beloved, very cuddly Golden Retriever under the covers, happily licking clean a dog food can. I vividly recall that many women in the class, visibly and some vocally, reacted to this picture. Some were shocked that a dog was in the bed. Many obviously did not hope to wake up in bed with a man and his dog. But I thought, "Wow, what fun."

THESE THREE MEN

The point I took from the professor's tale of his dog frolicking in the bed with humans, whether that was the professor's intention or not, was that while I was delighted at the mental picture of a man who loved a dog so much that waking to canine slurping entertainment made him smile, that there could exist some men or women who would be appalled at food can gravy on the sheets, dogs under the covers and other doggy activities.

Dogs are hairy. They shed. Dogs eat grass and leaves. Around two in the morning they wake  you with the "hurka-gerka" sounds of impending stomach upset. The dog lover learns to sleep with one ear vigilant to what their dog is doing in the night. If you hook up with a mate who is grumpy when you must fling off the covers and attend to the needs of your dog, save yourself heartache and arguments down the path to love, wonder if he is the mate for you.

A man who worries about your dog will probably gently and steadfastly care for you. A man who knows a little dog hair on his clothes means he has had the good fortune to be in your dog loving arms, will be a keeper.

There are neat, non-dog loving partners out there for the man who criticizes your dog house keeping or your dog responsibilities. Let the neat, dog-less women have those tidy fellows.

Love Test Four: Is he generous?

It is time for your dog's annual physical examination. Your veterinarian notes that your dog is now seven years old. He suggests that your dog have his first "Golden Age Check-Up."

Perhaps he recommends a urinalysis, a heart worm test, a very thorough blood screen test to check many blood values and give clues to how many body systems are faring and aging, a blood test called a "titer" to check to see  exactly which of the many vaccinations your dog may need this year, and a fecal exam. Cost for all this diagnostic wisdom will vary. It will be a valuable investment in the health and well being of your dog. Two to four hundred dollars of testing may give you vast insight into the health of many canine body systems. When you mention this expense to your would-be love interest, watch his eyebrows. Listen intently for his first reaction. If he expresses any scoffing or wonderment that you would spend hundreds of dollars on your dog: beware.

If he is a very financially cautious person, we will give him a little leeway if he appears appalled at the cost of high quality dog care. But, if you have seen him buy any pricey items for his enjoyment or convenience, perhaps for a hobby (computers, audio equipment, sailboats, ski vacations, professional sports tickets, entertainment toys, cars, dapper clothing, etc.), take time to wonder if your spending desires and needs will rank as high in his estimation as his own.

A man with a generous heart will be a joy to you and your dog. A man with a tightfisted heart is best left for those who want to be pet-less and cuddle up reading stock reports and bank statements. Good luck and high fortune to them.

Happy love hunting! Look well to how he puts his hands on the dog. Bide your time. Assess whether he is the dog-man of your dreams. Even if you choose to toss him back into the sea of auditioning boyfriends, you are not alone. You have the dog who loves you. If you are devoted to your dog, you need a partner that shares that huge and basic need. True love was never deeper than when hearts meet over the heart of a good dog.

9

A Father's Example:
Adored By Dogs
and Little Girls

"Great men have always had dogs."
Oouida

"**W**hy didn't you jump off the bus and save the puppy? Exactly where did you see the little puppy?"

We are sitting at the kitchen table. My mother is pouring iced tea. My daddy is surreptitiously handing a nugget of homemade biscuit to our dog Ruffles. Ruffles is fixated upon Daddy with expectant black eyes.

I am 8 years old, breathlessly describing a little pup I spotted on the edge of the road during my bus ride home from school. My lost puppy story has my father's unwavering interest.

 10

THESE THREE MEN

The next thing I know, we are all in the car, heading down Hickory Grove Road, all peering into weeds and fields, hoping to spot the puppy.

A Dog's Life Is Precious

I recall having the feeling that if we did not rescue the puppy I would somehow have failed my daddy. Little puppies were for protecting and bringing home.

Even at 8 years old, I was plenty big enough to understand that one responsibility in life is to protect creatures smaller and more defenseless. We found the little pup, a tiny beagle, muddy and cold, in a ditch. She came home with us.

We named her Raffles, and told her she was sister to Ruffles. She lived to be ancient, cherished and an accomplished rabbit hunter.

Live Your Values

I learned almost every necessary value and belief by watching my father live his life. He did not hold forth and lecture. He was a quiet, thoughtful man. He loved dogs of all sizes, shapes, purebred and mixed breed. I never saw him drive by a dog walking down the side of any road, busy or deserted, that he did not pull the car over and check the dog for tags and an owner. I have shared the back seat many times with dogs who needed a ride home.

Time Invested Equals Results

My father devoted time to training his dogs. He taught them to retrieve by playing fetch

11

with them before breakfast and before supper. Each time they ran back to him breathless and delighted with the game, he rubbed them, spoke gently to them and showed them they were the best dogs in the world. Never in my life did I ever hear my father raise his voice in anger to a dog. If the dog misbehaved, he got up from whatever he was doing, went to the dog and showed the dog what he wanted the dog to do. If the dog misbehaved, he blamed himself for needing to invest more time training.

First, Pay Attention To Your Student
When my father worked with his dog, he gave it his undivided attention. If company arrived while he was teaching the dog to sit or to come, he stopped his training until he could give as much attention to the dog as he wanted the dog to give him in return.

Respect Must Be Mutual
The best trait in his dog training was that his dogs knew he had unquestioned positive regard for them. He was a serious bird, rabbit and

squirrel hunter. He treated his hunting dogs with a respect that told them they had skills that he needed that were as valuable as any skill he had with his gun or with knowing when or where to look for game.

Daddy's dogs were his partners and his family. They were never live possessions.

Consistency Is Key

Daddy was consistent in his expectations and his rules. If a behavior was wrong some of the time, it was wrong all of the time. He could take his pristine dressed wife out to dinner riding on the front seat, with a large, panting bird dog riding on the back seat, and the dog knew jumping over the seat into mama's lap was not allowed.

He taught dogs and puppies lessons like this over and over in the driveway, with lots of praise, firm but gentle placement onto the back seat, and lots of repetition of the training. He did not place his dogs suddenly in untrained situations so that they could learn to fail.

Train. Don't Complain

My father did not nag. I wonder if he spoke so little because he expected listeners to be smart and respectful enough to be listening politely. Dogs will tune you out if you yammer, beg and whine all the time to them, night and day. 'Show,

13

don't tell' was the communication method my father used to raise dogs that were smart and gentle just like he was.

Love Is Always Remembered

Until the day he died, the most thrilling sound my father's dogs and I could hear was the crunch of his tires on the gravel as he drove up the driveway. The slam of his car door would bring us to adoring attention. Our eyes would be riveted to the back door as the great big, gentle man who always loved us filled the door frame.

He taught me everything I understand about the work required to deserve the adoration of a fine dog. He gave me everything I needed to go out into the world and recognize fairness, compassion and contentment.

The Reward? A Good Dog

If giving such a daddy up to death is ever bearable, I am at least comforted to say he died in his sleep with an elderly Scottish terrier named Daisy asleep in the crook of his arm. Such a parting from life may be as fine a leave taking as any of us can expect.

His lessons speak in my head and heart, ready to be passed on to new dogs he would have loved to train.

Will Rogers once said, "If there are no dogs in heaven, then when I die, I want to go where they went." I know I can speak for my father when I say I am sure he agrees with Mr. Rogers.

Attack of the Bladder Stones

"Blessed is the person who has earned the love of an old dog."
S.J. Seward

Abroham, my most senior employee, has retired due to health problems. He has never missed a day of work. A more willing worker I have not met.

Arthritis and just plain old age have forced him home to rest and he is dissatisfied with the lack of work. He tells me he is a working man. I tell him he is more than a retired worker. He is my best friend. Abroham, of course, is my dog.

 16

Since I teach obedience classes, he has had steady employment at my side for nearly fourteen years.

Rewarding Service With Service

What goes around does come around. Abe has assisted my work, by my side, all his life. Without question, I will be by his side as his assistant for as long as he can use the help.

Until a few weeks ago, Abe had only two needs for my service that he could not do without. He needed me to lift his rear end up off the floor on days that the arthritis in his hips called for help. Once the hydraulic lift of mother was applied, Abe could walk where he wanted. He also needed to go outside to use the bathroom more frequently than when he was an iron bladder'ed young dog. I arrange my schedule to report home to take him out onto the grass for nature's call every three to five hours.

Where He Goes, I Go

There can be a positive result to any inconvenience, I learned. Because I am so accustomed to being present for every potty break and outdoor outing, I saw trouble was brewing on the urinary output front.

Geriatric Emergencies Build Quickly

Abe suddenly went from needing to go out every few hours, to not going to the bathroom at all for thirteen hours and then for sixteen hours. Every dog owner knows that frightening symptoms always occur between noon Saturday and early

17

DEVOTED TO DOGS

morning of Monday when the veterinarian is closed, don't they?

Abe was diagnosed with an x-ray that showed his aging bladder full of bladder stones. Surgery was performed immediately. Stones removed were sent off for analysis, and the bladder and related plumbing flushed clean. Such an old dog is not a favorite candidate for anesthesia, but his surgeon warned we had no choice. The only alternative in this case was to wait until his urinary tract blocked completely and then have the surgery. Surgery before total blockage was definitely the safer choice.

Post Surgery Vigil
The first week after the surgery was agony for all of us. Abe came home wearing a pain relieving patch that drugged him into oblivion and was unable to walk or eat. Three days of day and night howling began. Twice, I decided he would have to be euthanized, since I never intended to let him suffer just because I would not give

him up. Our wonderful veterinarians calmed me down and reminded me that a very, very elderly dog had just survived major abdominal surgery with a great deal of anesthetic and analgesic drugs.

No one at our house slept over three hours at a stretch for nine days. When Abe recovered enough to ask to be taken outside, he had his days and nights confused. I began wearing sunglasses in public, night and day, to hide the fact that I had given up sleeping and was doing a great deal of crying over his suffering. I was also experiencing a glimmer of the agony of the grieving process as I looked face to face for the first time into the prospect that Abe could not live forever.

An Old Boy Revives

Good news. After two weeks, Abe began to eat real meals without hand feeding. He walked outside unassisted with me hovering behind him.

I had been supporting his rear section using a long towel sling under his stomach. Abe was glad to have me put away the towel. It is difficult and very undignified for a boy to try and urinate with his mamma holding a towel under the parts he needs to use.

Three weeks have passed and Abe is nearly himself again. Always the dog who wants to please, he is eating his prescription anti-bladder stone canned diet as though it is caviar. He is following all the do's and don'ts dictated by

19

the bladder stone analysis of 'calcium oxylate' stones.

I trail behind him every time he goes outside with a long, flat baking pan. I lurk to catch a urine sample twice a day. After I carry him back up the front steps, I rush into the kitchen and test the pH of the urine.

Our goal is to have the pH remain over seven; to have very alkaline urine and avoid new stone formation, if possible. Protein and all foods with calcium are limited. Abe loved tuna and salmon. No more of that for him.

A Dog Mother Has To Know
I am studying labels. Peanut butter has more protein than fat free cream cheese, but the cream cheese has more calcium. Abe had liked both foods for taking the several pills he has to take each day. Now, I am rolling the pills up in tiny, wet pieces of bread and he is eating the pills that way.

THESE THREE MEN

Abe and I urge you to keep an eye on your dog, regardless of his age and learn as much as you can about his regular habits. Go outside with him a few times a day and make sure all his plumbing is working properly.

Study the labels of anything you feed your dog. If the food is cheap, there's probably a reason. We really are what we eat. All dog foods, treats and nutritional supplements are not created equally and may not be healthy for your dog.

Don't give your dog any vitamin, nutritional supplement for joints, coat, or any reason without having your veterinarian approve and record the addition in your dog's permanent medical record. Keep his weight down so he won't wear his joints out any faster than he must. Walk him every day to build up his ligaments and endurance so when he is fourteen he will be a young fourteen and not an invalid.

Preserve his health and never doubt your veterinarian wants to hear every symptom and all your questions. Study his every habit now and you will recognize medical problems to prevent emergencies.

Honored To Serve

Is this constant vigil of the old dog an inconvenience to me? Not hardly. If only I could be promised the job would last forever. I am glad to serve. After fourteen years of faithful service, he has earned his keep and his right to nursing care.

21

2

Genteel Humans: Are You As Well Behaved As Your Dog?

"He who smiles rather than rages is always the stronger."
Japanese Proverb

When a Poodle
Invites You to Tea

*"It is fatal to let a dog know she is
funny, for she immediately loses
her head and starts hamming it up."*
P. G. Wodehouse

Humans only, s'il vous plaît. The rule of the day
is: "It's all about the poodle." The poodle deigns
not to share her limelight.

Your Fine Dog: Not Invited
Never take your own dog to another dog's
party unless the human host has begged you
to do so. Even then, the best-mannered guest
leaves other dogs at home. The poodle hostess
requires center stage.

Pay Homage With Material Goods
Come not empty-handed. The poodle requires
material, demonstrable homage. Bring a gift. Is
your gift edible? All the better.

Tap The Door, Do Not Ring The Bell
Experienced guests know to "tap" the door, gently, as a hummingbird wing beats the air. The poodle has already seen and heard you long before you stepped onto her walkway. Do not ring that detested doorbell and rouse the poodle to bark your arrival.

Enter Her Home With Quiet Grace
Enter quietly. Only the poodle makes an entrance. Surely to goodness your mamma reared you to "never enter a room talking." Manners, dears, manners. The poodle demands genteel guests.

Greet Your Hostess First
Be gracious to the poodle. Make a beeline for the poodle. She is your hostess. Exclaim her name in mellifluous whispers tinged with awe. Kneel down to her level. Do not hover over, nor lunge at the poodle. Keep your direct eye contact to yourself until the poodle offers to gladly wag her pompom tail with joy to see you.

Make Your Introductions
Introduce yourself to all present. It is rude to monopolize the poodle. After paying brief, heartfelt homage to the lovely one, take yourself around the entire gathering. Introduce yourself to all the poodle's guests.

Pleasing Conversation Only
Never find fault, nor offer obedience tips to the poodle. Even if the poodle were to lapse and behave a trifle badly, never offer a reprimand n or negative comment to the poodle. It is the height of tacky rudeness to criticize (thus

branding yourself a know–it–all) in the poodle's own domain. Unsolicited advice will brand you uncouth, a social outcast in poodle society.

Admire The Poodle
By the time you leave the presence of the poodle, you should be able to paint a meticulous word picture of the poodle. Admire her wise eyes, her boundless curls, her dainty manicured feet. What color was her topknot's bow? Study the perfection of the poodle. Reflect that perfection in your praise.

Give No Tidbits To The Poodle
Do not feed the poodle from the table. The poodle may have a special diet. Her manners may be too nice to allow her to beg. Her mamma may be too polite to admonish you to abstain from feeding the poodle.

Never A Braggart Be
No one wants you to hold forth on your own glorious dog. Dote on the poodle. When blessed to be guest of the poodle, talk only to and about the poodle. Give your own fine canine companion his or her own party. Wait to sing your own dog's praises when she or he is guest of honor.

Soak In The Glory of the Poodle Home

Notice and admire all family pictures that include the poodle. Before the soiree concludes, be sure to walk about the poodle's charming domain and admire all the poodle's photographs, portraits and life memorabilia.

The poodle probably has an extensive poodle figurine and collectible display. Be sure to ask questions about her collected treasures. Does she have a scrapbook? Beg to be allowed to sit captivated with the scrapbook, and perhaps the poodle, on your lap.

Do not handle the toys, or possessions, of the poodle unless the poodle presents them to you. Do not rudely touch the poodle's treasures. Let the poodle make the first move toward any sharing.

Depart Before You Tire The Poodle

Take your leave while the poodle still finds you captivating. The poodle pampers herself with beauty rest. Short poodle parties are the best parties. Leave before the poodle leaves you for a nap.

Thank the poodle for her glorious company.

Go back down to your knees. Thank the poodle for the delight of her company.

Leave promptly. Never linger. Farewell. Now.

The poodle must get back to being the center of attention for her remaining company. Or, she may need to retire to her boudoir to rest her tiny paws.

Close All Doors and Gates
Close the poodle's gate. If you do one thing correctly, the poodle and every other canine blessed to abide within a fenced yard, pray you do this one thing: shut and secure the gate.

One gate left open. One poodle escape. You will never be invited to any poodle's party again.

Rue The Day You Are Labeled A Slacker
Word will go forth to canines and their companions everywhere that you committed the quintessential faux pas. Leave the poodle's gate open and all dogdom will brand you a slacker.

These Rules Apply To
All Canine Celebrations
What if you find yourself invited to tea for a terrier? Or to take libations with a Labrador? Or to mingle at a mixer for a mixed breed? Rest confidently, gentle reader; follow these poodle party rules and you will always listed on all of dogdom's 'A' guest list.

Party on.

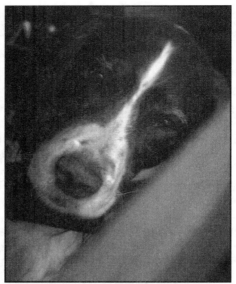

Mr. Quinnton's Quintessential Code for Companions

"If you get to thinkin' you're a person of influence, try orderin' somebody else's dog around."
Cowboy wisdom.

Last week, my mother and I visited my friend the veterinarian. I have been on a diet. We were invited to visit my doctor's hospital and weigh my diet progress.

Dog manners, and the manners of a dog's human companion, are a subject of continuing concern to me, as a springer spaniel. My mother,

 30

GENTEEL HUMANS

Sarah Ferrell, has consented to let me be her guest columnist so that I may hold forth on a subject even more pressing in my mind than dog manners: human manners.

Let Your Good Manners Make Your Dog Proud
A dog cannot rise above the manners of the human attached to his leash. He may be brilliant, well versed in the do's and don'ts of polite company, but if he finds himself connected by leash to a human who is less than genteel, then my, my, pity the dog.

An Aged Dog Is A Wise Dog
I am 12 years old and thereby I have the sanctity of age that opens the door for me to hold forth on etiquette. I realize that grannies and refined aunts formerly performed the service of setting folks straight when their manners were in disarray, but I find a sad few elders offering discourse on how to go forth into polite company.

Humans Embarrass Their Dogs
May I relate my afternoon observing the humans at the veterinary hospital? Several dogs cringed and rolled their eyes and hid their heads behind chairs and potted plants, so mortified were they to see their humans misbehaving so badly.

I must applaud that the cat owners were quite well behaved. I credit this to the fact that the three cats present were politely resting in their traveling cages. A pet in a carrier is usually safe from aspersions from the manners police.

31

Code Of Conduct For Humans

Rather than tell each tale of manners gone awry, I have laid down the following "Out In Public With Pets" code of conduct. I realize that you, gentle reader, do not need these rules since you are perfect pet-owning humans. Perhaps, you could clip out my rules, carry them in your wallet, and if you see a mishap in manners, you could surreptitiously place the rules on the offender's windshield? It never hurts to anonymously attempt to help one's species evolve. Aren't manners, or the lack thereof, surely an indication of civilization's progress?

No Naked Dogs In Public

Your dog needs to wear his collar at all times. All dogs should be on leash when they darken the door of the veterinarian, or when they stroll

the public streets. Since I am older and am apt to speak my mind, I will leave the 'always on leash in public subject' with a sharp question: Do you know what the folks who work at the veterinary hospital should call the dog owner whose dog dashes into the reception area without a leash? Inconsiderate brutes. A dog owner whose dog leaps through the door, off-leash, yards ahead of the owner, makes a very bad impression. First impressions count.

Uninvited Kisses Are No Delight

Owners must accept the fact that not every strange dog wants to kiss their dog. Some

 32

dignified dogs will take great, snarling offense if your precious bouncy dog hurls his wriggling self over to plant a kiss or sniff a bottom. When in public with your leashed dog, control your dog's affections, greetings and friskiness.

Dogs are pack animals. This means each one has an opinion about who will and who will not be allowed to take physical liberties with his body parts. Pack does not mean, "we dogs are all one happy family longing to have physical contact with every dog we meet." Many dignified dogs do not want to play with pushy, untrained dogs.

Let Resting Dogs Rest
A dog resting quietly in the veterinarian's lobby may be there because he feels bad. Be considerate. Find a seat farthest from the other dogs present and sit quietly with your dog. No sniffing of cat cages. Allowing a rambunctious dog to harass a captive cat is not cute, it is unkind. Cats who do not live with dogs may be terrified of that big, wriggling nose invading their space.

Ladies and Gentlemen
Do Not Groom In Public
I am a long-haired dog. I have submitted to, and sometimes enjoyed, endless hours of brushing, clipping, toenail trimming, ear combing and undercoat stripping. However, I am appalled and so embarrassed for the dog whose human companion hauls out the brush or comb in the veterinary lobby.

One of the reasons that many non-dog-loving people complain about dogs in public is that they feel that we shed. Some humans feel dogs are dirty. But just as your human granny should have taught you that to brush one's hair in public is rude, so it is to brush the dog in public.

Brushing should bring about varying degrees of hair shedding. No one wants your dog's fur wafting across their floor. If you feel your dog needs a sprucing before he greets the veterinarian, for goodness' sake, do brush him. Brush him at home. As you brush him, get your hands on him and feel him all over for lumps, bumps, scabs and tiny creatures that crawl and attach. This home-grooming exam will make you a better conversationalist with the vet. My mom says that every lump she has ever found on me she discovered while I was lathered up in the bathtub. Brushing and grooming are good. Confine them to the home or the outdoors.

Arrive Early
Make it a rule to arrive early at the veterinarian's office. If early, you will have time to give your

dog a once-over for grooming embarrassments. If he needs a meeting with the dog brush, take him outdoors and brush him outside the doctor's waiting room. This is also a good time to walk the dog around and let him sniff and add any of his own bathroom contributions to the outdoors.

Poop: Pick It Up

Speaking of poop: Outdoors or indoors, all excrement that plops in public places must be picked up by the human. None of that staring vacantly off in the other direction while the dog eliminates on the vet's sidewalk, a neighbor's lawn or any other public spot. Ignorance and indifference to dog waste pickup responsibility give dogs a bad name, one more reason many dogless humans do not like dogs and do not want them out in public.

A dog has to "go to the bathroom." We do not have hands to pick it up. A few dogs will eat it, and that certainly takes care of the pickup problem. However, it has been my experience that dog owners really do not like that disposal method.

If you are going out with your dog, no matter where, realize that the dog may have to eliminate. Take a plastic bag with you. Grocery, drug and discount-store bags are perfect pickup bags. My mother stuffs them under the front seat of her van, and there they wait until I am taken for a walk. Take extra bags. Be ready to share a bag with a dog mom or dad in need.

Be Quiet While You Wait Your Turn

My grandmother once told my mother, "Never be a respecter of persons." She did not mean, "Do not respect people." She meant, "Treat the staff as nicely as you treat the doctor." This point of etiquette is too broad for a little springer like myself to discourse upon. Let me try and explain with an example I witnessed while waiting in the veterinary lobby for my recent weigh-in.

Mama! Behave!

A lady came in, expensively dressed, bejeweled, and having leapt from a pricey, late-model foreign car. She flounced into the hospital lobby. She was either visually challenged or just plain rude, since she did not get into the line of three waiting clients. No, she formed her own line beside the true line and said in a demanding tone, "I don't have time to wait. I'm on my way out of town."

I was so embarrassed for the little corgi unwittingly leashed at the side of this paragon of pitiful upbringing that I cannot tell the entire story. Suffice it to say that she wanted to board the dog that very day, and raised her voice and her haughty demeanor when she found there were no boarding openings. Next, she lit into

36

the always polite, soft-spoken receptionist demanding to see the doctor, "just for a minute, right now, to ask one question." Throughout the avalanche of dog-mistress misbehavior, dogs and waiting dog mothers watched, captive witnesses to this rude performance. Finally, she stomped out the door, dragging the surely mortified corgi with her.

Secret Codes Label Misbehaving Owners

My mom and I discussed this rude behavior
 performance as we sat at a local drive-through having a very small milk shake. Mom can read and I cannot, so Mom told me a secret that brought about my private doggy smile. Mom has worked in veterinary offices, and she whispered to me that there are secret codes that can land on the charts of unsavory, rude patients.

There is the 'UNC' code. This does not mean that the doctor or staff knows the 'UNC' patient is a graduate of the great Tar heel mecca in Chapel Hill, N.C. No. It means: "Under No Circumstances."

A 'UNC' client may have felt important abusing a receptionist or technician, but most doctors protect their valuable staff. Abuse them once, maybe. Twice, probably not. When this self-important, loud, demanding woman calls again, the doctor will be "so very sorry to have no appointments available." She will be branded: 'UNC', Under No Circumstances.

There is one more secret rude label that I pray no one I know ever has inscribed on their veterinary charts. That is 'OPIA'. My mom says that even though I am an older dog, I am still too young to know words that she refers to as "unseemly." She says that 'OPIA' translates roughly to "Owner Is Pain In Derrière." I know the "A" part of the label is a bad word my mother is keeping from me.

Make Your Dog Proud To Be Your Dog

When you go to the veterinarian's office, be gentle with the staff. Polish up your manners. Remember that the doctor went through all those years of study and expense to have a pet hospital because she or he wants to help pets. Dogs misbehave when they are untrained. Humans misbehave even though they know better.

Thanks for letting me speak my mind on manners. My momma says I have said quite enough for one day. She says it is time for a little boy dog to be seen and not heard. I am going out on the deck to supervise the hummingbirds.

Good Manners
Not Just for Dogs

*"Properly trained, a man
can be a dog's best friend."*
Corey Ford

"**P**ardon me. I am about to get on my high
horse." My grandmother would say that just
before she would sit her grandchildren down and
hold forth on etiquette and the ways of getting
along with grace and humor in the world.

My own mother followed in her footsteps, giving
lessons describing how to behave in company.
Before and after any social gathering, Mother
would launch into her assessment of the good
manners that would be called for by the occasion

39

or that she saw to be lacking once we returned home behind closed doors.

Recently, my dogs and I attended six days of dog shows. We enjoyed a barking good time and admired dogs turned out to perfection: brushed, blown dry, white dogs chalked to dazzling whiteness, and fluffy dogs trimmed to perfect outlines of their breed standards. These willing canine companions were on their best behavior, unhesitatingly participated in these bizarre dog show activities purely because masters they love wanted to win at the dog show.

Consider Your Own Temperament

I heard a great deal of theory about dog temperament. Dog owners and breeders don't hesitate to cast harsh judgments on dogs who have bad manners, snarl, bite, fight and are not a credit to the gentle temperament that makes humans adore dogs.

Before we ask good manners of our dogs, it is best we master good manners for ourselves.

Everyone entered in the dog show hopes to win. Only one dog of each sex of each breed is going to win each day. That means that there could be 150 Rottweilers exhibiting on one day, but only one dog (male) and one bitch (female) can be the day's winners and take home championship points. There will be 148 losers. Anyone with any math and statistical savvy should not be too dumbfounded, angry or feel robbed when they fail to win.

GENTEEL HUMANS

Since only two dogs from each breed will win,  you witness a great deal of disappointment at a dog show. But even if the judge did not like a particular dog best, it does not mean that dog is not a beautiful, spectacular dog. I saw competitors throw their second and less than "winners" ribbons on the ground. I watched competitors exit the rings with red faces, dragging their dogs, and looking like the storm clouds.

I wondered how on earth did all those kind, willing dogs, who had endured hours in the car, days of brushing, shampooing and all kinds of primping and lack of freedom, feel when their mom or dad stomped to the van looking like a terrible disaster had befallen them. These dogs deserved better.

How wonderfully pleasant and striking it was to see dog handlers who did not win reach over and offer a congratulatory handshake or a pat on the shoulder to the person who had just beaten them. True class and good breeding can be seen in humans as well as the dogs in the ring.

41

Make Eye Contact When Any Person Speaks To You.

I watched several people lean over to congratulate those who had beaten them only to see that the winner did not even turn to look into the speaker's face, nor receive the well wishes with any grace at all. Terrible to watch. I hoped my granny in heaven did not see any of these folks who had no doubt been pitiably dragged up without manners.

Good Manners Open Doors To Future Success

When grandmothers gathered little faces to their knee to pass on lessons of civility they were doing this to not only make the world a more gentle, enjoyable place to pass a few scores of years. They were building a foundation of knowledge of how to get along in the world and prosper. Even if no one holds forth on etiquette very much these days, we all know it when we see it. We enjoy the company and try to ease the paths in life of those who have been kind and calm to us.

Introduce Everyone In The Group

Not much introducing seemed to go on at the dog show. Newcomers joined groups and either were already known to the group or were often ignored. Heavens! Where were their manners? Even the joy of victory or the frustration of defeat does not suspend the cardinal rule that civilized people introduce others who enter their conversation.

GENTEEL HUMANS

Didn't everyone's granny teach them that any time you enter a room or a group, you must greet those already present and that they will introduce you to everyone present? Even dogs stop to sniff and welcome newcomers to their groups.

No Shoving! No Crowding!
Hard to believe. I know it is nearly impossible to think a grown-up person might physically shove another out of the way, but I saw this happen. I felt it happen.

My dog and I had won first place in our age group of dogs. The ring steward was calling out armband numbers as we entered the ring for the final judging. Before we could even stop walking and stake out our spot to wait for the next round of judging, a rotund woman in a hurry took her beefy shoulder and shoved us

with startling might, saying, "The Open Class winner goes first."

I was so dazed to be shoulder-to-shoulder with such a rude woman that I was speechless. I thought, "Oh my goodness, I have ventured out to be touched by a graceless ruffian!" But I smiled and nodded and let the rough woman trundle on toward whatever spot of Earth her trajectory hurled her.

When I left the ring, a bystander came up to me and said, "That woman shoved you!" We laughed and wished her well. We wished her well from a distance, mind you, and gave her a wide berth for the rest of the week. We also watched as her dog did not win. Did the judge mark her down as rude? Perhaps so

It Is Tacky To Wheedle Free Advice

I happened to be standing in a group in which a lovely woman was introduced as a veterinarian. This poor doctor was bowled over with medical questions. Where were these people reared? There is nothing more rude, in a social situation, than to try and dig up free advice from a doctor, lawyer, plumber, electrician, psychologist (you fill in the profession). Talk about rude!

If a professional holds forth on a subject in her field and everyone gets to enjoy and benefit from her knowledge, that is wonderful for all present. But to ask for free advice in any social situation is the height of rudeness. If my mother were alive, I would have to ask her to comment on the shades of "tacky." Seems you don't hear much about things being "tacky" anymore. So much the pity for children and folks looking for guidance in the graces of making others comfortable and welcome.

Bite Your Tongue

My daddy wisely taught, "If you can't say something nice, keep your mouth shut." Standing in a large group outside a show ring that my dog and I had just left, I heard a woman moan in a loud, whining bray, "I didn't mind losing, but did you see that the winner was the ugliest dog you ever saw?"

Surely this woman did not know that standing right there in her large group of listeners was the husband of the owner of the dog who had won and the wife of the judge of that breed.

The person, unfortunate and unschooled in social graces who made this mean statement, became a legend for the rest of the dog show week. The story was told and retold. By the end of the week her one poorly chosen declaration

had offended several dog breeders, many people whose dogs were related to the "ugly" dog and all the friends and relations of the dog.

A wise and genteel friend of mine likes to quote Abroham Lincoln's advice, "It is better to remain silent and be thought a fool than to open one's mouth and remove all doubt."

Would that we could all be as gentle and well meaning as our dogs. We have been entrusted with dogs to teach us kindness and that life is about feeling good and sharing happiness.

The next time you rub your dog, thank him for his good manners. Mind your p's and q's at your next dog show and perhaps if you demonstrate you are of gentle, well-mannered temperament, someone will trust you to hold their puppy.

Holding a puppy is one of life's best rewards. And every little puppy life offers us a new chance to be kind and well-mannered and to lead by example.

Pass The Green Beans Please

"Life expectancy would grow by leaps and bounds if green vegetables smelled as good as bacon."
Doug Larson

Have you noticed that human strangers feel no reluctance to prance right up to your dog while the two of you are cavorting in public and point out that your precious companion is fat?

You may be sitting on a bench, delightedly sharing an ice cream cone. Are these strangers jealous that they have no one to ride them around, buy them frozen delectables, kiss them all over the muzzle and adore them? Could be they are just busy bodies?

Are these strangers merely afflicted by having horrendous conversation skills? Is calling my dog fat a scintillating discussion gambit?

47

Rude Comments Force Facing Realism

In truth, I have to crawl from my pit of denial and blaming and admit the truth: my dog is fat. Twice in one week persons known and unknown to me have regaled me with the 'fat dog' lecture.

The first person to offer a fat dog intervention was someone beloved to me and to the dog. With the utmost respect and horrified realization that she was accurate, I cringed an 'oh, I am a neglectful, self indulgent dog mother' cringe. I have allowed my lovely formerly little Vivien to become Big Vivien.

Are You're the Big One
Or The Little One?

Fat accumulation sneaked up on me. It is a Southern tendency to have 'Bigs' and 'Littles' in one's family. I had a "Little Sally" cousin, whose mamma was "Big Sally". A "Big Jack" uncle, who's son was "Little Jack". It may be a Southern custom to be so busy rewarding our loved ones with fresh baked chocolate Bourbon pecan pies, cornmeal dumplings, collards, pot liquor, sweet tea, chicken and pastry that we turn each generation of slim "Little Viviens" into "Big Viviens" by the time they are matrons. I have fattened up even my canine 'Little Vivien' in my misplaced, ill-advised, food centered joy to over love her.

"Madam, Your Dog Is Fat!"

The next "you have a fat dog" slap in the face struck its mark while we were heeling around a big grassy field with a bunch of strangers. Every

 48

woman present had an advanced obedience goal on her mind as the teacher shouted commands to us .

"Halt, and straighten up those crooked sits!", "Forward, Fast! If you or your dog can't run, go stand in the middle of the circle until you catch your breath." When you hear that sort of permission/prediction to leave the athletic woman heeling group, you might as well figure some sort of fat lecture is coming.

My young dog and I were relaxing by the field's fence when a woman (thin and very pretty, honesty demands that I add) glides over to us with the boisterous greeting: "Does that dog have a real thick coat, or is he just real fat?"

I wanted to retort, "You must not know this is the Angel Gabriel and he is perfect any way he deems to be." Manners clamped down on my tongue and I offered sweetly, "I just don't know. Would you like to feel him?" The sweet cloy of mannerly sarcasm was wasted upon this emissary of the fat dog gestapo.

Thank You, Mary, Jesus And All The Saints

Silently, I thanked all the saints in heaven that I am a lifetime Weight Watchers member at "goal" and happened to be on a thin downswing at that moment. Had I been ten pounds heavier, this helpful dog watcher's fat assessment of my dog would have gone straight to my defensive fears of whether I was fat or just fluffy, too.

49

Two truths were impressed upon me after my encounters with fat dog reality and a desire to mend my overfeeding ways.

Sugar Coat That Insult, If You Please

One, sugared words and gentle suggestions are far more readily received when one is about to tell someone their dog is fat. To alienate the listener is neither graceful, nor helpful, when trying to impart wisdom.

Two, where there is rude finger-pointing, there is liable to be a basis for the unwanted attention. In other words, when the word 'fat' comes up, it is time to take a hard look at the dog.

Hop On The Scales, My Lovely

Enfold your trusting canine in your arms and step on the scales. The truth will set you free from giving your beloved dog too many biscuits, indulging her with human snacks and promoting unhealthy eating that never translates into "food is love."

Food Is Not Love

Food is food. Too much food is fat. Fat will shorten and limit the life of the dog you want to love for many, many years. The support and advice of wise dog lovers was the solace I sought for dog diet encouragement.

Marge Brandel, long-time supporting member or the Greater Fredericksburg Kennel Club, and devoted mother of very fine Rottweilers, Border Terriers and Schipperkes offered canine dieting experience saying: "I have had several Rotties

who needed to watch their weight. This can be hard, they start to tear up things in the yard or pester the daylights out of you if you cut back their ration of food too quickly. I reduce their meal size gradually. I reduce their food by a teaspoon at a time, without increasing their treats. I give small treats whenever they come in from outside and when we leave them alone I hide a treat or two in a 'molecule ball'.

"Cheerios are a good substitute for biscuits. The dog sees that he is still getting a treat, but a Cheerio is tiny compared to a whole dog biscuit. I add French cut string beans to the reduced size serving of dry kibble for one of my Border Terriers to fill him up.

"I think weight gain is breed-related to some degree, like human families: some families gain weight more readily than others. Some seem to be far more efficient in burning calories, sounds like a survival trait to me. And some breeds are more active and burn it off more readily, i.e. Border Collies."

Bulldogs Often Boast Portly Dignity

Next I asked two Bulldog owners how they attacked the battle of the bulge. Susan Rodenski of Semper Fidelis Bulldogs, shared her canine weight control tips, saying, "Bulldogs (especially as they age) tend to put on weight. This is particularly true if they are the only dog in the house. Allowing a dog to eat too much is literally 'killing them with kindness'.

"With our bulldogs, we start them on a 'reduced calorie' or 'senior' dry kibble at one year of age. When a dog is not an active dog, the reduction

of calories seems to keep extra weight from piling on as he ages. If our dogs, who are on this low calorie diet, act hungry, I add a can of green beans or a non-starchy vegetable that is in season."

"For treats, I tell advise dog owner's to measure out the dog's daily portion of dog food and to use the dry kibble as a training treat. It never hurts to make them work for their treats: "sit" or "lie down" for any treat teaches the dog his manners while he gets a reward. "

Another dog mom known for Bulldog love offered 'the mother is in charge of the food bowl!' advice. Cathi Allison, who owns Dog

GENTEEL HUMANS

Dayz of Fredericksburg, and is owned by four pleasingly thin canines told me: "My dogs aren't overweight. They give me sad eyes asking for treats, but I don't feed them all that much. If they do get a lot of treats (due to training or an especially generous cookie-giving customer day at the shop) I cut their evening meal back.

"Benedick has been forty-five to forty-eight pounds his entire adult life, and Bulldogs are one of the breeds that a lot of people allow to get fat. I firmly believe that his staying thin is one of the reasons he is so healthy at age eleven.

"Pumpkin is on strict rations as well, since due to auto-immune related joint problems, she cannot exercise much. At fifty five pounds, she gets a strict 2 cups of high quality food a day with a few smaller biscuits for treats.

"All of my dogs are spayed/neutered, and still, no one is overweight! I think the idea that 'spaying causes weight gain' is too often used as an excuse to over-feed the dog. It's like dieting for people, if you are gaining weight, you have to eat less and exercise more.

"I see so many overweight dogs come through my store and I feel bad for them. Even though I sell treats and I know that dogs love the treats, treats are best given in moderation. Food is not love at my house: belly rubs and butt scratches are love, and calorie free!"

Sometimes The Truth Does Hurt

I am taking to heart the weight control advice of strangers, loved ones and experienced dog mothers who know how to raise a healthy, carefully fed canine. Good luck to all of you who take up this dog love commitment with me. Less snacking. More walks.

Hand us a green bean, will you?

3

Your Dog Is Watching: Dogs Have Told Me This

"Good friendships are fragile things and require as much care as any other fragile and precious things."
Randolph Bourne

Humans Behaving Badly:
A Dog's Eye View

"Heaven goes by favor. If it went by merit, you would stay out and your dog would go in."
Mark Twain.

I recently invited four dog friends to cast an appraising eye upon a class of dog obedience graduates. My dog-wise judges were: Duffy C., a Springer Spaniel; Sibelle W. a Toy Poodle; Pumpkin A., a Pit Bull Terrier; and, Maggie and Mollie R., Toy Poodle sisters.

Dog judges were asked to make notes of any misbehavior that they believed called for retraining.

To my surprise, when I collected the score sheets, I saw that the dogs had evaluated the human dog trainer's behavior at the graduation, and had not been moved to comment upon the work of the graduating canines. Here lies lesson one:

Point of view lies with the beholder. Never take for granted that the behavior you, the human, sees is the behavior being acted upon by the dog.

For every human who has announced in a dog-obedience class, or anywhere else, "This dog is stupid", let me put you on notice that, while your dog cannot speak up to comment on his assessment of your understanding of the dog's viewpoint, your timing and praising skills, or all the other capacities and failings that only our dogs se, your dog is listening. Your dog is reacting to your actions. Here are a few behavior assessments and suggestions from a dog's-eye view.

A Dog Is Listening, by Duffy C.
What's with all the insults to these nice dogs? No one ever looks smarter when they cast aspersions on the dog at the other end of the leash. Like your granny surely said, "If you can't say anything nice, don't say anything at all."

Calling a dog insulting names and belittling his intelligence makes the owner look bad. Speak kindly. Offer commands firmly and gently. If the dog stares at you as though "sit" is a mystery to him, raising your volume will not teach him the command. Gently, with your hands on the dog, guide the dog's back, head, feet and bottom into the position. When your dog does not respond to your words, assume that you need to show him what to do. Dog training takes as long as it takes. Shouting, belittling, shaming

YOUR DOG IS WATCHING

and blaming will only teach your dog that he would rather not be trained by you.

Quit nagging. Stop begging. Resolve to ask the dog to do something one time. If the dog does not do what you asked, assume he does not understand the words you are saying. Get down on the floor and show the dog.

If you are in a class situation, make sure you are really talking to your dog and not chatting with another dog's owner. Ask yourself, "Am I paying the dog as much attention as I am asking him to pay to me?" Show him. Praise the dog. Reward the dog. Stop talking to him in whines and wheedles. Your voice tells the dog whether you are the leader. If you are a whiner or a beggar, your dog will learn to tune you out. He may also show you that you are not worthy of his attention by being more interested in other dogs or in strangers. No one voluntarily listens to a constant whiner.

Don't Judge A Dog By Outside Appearances, by Sibelle W.

I was not able to concentrate on this batch of graduates because the humans had very poor social skills. Several of the humans allowed their dogs to invade my space and frighten me. This happens to me so many times when I am out in public that I have told my mother that this will be my last outing as a judge. Just because I am small, cuddly, have a waggy tail and soft, brown eyes does not mean that I welcome unknown dogs kissing me in the mouth. Who knows where their lips have been? Not on me, please.

Dog owners, please do not assume that every dog you meet wants your dog to kiss him, nudge him, pant on him, nor sniff his bottom. Sometimes the most cuddly–looking fluff of a dog would just as soon bite your dog's nose off as look at him. Many dogs, whether they are huge or tiny, can be very protective of their body space and pecking order among strangers. Just because your dog plays well with others does not excuse the very bad manners of kissing and sniffing every dog he passes. Keep him on leash, a short leash, not one of those cursed reel out and misbehave flexible leashes. Your eyes and your attention are best placed on your dog in all public settings.

Better Speak with Your 'Outside' Voice by Pumpkin A.

I enjoyed seeing the humans concentrate on their tasks. I find humans to be trainable and affable.

YOUR DOG IS WATCHING

My pet peeve for this class of Homo Sapiens had to do with lack of discretion and a sad state of social, communication skills.

I am acquainted with a wise woman who coined  the admonishment, "You are talking with your 'in your head' voice'. Better speak to me with your 'for the public' voice'." Gentle human, when you are out in the wide world discoursing and sharing opinions, what comes into your mind does not always have to be spoken to your unsuspecting listener.

It is rude, and sometimes 'fighting words' to approach a stranger and state an unfavorable opinion or assessment of their dog. As a Pit Bull Terrier, even though I have graduated from obedience schools, earned my canine good citizen and therapy dog titles, I often hear insults to large and powerful breeds when I am out in public.

If you are afraid of a certain breed of dog, or you have had a bad experience with a specific breed, please keep 'inside your head' thoughts to yourself when you are outside your personal circle of acquaintance.

My mother should not have to tie bows to my collar to try to shape other humans' behavior to

approach me with a smile on their faces. Please treat every dog you meet as you would have others treat your nice dog.

Body Language Speaks Volumes
by Maggie and Molly R (canine sisters)

It was our pleasure to watch the dogs walk beside their owners on their loose leashes. Some of the dogs and humans were so in tune to each other that it was obvious that they had done their homework, and that they enjoyed their training partnership.

Owner body language is the behavior skill that these humans could improve. As 5 pound dogs, we are most sensitive to what the giant humans do around us.

Human trainers, especially those who have made the excellent choice to live with and train a tiny dog, must constantly remember that we may be huge in character, but we can be very fragile.

We are breakable. We may have fears of self-protection.

No dog enjoys a big human looming over him. Get down on a dog's level when you interact with him. Consider whether your movements or body posture could threaten or worry a dog.

We have learned to be wary of small children, who can be too rough, too frenetic in their movements, and often just plain inconsiderate. We are not pleased when strangers pick us up and wave us around in the air like stuffed toys. We are all dog, with all the dog worries and territory concerns of bigger dogs. Many small dogs learn to bite because they are forced to remind inconsiderate or ignorant humans that being small does not invite being treated like a plaything.

Thank You, Wise Watchers

The dogs who came to judge the humans taught me that a dog is always watching. Watching for cues, for training, for invitations to play.

Listen to your dog. He does not need human words to teach you all you need to know about being his best friend.

Comb
Your Beard
And Sit
Real Still

*"I would rather see a portrait of
a dog that I know, than all the
allegorical paintings they can show
me in the world."*
Samuel Johnson

Whew! It was too scorching hot to run into the backyard and hunt for turtles. All I, a little gentleman dog, wanted to do was stretch out on the cool, leather sofa and stare at the front door. Maybe Lorin, our UPS man, would ring the bell and bring us a box of dog goodies.

Speaking of boxes, as hot as it was this summer, do you think my mother would sit still? The dog days of summer didn't wilt mother's search for dog activities. Even if I could talk, I wouldn't have let her down and said what I was thinking: "Please, Mom, let us lie here and rest until the heat wave breaks."

That very moment, I saw Mom huffing, tugging and perspiring while she dragged a big box from the attic. My older canine sister, Vivien,

 64

dogged Mom's heels. As a spaniel, I was blissfully content to lounge on the davenport and await instruction. Vivien, a herding dog, demands to be right in the midst of all plans as they unfold.

What Lurks In Yonder Box?
"Dog Hats," the box says. Vivien told me that. Viv predicts that the dog hatbox can mean only one thing for us: We might as well prepare to have our picture taken.

Dogs experienced in being photographed recognize a Halloween picture shoot in the works. We can expect the fall portrait session early this year.

Quinnton says that more than boredom has triggered hats, cameras and backdrops to appear: "Mom judged the Fredericksburg Parks and Recreation Department's annual photography show and contest, and she has had dog pictures on her mind ever since."

All the dazzling poses of Shetland Sheepdogs leaping in snow, Shih Tzus with elaborate hair-do's, and cats in action set Mom afire to photograph us.

Dressed For The Camera
Quinnton has posed as a pumpkin, a Santa's elf, the Easter Bunny and Cupid several times over his 12 year partnership with our mother. My first year on earth, she dressed all of us up as shiny Christmas-tree ornaments, attached us by ribbons to the tree in the front yard, and

impressed upon us what fun it was to be stars on a Christmas greeting card.

If you live in a home with a human caretaker and a camera, you must know the signs that you are about to startled with flash, laughably costumed and wheedled sweetly to "Sit pretty!" Quinnton, Vivien and I offer you these clues that your time for a portrait is approaching.

Prepare For The Bath
The telltale bath tip-off is when Mom rolls a big, rubber nonslip bath mat into the tub, then covers the bathroom floor with towels. If an unsuspecting dog, lacking powers of observation, has followed her into the bathroom during this preparation, woe unto that canine when she closes the door. You might as well jump into the tub, pal, because a shampoo is coming. Be sure to clean the corners of our eyes to make us close-up ready.

Create Open Space For A Studio
Mom's idea of home decoration includes no less than twenty books stacked around her chair, six or eight stacks of books on the hearth near her chair, with piles of magazines spread around her. When you waggle up to kiss her on the knee, you have to tread watchfully or you will ski across the rug as the magazine mountains slide beneath your paws. When our mom begins de-cluttering, we know a spectacular event is going down. Neat is not a word Mom has much use for, nor aspiration to become. We have heard her exclaim when returning home from a tidy

home, "Wonder how they find time to play with the dog?"

Clutter, hair balls, scattered dog toys and the general detritus that accumulates while communing with dogs can make the backdrop for one's portrait too distracted.

The wall and floor around our posing area is clean, and free of distractions. Mom is partial to anchoring us to our ancient ball and claw-foot dining-room table. She says that generations of Ferrell dogs have been tied to these massive legs and corralled for portraits. Thank goodness we do know what "sit" and "down" mean.

The Right Light
A velvety marine-blue blanket goes under our paws as a clutter-free backdrop. Windows that would shine light behind us are covered. Backlight is a tricky component to use in the home portrait.

We do need as much light as we can get to light our eyes and keep our faces from looking flat and bored. We are not solid black dogs, thank goodness, as Mom says taking a great picture of a black dog is a feat to challenge any would-be portraitist. In times of concern regarding "will the light be right?" we advise you to set up your posing station outdoors in early-morning or in late-afternoon light. Soft light with a bit of fill flash illuminates details and produces delightful color reproduction.

Look Into The Camera

Our photo advice to dogs is, "You might as well look into that lens and get it over with!" Fast is a key word for photographing your canine pal. No yelling. No name-calling. Your dog wants the photo project to be finished way more than you do.

Make dog-captivating noises. Squeal, sigh and whistle. Wave squeaking toys. Toss toy balls or interesting objects high above your head. Have an assistant stand or kneel behind you to call our name. Make sure the assistant has a willing personality. Unwilling, sullen assistants do not amuse dogs.

Get A Dog's Eye View

Look us in the eye with your camera. Either get down to face-level, or elevate your dog. Can't put your finger on why your dog pictures never quite thrill you? Probably, you need to get the camera lens straight across from our doggy eyes.

Peanut Butter Ends Panting

"Please shut your mouth!" Vivien always whispers to me. Humans prefer a picture with the dog's tongue tucked inside his mouth. Panting shots are rarely attractive. A dab of peanut butter on the roof of the dog's mouth will often make for a pleasing closed lip expression. Have your assistant dab the peanut butter while the photographer squats eye to lens, ready to snap the picture.

Costumes, Props And Disposition

Many dogs find that their owners are not temperamentally suited to crawling around, repeated gentle posing, light placement, dog attention captivating and pose designing that we dogs require from our canine photographer. Our tip: If taking the dog's picture makes you anything but delighted, do not undertake the canine portrait shoot. Gather your props, holiday decorations, hats, fake flower arrangements, favorite dog toys and delicious biscuits and transport your gorgeous canine to a professional.

As for me, my mom is calling my name. I have to go and let bumble-bee antennae be tied to my head. Looks like I am going to be a bee. Vivien gets to be a flower. Quinnton announced he is wearing a crown and is going to be the king bee.

We dogs do a whole lot to keep our mother entertained. That's our job, and we are going to do it.

Should Your Dog Like You?

"In order to really enjoy a dog, one doesn't merely try to train him to be semi-human. The point of it is to open oneself to becoming partly a dog."
Edward Hoagland.

What does your face look like to your dog? Our dogs spend most of their lives staring up into our faces with 'What will you do next?' expressions. Your dog is probably watching you right this minute.

Try this: Look at your dog. Stand up. Did your dog turn his head toward you? I tried this behavior–reaction experiment. All three of my dogs disrupted their endless vigil hoping a squirrel would scamper across the deck. Three faces turned rapt attention my way and stood up in anticipation that Mamma might leave the room.

Your facial expressions mean the world to your dog. If you look like a storm cloud, your dog may perceive threat in your expression. Worried dogs often respond with canine behaviors that

 70

reflect the stressful emotions they read from their humans.

Your Dog Is Always Watching Your Expression

When obedience and behavior consultation clients tell me, "He knows exactly what he did wrong" or, "He knew he'd be in trouble," I know that the dog in question probably lives with a person who has an expressive face that the smart dog has learned to read. Imagine this: You walk in your door, see a chewed belonging or a puddle of urine. I doubt you begin to smile and coo at your dog.

Only a very stupid dog has not learned by early puppyhood to know what an angry human face looks like. How do dogs learn what other dogs are thinking and what they are about to do? They learn to watch and respond to every nuance of lip curl, tooth display, eye contact and head and body posture.

Consider what your face looks like to your dog. Smile at your dog. Beam at him like you love him. When your dog pleases you, make sure you give him just as many smiles and kind words for good behavior as you ever give him reprimands when you are not pleased with him.

Obtain a copy of "On Talking Terms With Dogs: Calming Signals" by Turid Rugass for an eye-opening, relationship–building understanding of learning to read your dog's facial expressions.

How Does Your Voice Sound To Your Dog's Ears?

After your dog sizes up whether your eyes are staring and your lips are pulled straight in a grimace, he listens for obvious cues to your mood demonstrated by your voice. *Dictionary. com* defines 'paralanguage' as "properties of speech, such as speaking tempo, vocal pitch, and intonational contours, that can be used to communicate attitudes or other shades of meaning."

Dogs, since they do not speak in human words, are very dependent on their interpretation of their humans' 'paralanguage.' Pity the dog that lives day in, day out with a dog owner whose voice is nearly always a whine. Resolve to stop whining at, pleading with or begging your dog. The dog probably does not understand your actual words, but he may be stressed by tones that say his pack leader thinks we are all in trouble.

Dogs live in constant stress if their owner's voice signals to the dog that he has to shoulder the burden of taking charge of his should-be pack leader. Make sure that your tone, when speaking with your dog, does not sound like you are a littermate pleading for the dog to take charge. Leaderless dogs get into trouble trying to lead the pack.

Develop your calm, upbeat, happy voice in your daily talks with your dog. Try not to coo or beg all the time. Use your voice to let your dog know that life at your house is safe and good.

How Does Your Body Language Look To Your Dog?

Human height is overwhelming when you are dog-sized. A dog may feel anxious or threatened by some body postures. When your veterinarian places your dog onto an examination table, he is accomplishing more than saving his back from bending over to examine the dog. He is keeping his body straight and refraining from hovering over the dog. Your vet is probably not going to suddenly lunge down and stare into the dog's eyes.

All of us want to train and own dogs who are so well socialized and sound of temperament that hovering, staring and confronting do not bring about a dog bite. We must acknowledge realistic dog-reaction tendencies. Canine behavior observation teaches that a dog needs

and deserves respect for his personal body space. I don't want a stranger to hover over me and stare into my face, do you? I don't want an unknown person to run up and kiss me on the mouth while I stand in line at the movies, do you? Dogs are living creatures. Dogs deserve respect for their space.

Can You Be Still?

Where your body, especially your hands, are in relation to your dog is a big deal to your dog when he considers whether an interaction is safe and acceptable. Dogs were bred to do jobs: hunting, chasing, herding, guarding, etc. Most of these jobs have honed dogs' visual acuity to moving objects and sudden motion. Respect a dog's sensitivity and likely reaction to motion. Consider where your arms and hands are and what your hands are doing when you train him, walk him, interact with him.

Learn to fold your leash neatly, rather than allow it to flap around beside his face, when you walk him. Keep him on a very short lead in public. Realize that you are teaching him to pull you when you allow him yards of leash for pull distance.

Guard your dog from the running and whirling of small children, especially if he is unaccustomed to the motion frenzy of child's play.

YOUR DOG IS WATCHING

Never swat at him with your hand, foot, nor a rolled-up newspaper. Threatening, sudden movements entering your dog's keen peripheral vision can be frightening. A dog that has never offered to put his teeth on anything other that a biscuit or dog bone may be triggered to use his teeth to stop a moving object that suddenly appears to rush past his head. "Slowly" and "calmly" are the key words for how to approach and touch a dog.

Does Your Dog Feel Pushed Aside?

Honestly, how many times a day do you take a minute of two and talk to your dog? Not talk at him, but stop, make pleasant eye contact and let him hear a voice that sounds friendly?

Too many dogs are starving for their human to let them know with a bit of time and action that the human is so very glad this dog came to share their life. Pledge to put a minute or two into your morning, evening and bedtime routine to stop and talk with your dog.

Put on your coat and walk around the edges of your fenced yard with him. If he relieves himself, praise him as though he has created gold from base metal. If you have a little scamper in your own soul, skip over to him, frolic away from him. Invite him to chase you to the door. Stop and magically produce a cookie from your bathrobe or coat pocket. Think less about your dear dog acting human. Meet him more than halfway: Show him you know a thing or two about playing like a dog.

Walk A Mile In His Paws

Make a promise to your good, faithful, adoring dog that you will try to be more doglike and that you will expect him to be less humanlike. Ask not what your dog can do to please you. Ask what you have taught him by your own behavior that has made him more pleasing to you. If ever you are on the brink of yelling at him for a mistake, stop. Chastise yourself for reprimanding when you could be training. Remember this dog wisdom: You get the dog you deserve.

Cat House Rules:
Sam the Cat Speaks Out

"Every animal knows more than you do."
Native American Proverb.

Sam, watches for dogs, high atop his favorite perch. With home made cat tree, cat-perfect water fountain, and dinner at the ready, life is good; even if dogs are watching.

My mother has taken my abominable canine companions, Vivien, the incessant herder-barker, and detestably curious Gabriel away to a dog show. The elder dog, Quinnton, is my friend and he has stayed here with me. While my young tormentors are gone, and since I hide behind my mother's desk most of the time anyway, tonight I have found the coast clear of canine poking paws and sniffing noses and shall speak my feline mind.

77

DEVOTED TO DOGS

Being a cat, I am smarter than dogs. I scoff at how easy it is to outwit my canine halfwit house-mates.

Why would my nice, seemingly intelligent mother and father, want to share my home with silly, troublesome dogs? 'Tis a puzzlement to a cat. Alas. Looks like the Spaniel and the Collie are here to stay. I intend to present my human parents with my "Cat House Rules" as soon as I see them again.

Rule One: My Litter Pan Is Not A Dog Buffet

What's up with these nasty dogs who cannot pass by my toilet without confusing it with a fast food drive through? I accepted long ago that the canine race could not be fathomed, but their invasion of my personal litter box leaves me hissing and stomping my paw.

Mother has attempted to remedy this invasion of my personal space. She has given me a covered litter box. Our family room has a long built-in bar, where thank heavens, my covered litter box now rests. A sturdy baby gate denies dog access behind the bar, and finally, has thwarted those black dog noses that so love to snuffle in my clumping clay.

Mother learned that the box needs to be emptied every day, without fail. A clean litter pan offers nosy dogs less interest to sniff and snack in my private box.

A clean litter area prevents me from having to seek a dry, hygienic place of my own choosing to relieve my kitty needs. Mother trains quickly. I was forced to urinate on the clean floor under her desk when my box was not cleaned daily. A quick read of "Clinical Behavioral Medicine for Small Animals", by Dr. Karen Overall, retrained mother to have a better understanding of why I was not using my litter pan, and how to entice me back to more acceptable behavior.

Rule Two: Give A Cat His Privacy
Some cats, especially if they grow from kitten-hood with polite dogs, may love their dogs. I am not one of them. I was here when the new dogs arrived. During my kitten youth I had an older dog brother, Abroham, who was a prince among dogs. He left me alone. I left him alone. Mornings, if the sun shone just right through the glass front door, Abroham and I would find ourselves sunning and napping, butt to butt. We did not cavort together. We did not cuddle, nor forget that we were cat and dog. Abroham had dignity. I had my space.

The young dogs do not have a speck of cat sense. They worry me. They have no regal bearing. A dignified, brilliant cat such as myself deserves privacy and to be admired from afar. It took my mother a few chewed plants, scratched sofa arms and hair-rubbed chairs to get the message that I was stressed and speaking ill of her young dogs.

Mom procured a tall, heavy, industrial shelving unit at a discount store. The shelves were made

79

of a lightweight, but very sturdy PVC material,

that assembled easily. My human dad used his saw to cut cat–sized square openings in the center of the top two shelves so that I can climb from shelf to shelf. Mom used the hot glue gun to stick shelf–sized pieces of carpet remnants to my shelves. Holes cut into to the carpet, turned the big five shelf storage unit into a very affordable, cat friendly cat tree.

Privacy at last. Try as they might, those pesky dogs cannot climb my tree, nor sample my food. I perch on the top of the carpeted top shelf and smirk at the silly dogs who come and sit and stare at me.

Rule Three: My Food Is Mine

Dogs try to steal my food. Cat food smells yummier than dog food, I admit. Dogs will eat just about anything. They are not subtle in their tastes. Cats are. Do not let your dogs eat your cat's food. It makes for bad cat relations. The cat food is not formulated for healthy dog nutrition.

Rule Four: High Places
Are Good Cat Spaces

Surely, if you have cats and dogs, you can find one high spot for a cat to find peace from dog curiosity.

The top of the washing machine or dryer is a nice high spot for a cat food bowl. A bathroom vanity offers a tall protected cat place. Walk around your house and make high nests for your cat. Give in to the cat's will to jump and rest in peace. Add a small rug for cat comfort. Make it easier for the cat to take off and land. Every cat needs his own elevated resting place.

Rule Five: A Cat Demands Cleanliness

Face it, dog lovers, those pooches that you pander to can be paragons of pools of leaves, puddles of mud and piles of odiferous dog hair. Many smelly dogs will roll in putrid remnants of foul offal.

Not only am I willing to keep my cat self clean, but I would appreciate it so much if you will keep pristine all my food bowls, water containers, potty areas and sleeping mats. Running water for my drinking needs would thrill me. Have you seen those kitty water fountains? Better than a dripping faucet and just my cup of tea.

Rule Six: Protect Me From Danger, Please

I cannot be responsible for the boundless curiosity and often brainless wild antics of dogs. But I can ask that you protect me from the many cat dangers that lurk in home, garage and yard.

- *Antifreeze*
  Check everywhere you park a vehicle that uses anti-freeze to make sure that none of this deadly liquid calls to me. Anti-freeze is deathly sweet and has needlessly killed many of my cat brothers and sisters. Protect me from it. While you are thinking about this liquid danger, make an appointment with your car mechanic to change your anti-freeze to safer formulas created with cats, dogs and human children's safety in mind.

- *Choking By Hanging and Tangled In Cords*
  Walk about your home checking for long or loose cords. Blinds, pull up shades, electrical cords. Many cats die from choking on long cords. Paws caught in cat-tantalizing strings and loops make for emergency situations. Protect me from hanging myself with my own collar. Make sure my collar is a "break-away "or elastic design.

- *Suffocation in Clothes Dryers and Trapped in Washing Machines*
  Teach everyone in my cat home to close all doors to washers, dryers, cabinets, closets, and discarded appliances. Make sure that no cat is cat napping inside.

- *Maimed and Killed By Dogs*
  Some dogs are deadly to cats. A cat may seem no different than any other prey animal to some dogs. Cats need fences, too. Supervise us to see that we do not jump over our fence. Make sure that no unknown dogs can enter our yards and homes. The most brilliant cat is no match for teeth and paws of a dog that is ready to chase him down and tear him to bits.

Rule Seven : I Am Not A Dog
Please do not treat me like a small, smart, agile dog in a cat suit. I must never take medicines that the veterinarian has prescribed for a dog in the household, unless the veterinarian has given his advise to do so. Many medicines that heal the dog may kill me.

Usually, I do not want to rough house and be played with as you would those goofy dogs. Be gentle with me. Let me decide how and when to play. Buy cat toys, cat food, cat products for me. Protect me from untrained human children. A cat word for human children may be: enemy.

Rule Eight : When In Doubt, Ask My Veterinarian
Never guess about whether or not I am sick, or why I am behaving in any suspicious fashion. Take me to my veterinarian.

Rule Nine : Blame is a Losing Behavior Game
You say misbehavior. I say stress and anxiety. I cannot speak human words. I am uable to tell

DEVOTED TO DOGS

you that dogs are tormenting me, or that a too-full litter box has made me refuse to use the box, or that I am lonely, frightened, or bored. To communicate my needs, my dislikes, and my anxieties, I will have to use my teeth, claws, voice, and bathroom choosing abilities.

If I appear to be misbehaving, please try and understand me. Do not blame or punish me. I am a brilliant, affectionate creature and need your devotion to my opinions and needs.

Read my cat rules, to your dogs, will you? Not that I think those silly dogs will understand the rules; but at least you can reprimand them for breaking the rules since you, the human, are in charge of all of us.

4

Especially For Old Dogs

"The bond with a true dog is as lasting as the ties of the earth can ever be."
Konrad Lorenz

86

Old Dog Comforts

"When all is done and said, in the end
thus shall you find, he most of all doth
bathe in bliss that hath a quiet mind,
clear from worldly cares, to deem can
be content, the sweetest time in all his
life in thinking to be spent."
Lord Thomas Vaux

Have you searched the clouded eyes and grizzled muzzle of a dear, elderly dog and wished for more time?

We cannot indefinitely prolong our dog's number of days. We can pledge to enhance our old dog's enjoyment of the time he has left.

There is no finer solace when his time comes to die than to realize that you demonstrated that nothing came before his comfort, his health care and his peace of mind.

Old Dogs: Our Friends, Our Protectors

When you look into the face of your old dog, you see more than trust and a gentle heart. You see your life with him reflected back to you. Old dogs have loved us when we were sad, steadied us during life's turbulent challenges and watched us age along with them.

They have enjoyed, endured and enhanced every part of our human family's history. An honest heart demands that we give back to our old dogs in their dotage the attention they unfailingly gave us every hour of their lives.

Old Habits Offer Comfort

Old dogs find comfort in habits and experiences that require our time and commitment to guide them gently into comfortable old age. As canine friends approach the end of their gentle lives, they require more of our attention to their comforts. They need more time for settling in comfortably beside us, content to know we are there.

The Best Care: Your Gentle Hands

Old dogs like hands-on love. Carve 10 minutes from your hectic day to get your hands on your old dog. Make him comfortable on or near your lap. Gently groom him. Feel for lumps, bumps, heated areas, painful spot, any signals that a veterinary checkup could improve his health and your peace of mind. Your veterinarian has known him all of his life and is the person who can assess changes in his teeth, body systems, metabolism and general vigor.

Let Your Veterinarian Help

Perhaps your dog is troubled by aches and pains that could be alleviated with a prescription the veterinarian recommends. Every six months is not too frequent to visit your trusted dog doctor for guidance to lead your geriatric friend into a healthy and pain-reduced old age.

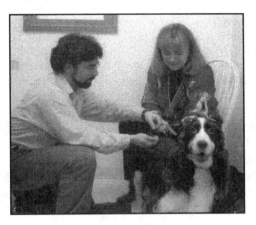

Acupuncture: Relief and Comfort

Consider acupuncture and other auxiliary therapies that your veterinarian may recommend to ease geriatric aches and complaints. One day every month, my older dog, Quinnton, and I head to Northern Virginia for Quinnton to enjoy an acupuncture treatment at South Paws Veterinary Clinic by Dr. Jordan Kocen. The acupuncture treatment certainly eases Quinnton's increasing creaks and pains. Dogs are forthright in their reactions to their caregivers. The moment Quinnton sees Dr. Kocen, he wags his tail and sidles up to him with a dog smile on his face. (If you have any doubt that dogs are capable of showing emotion by facial expression, I would refer you to a fabulous book, "On Talking Terms With Dogs," by Turid Rugaas.) Our monthly car trip is an opportunity for Quinnton to be the center of attention with his mom. We call his acupuncture trip his "orthopedic tune-up."

Acupuncture Day Is Quinnton's Day

I have chores I should be doing or other ideas of entertainment. But I will have only one Quinnton. Everything else that calls for my attention can wait. One day each month, I attempt to make a payment of my time and attention for all the devotion and companionship the brown-freckled sweetheart has given me. He has taught hundreds of obedience classes at my side. He has graciously, patiently, posed for thousands of photographs. He has been my work partner and has never called in sick or bored. He always shows up ready to serve and befriend.

Quinnton is 11. There is no turning back to add activities to his youth and middle age. There is time to let him know that he is everything to me. One trip per month for his acupuncture therapy is my gift of attention and care to him.

Investigate and Celebrate: His Health And Nutrition

Although his hearing is diminished and he creaks when he rises, the elder dog can often hurl himself up off the floor with determined and delighted effort when he hears the food pan rattle.

FOR OLD DOGS

"Here comes the highlight of my day!" is his response to impending dinner. Ask your veterinarian about geriatric foods, supplements and other ways to tantalize his elderly palate. How much bother would it be to stir-fry lean turkey, if your veterinarian feels his nutrition could benefit? Lackluster appetite may experience a new lease on dinner with a few minutes of culinary care. Be scrupulous regarding whether health information actually comes from a medical/scientific source. Act upon all unusual behaviors and discomforts. Let your veterinarian decide if he is sick. Old dogs deserve immediate care.

Take Care Where Your Old Dog Sleeps
Give your venerable companion the best bed in the house, not necessarily your bed. Does he prefer to throw his head up on a bolster, or a thick orthopedic bed? Is he less restless if his bed is next to your bed? Are his old joints warm enough? When sleeping is an aged friend's primary activity, a special bed is his due. If he

can no longer hop onto old haunts, the sofa (if he is allowed to go there) or your own bed, consider a step to make his leap less taxing to his aching joints.

Steps, Ramps And Brainstorming For Comfort

Robert Johnson, fine dog daddy and wise dog man of Spotsylvania County, Virginia heard me moaning about needing a step for Quinnton to use to jump onto my high bed. Johnson smiled and explained I didn't need a special step. He told me to move an ottoman from a chair in the den next to the bed. Eureka! A perfect launch pad for Quinnton to regain the bed that serves as his squirrel and driveway lookout station. Survey your dedicated dog–loving friends. Ask them, "What did you do to make your old dog more comfortable?" Hints from dog dads and moms may surprise and delight you.

Nourish His Spirit

What does an old dog want? You and your undivided attention. Keep an old–dog diary. Start his "Life Story" scrapbook. Record your thoughts about him, his responses to bodily changes, weight, appetite, toilet habits, environment. Talk to him. Be quiet and listen to his breathing.

Old Dogs Are A Breed's Future

When you buy a puppy, ask the breeder how old all canine grandparents lived to be. Inquire about the health, vitality and current life situations of the breeder's old dogs when you interview breeders or consider breeding to their dogs.

FOR OLD DOGS

Remember the sage advice: As trots the mare, so goes the foal. Often the best insurance that a pup will age to be healthy and happy can be seen in the way the pup's mother and father have fared with the passing of time.

A responsible breeder who has dedicated life, finances and hopes to making a breed healthier and happier will welcome your health questions. If a breeder cannot tell you about the old dogs in the family, you may want to continue your search for the healthy puppy who will one day be your old dog.

Dedicated breeders often ask would-be puppy buyers, "How old did your last dog live to be?" Or, "Tell me about the dog you lost. How was his health in old age?" An inquisitive breeder is not trying to stir up sad memories. That wise breeder knows there are puppy buyers who will treasure a dog to the very end, and then there are less-careful owners who will discard, euthanize or neglect an old dog for reasons as shallow as, "He began to urinate on our good rugs. And we couldn't have that." If a breeder grills you with questions, count yourself fortunate. Chances are good you have found a breeder who will want to help you care for your dog till death do you part.

A Gentle Goodbye Is The Final Great Gift
Releasing an elderly canine friend to death will break your heart. Grief is easier to endure if you can envision his merry, old tail wagging as he watched you prove your esteem by your actions. Love him today like there is no tomorrow.

Battling The Bulge:
The Hips You Save May Be Your Dog's

"I came across a photograph of him not long ago. his black face, the long snout sniffing at something in the air, his tail straight and pointing, his eyes flashing in some momentary excitement. Looking at a faded photograph taken more than forty years before, even as a grown man, I would admit I still missed him."

Willie Morris

Is your older dog fat? Do you wish he could live forever?

Dog owners who strive to give their dogs long and pain-free lives must not over feed their dogs. Human table scraps, or feeding too many treats, adds more calories that most adult dogs can metabolize.

Repeat After Me, Please:
Food Is Not Love

Overfeeding our dogs is not kind. A fat dog is fat because an owner feels happiness seeing the dog respond to food. Food is not love. Food will ultimately make a dog fat. Obese canines often have shortened lives.

I enjoy nothing more than watching my Quinnton's face when he discovers a new food. He looks at me as if to say, "You humans are mystical beings. You have hands that can open the magic refrigerator. You stuff yourselves with abandon at will."

Fat Old Dogs: Painful Old Hips

With every extra ounce we allow ourselves to feed into our sweet, defenseless fat dogs, we may take days off their lives.

What wears out most often on a beloved old dog? His hips. Maybe his elbows. Often his spine, if he is a long backed breed.

The terrible day dawns when the geriatric dog's hips wear out. If there is anything worse than to have to make the decision to end the life a dog who just absolutely cannot hoist himself off the rug, nor take one more step into the yard he once commanded, I do not know what it is.

For a fat dog, hauling around extra blubber is a burden that limits his activity in the short term and steals time away from him in the long term.

My dog Quinnton is eight years old. He has had a cruciate ligament replaced. He has arthritis in his shoulder and elbow. He also is slightly dysplastic in one hip. My veterinarian knows that I want him to live forever.

Thin Is Good Active Is Great
Most weeks Quinnton gallops after squirrels, allows himself to be herded across the yard by a young Bearded Collie, and will chase his ball until human judgment is required to halt the frenzy before he collapses from exhaustion.

But some nights, he stands and stares at my tall bed and looks to me, as though to plead, "Could you put me up there? It's time to go to bed." I lift him up and I wonder, "Will he be limping tomorrow?"

I let him limp no more than one day, until I take him in to his doctor for a check up. Lately, we

drive home with a little bottle of anti-inflammatory pills. I give one a day for five days and then one every other day for five days. So far, the ten capsule regimen alleviates the pain for the little limper and he resumes romping, stomping and retrieving for a few months before stiffness and pain strike again.

Face Reality: Weigh Once Each Week
Each time we go to the doctor, I am reminded that is critical to his health and mobility that this dog stay trim and lean. Once a week I heave

him into my arms and the two of us step onto the scale.

With A Big Calendar Taped to The Side of My Refrigerator,

I record our weekly weigh-in. Quinnton's goal is to hover just under fifty pounds. Forty eight is our ideal. I know that every pound over goal weight will take weeks, months or more off the days this dear companion will be alive padding behind my every step.

Vegetables: Add Bulk To The Bowl, Not To The Dog

In order to cut back on the dry food ration and not face a starving dog, I serve three quarters of a cup of dry food, with a half cup of warm water mixed in. I deliver the bowl to Quinnton with a whole raw carrot, or a half cup of canned French cut green beans on the side.

Reducing the weight of your dog must be supervised by your veterinarian. Every dog needs a correct mix of nutrients and fresh, clean water. Let your veterinarian decide the ideal weight for your dog and help you formulate a weight loss and maintenance plan.

Danger: Don't Reduce The Dog Too Quickly

Often, pounds need to come off, but a dog must not loose too many pounds too quickly. Medical supervision is very necessary. Starving a dog is never, never safe nor healthy.

Carrots, green beans, canned pumpkin, frozen squash, and watermelon pieces are a few of the things that many dogs will wag their tails about and feel they have been given a treat. Many veterinarians sell reduced fat, high fiber dog treats for their dieting patients.

Lick Your Lips For Liver Dusted Diet Fare

For training treats, I have used low calorie human cereals: Cheerios, bran or rice squares, coated with a light dusting of freeze died liver.

Buy a very small container of freeze dried liver treats. Beat them to powder with your hammer or other smashing tool. Place a box of the low fat, plain cereal squares in a big bag or container and shake the liver dust onto the cereal. Suddenly you have a treat for training that smells like heaven to a dog but won't add as much fat to the unsuspecting dieter. Keep treats in an airtight container.

Treats: Smaller Pieces Are Best

Remember the rule for using treats as a training tool: the smaller the treat, the harder the dog will work to earn another.

Will your dog like healthy snacks more than pie, knockwurst and cookies? No, and neither do I. But as the dog mom I am capable of retraining the palate of the dog.

We, the owners who love dogs so and try to prolong their time on the Earth, are the ones who must feed them cautiously.

Protect The Dog You Love
With Healthy Feeding

Can we stop ourselves from the selfish gratification we feel when we see those eyes light up for a bite of bacon or one last bite of the pie we enjoyed? We can and we must.

The little dear soul that has been taught to beg, begs in ignorance. We know that excess fat will grind away his joints and shorten his cherished life.

Train your dog to love healthy snacks. Once the potato chips, steak fat, leftover sausage, and all the yummy human fattening foods vanish, a carrot stick will commence to look indescribably delicious.

Protect your dog from his joy of over eating. Soon, he'll be leaping into your lap and hoping for a salad.

Reawakening
The Old Dog

*"Treasure the love you receive above
all. It will survive long after
your good health has vanished."*
Og Mandino

Dogs love Easter. I have seen it in their faces. They know the crinkly cellophane–wrapped Easter baskets are being made for them. Surely the humans hiding treasures in the grass are thinking of a dog's natural talents for sniffing, finding, and retrieving.

Stuffed ducks and bunnies fit nicely in the jaws of good dogs who love to carry gifts from room to room thinking thoughts of spring.

"The English word 'Easter' and the German word 'Ostern' come from a common origin (Eostur, Eastur, Ostara, Ostar), which to the Norsemen

 100

meant the season of the rising (growing) sun, the season of new birth. The word was used by our ancestors to designate the Feast of New Life in the spring," says Francis X. Weiser in "Handbook of Christian Feasts and Customs."

Still Looking For Fun
Old dogs may have gray on their muzzles. Some have slowed their bunny–chase habits. But deep in a senior dog's heart there lives a pup ready to celebrate the coming of spring.

This Easter, mark your calendar to begin an "Old Dog Rejuvenation Program."

Plan At Least One Invigorating Activity Each Week.
By the time the heat of summer arrives to make all of us want to lie wilting on the lawn, your dog will be feeling the joys of the rites of spring.

A Warm, Gentle Bath Is Therapeutic
I have rarely seen an old dog (or a young dog) who did not perk up to scamper and frolic after a good, peaceful bath. "Peaceful," however is the key. If bath–giving makes you and the dog wish you were anywhere but in the suds, do not give the dog a bath as a pick–me–up.

Make sure there is a big rubber, nonslip bath mat in the bottom of the tub. Many dogs hate baths because they panic on slippery tubs. Keep the water temperature warm. If someone assures you, "dogs like cold water!" ask them how much they enjoyed times that the hot turned to cold and they landed with a surprise with their own tender parts sitting in cold bath water.

Use a mild, conditioning shampoo made for dogs. Human shampoo is not formulated for the pH of your dog's skin. Sure, some dogs may do fine with human shampoo. But why take the chance of irritating your old guy's possibly more delicate skin ? This is the rejuvenation and joy program, not the experimentation and convenience approach to dog care. If you have doubts about a gentle dog shampoo for your older fellow, ask your vet.

If your dog despises water in his ears, place a small cotton ball in the ears and you may see a much more cooperative bather.

After you have lathered him up and massaged him and coo'ed at him and kissed him on the head a lot, it is time to rinse. Rinse. Rinse. Rinse. The most important task in giving a shampoo is to make sure that no suds remain on the dog. Rinse for as long as you think necessary and then rinse some more.

Using a conditioner? Great. Make sure the conditioner is made for dogs and that you rinse completely.

Lift the dog from the tub. Stand back and let him shake. Cover the bathroom floors with layers of towels. Once he shakes to his fur's content, gather him up in a bath sheet and rub him all over. More head kissing is allowed during this rubbing extravaganza.

Now he will fly around the house. Rubbing his nose on the sides of sofas, chairs and bed skirts is an absolute must. If you worry about him getting your bed damp, cover it with an old bedspread or sleeping bag before the bathing celebration.

While the dog dashes about the house, rubbing, shaking and generally comporting like a young dog, you can use the wet towels in the bathroom to wipe dog–shake splatters off the walls, mirrors, doors and floors. You are rewarded for giving the rejuvenating bath by a cleaner bathroom and a happy, clean dog.

Now that you have a sparkling, frisky dog a few social activities may lift his spirits even more.

Invite Your Human Friends Who Love Him To Come And Visit

Most dogs have human friends they love to see. These are the humans who get down on the floor with them and talk to them as if they were better than human company.

I have a few friends whom I sometimes think come to my house just to rub my dogs and tell them dog secrets.

That is fine with me. These are the friends I like best, too. "Love me, love my dog" is the

DEVOTED TO DOGS

unvarnished gospel of how to be popular with dog lovers.

Never doubt that wisdom or you will not really have any dog-lover friends. We dog lovers may bite our lips off before we speak up in an angry retort, but criticize, repel or insult the dog and you will become a pariah at that beloved dog's house.

When the special dog-lover friend visits, make sure there are baked goodies for dogs and humans. Turn a blind eye if the friend feeds the dog a miniscule smidgen of cake, or a bitsy morsel of cookie. Cut back on his dinner after he enjoys a tea party afternoon. Put the other dogs in the house in their beds or crates. Let the older guy have the lovely human all to himself.

Shell Out Big Bucks For An Exquisite Bed

Old dogs love the new-style beds that have a bolster around three sides, or the beds that are a luxurious cushion within a stuffed circle. Old dogs like to lie out and fling their heads off to the side for support. They can regally watch the household activities without wasting the energy needed to raise their heads. Ask anyone who has a fondness for their recliner why they like that chair best, and you will get the dog's idea of why a bed that supports the head is better.

104

FOR OLD DOGS

Many a dog who has never owned a bed will demonstrate that he always wanted one when a bed appears in the den or the bedroom.

Once A Month (At Least!)
Devote A Day To Your Old Dog

Write his name on your calendar and devote that entire day to him. Maybe you would both like to lie on the bed while you read and he sleeps with his head thrown across you. You probably need a day of rest as much as the dog.

Maybe you will go for a walk in the woods. All dogs love the smells that leaves and squirrels and rabbits and birds have left waiting for them to find. Maybe you will go for a car ride and let him shop at his favorite dog store.

As spring comes back with sunny days and the pleasure of another season to pass with the dog that loves you, mark your calendar to put your old dog on a program to celebrate having him with you another year. Young dogs will not mind the springtime rejuvenation regime either. Too soon, much too soon, young dogs will be old dogs, too.

5

Never Can Say
Goodbye

*"I think God will have prepared
everything for our perfect happiness. If
it takes my dog being there
(in heaven) I believe he'll be there."*
Reverend Billy Graham

Love Her Like There Is No Tomorrow

"She who died as she had been born and as she had lived, in my care, and surrounded by those who loved her."
Vicki Fowler

Izobel woke up, ate her breakfast, collapsed and died. She was eight years old. Merry and gentle best describes her short life.

As a tiny puppy she chewed two things: corners of wash cloths, and her mother's underwear. The underpants went into the trash, but the wash cloths remain with us.

At the time of the tooth inflicted crimes, these terry cloth squares were damaged, but serviceable. Now, several years after Izobel's dying, they are treasures. When I retrieve a washcloth with chewed corners, a vision of the tiny Izobel explodes on the screen of my memory. There she is: eager, willing, completely lovable.

Where Do You Cry?

The bathtub is a fine place to cry. I miss her today as much as when I gaped in broken hearted disbelief the morning she died.

Losing an elderly dog is a totally different onslaught of grief than sudden death of a young dog.

There is no easy way to experience the roller coaster of emotion between an elderly loved dog and human caregiver–companion. How do you face the end of life for a dog that has loved you so? I have lived through weeks treading on months of despair, obsessing over the question, "Is today the day I must let him go?"

To be the best steward and companion of an old dog, whom you know must be released from an aging, pain–tortured body, wrings out your heart on a moment to moment basis. But you do see the loss coming. You can take care to give him perkier days on his up days, and to be at his side, silent and attentive, on his frail days I used to ask myself, "Is there anything worse to endure than ending the life of an elderly dog friend?"

Gone Forever In An Instant

Then, Izobel died. As we say in the South, "She up and died!" Suddenly, our family could compare and contrast the types of sadness to gradually give up an elderly, beloved, wise old boy who had lived his life to the very edge of frailty; versus the shock of not having one moment

to prepare to say goodbye to a little, smiling female dog who had lived to please.

Our Izobel died without a day of illness. She died within one month of the death of our aged and treasured 14 year old dog, Abroham. Our grief was crushing beyond description. After post–mortem examination, we learned that Izobel suffered from a cancer called a hemangiosarcoma.

No Schedule For Grief
Three years after her sudden death, my heart still lurches and I feel nearly faint if I try to examine how it felt to be slammed into the reality of accepting that the two dogs we loved so completely were gone.

Two grieving truths have come to me.
One: Dying from the pain of a broken heart just does not happen. The longing of willing Izobel to come back, for even an hour, throbbed with a physical pain in my chest. Surpassing the emotional trauma, I experienced a physical

111

reaction to grief that showed me why the phrase, "a broken heart", is understood by anyone who has ever had such sorrow cascade over them.

Two: My grieving recovery was based on reflection and celebration of her life. Not finding her in her bed in the sunshine when I came home for lunch brought daily sadness. To miss marveling at her joy as she would fling herself above my shoulders when she saw her food bowl arriving was nearly unbearable. Worst of all, was the unrelenting emptiness of not feeling her little Spaniel self mashed warmly up against my chest in bed at night, guarding my dreams, always there.

The Sadness Is Inescapable
Eventually, I realized that sadness is better explored than suppressed. Finally, I found a peace that came from letting my broken heart go ahead and probe the depths of the friendship wrenched from me.

Izobel's Journal
Night after night, when I could not sleep, I began a journal of Izobel's life. At first I wrote her long letters, talking to her as though she was not gone. I told her how I missed her. Next, I made a list of every good time I could remember her having. From puppy kindergarten class through two weeks before she died when she pranced and heeled, competing at the English Springer National show.

Happiness Relived
Memories unleashed an unfolding of nearly forgotten happiness. I remembered the instant that I met Izobel: three days old, tiny like a brown and white hamster, tucked against her mother, "Ringer". I drove to Manassas, VA, to breeder, Julie Hogan's kennel every Wednesday for six weeks until Izobel rode home seat belted inside her tiny blue dog kennel.

On the bookshelf before me sits the Izobel life journal. I have not allowed myself to re-read those pages examining a life so jubilantly lived, but that feels so unfinished.

She Will Always Remain
I did not willingly part with my Izobel. But I have total control over not ending my celebration of her life.

This very moment, with three young dogs piled under my desk, I look at them and wonder, "What would you like to do for fun tomorrow?"

DEVOTED TO DOGS

If I had to lose any one of them, what are the joys that I know they would like to have today?

Wise Dogs Teach: Live For Now

Find a blank book and make a "Live For Now" list of things to do, things to say, things to teach your dog. Maybe you want a perfect professional portrait of her? Make an appointment today. Perhaps you want your gentle dog to share his grace with nursing home residents who would give all they have to rub one more nice dog? Maybe you just want to mark a day off your schedule and spend a day on the sofa with her head in your lap?

Whatever you and your dog look forward to, make a plan. Make a promise. Live all the life she has.

"Grieve not.
Nor speak of me with tears.
Laugh and talk
As though I were beside you.
I loved you so,
'Twas heaven there with you."
Isla Richardson

Abroham's Legacy

"I have found that when you are deeply troubled, there are things you get from the silent devoted companionship of a dog that you can get from no other source."
Doris Day

One year has passed since my dog Abroham had to say his good byes and make his way to where ever it is that beloved dogs wait for us to find them and follow.

I can say without reservation, that if the key to the magic door to go where ever it is that my brave and gentle Abroham went was offered to me this minute, I would grab that key and unlock any door to join him.

I would not hesitate with worry that my human loved ones and other dogs would feel abandoned. I would invite them to go with me, over to where Abroham waits. If these loved ones decided they had things to do in the life we are living now, I would kiss them all goodbye and go on with Abe. That is how much I miss him. I can spend hours deep in the fantasy of joining him again.

He Comes In Dreams

Sometimes these reveries feel very real. Sometimes I get to touch his warm brown head and lay my cheek on his big velvet muzzle. He comes to me in dreams.

I cannot will these sleeping visions to come. I do not analyze when these visitations will transform a night of sleep to the realization of my heart's desire.

Sleep opens the door to a place where Abroham lays across my lap and it feels to me that I hear his thoughts. I see his short, merry Springer tail flutter in the glee that used to greet me afternoons when I unlocked the front door and he would raise his handsome head and recognize with delight that his friend was home again.

I have a dear friend who will occasionally ask me, "Has Abe come to you lately?" She says she would give anything to have these dream world meetings with a long gone, but hourly remembered, dog that left her too soon. I can tell from the way she asks her question that these lucid dreams of Abe's return to me feel like treasures to her and not like the ravings of a still grieving dog owner.

How Best To Say Good-Bye?
No matter when our dogs leave us, they leave too soon. Months before we knew it was time to part with Abe, as his body failed him and his devoted spirit clung to our hearts, my husband and I would drive around discussing the never answered question: "How is the easiest way to give them up?"

It is easier if they die in their sleep? Is it gentler on the hearts left behind if they are very sick and you know there is no choice but to let them go? Is it easier to part with them if death takes them suddenly? On and on.

The more dogs that love you, the more agonizing ways you face that you may have to part with them.

Hold On To Their Gentle Spirits

My conclusion, after great obsession on these quandaries, is that there is no easy way, no way without heartbreak, no way on Earth to part with a dog who has given his life to you.

They leave when they must. They wrench huge, gaping holes out of our hearts, out of our day to day reality and from our desire to continue loving them when the time dawns that their lives with us must end.

Perhaps our dog's shorter life spans teach us that physical life must recycle, must be born and die, but that memories and gifts of the spirit are the jewels that will always shine before us while we remain behind.

Surviving The Sadness

It seems to me that we can close our eyes and see any reality that we choose. The memory of Abroham makes me believe that surviving sadness and searching out dogs who also need us is one of the great responsibilities of those of us who love dogs.

These days, I am teaching my little Springer pup, Gabriel, to dash around the yard proudly carrying Abroham's hula hoop. Our other adored addition, Vivien the Bearded Collie, recently went downtown to the dog store and choose the biggest toy there to drag home and around the house. I can remember Abroham dragging huge toys with the same pride and I wonder if Abe's always whimsical spirit came to Vivien, saying ,"Mom will like it if you romp and frolic with giant toys just like I did."

Quinnton, our seven year old Springer, lays on the bed, his freckled muzzle warm on my knee, and watches the two young ones as they investigate the life before us. I lay my head on his and say to him, "Live forever and ever little one. You are the Springer trust."

Quinnton is the only one here trained by wise and devoted Abroham. He appears to be assuming his daddy–dog responsibility with an aptitude that would make Abe proud.

Abe is not gone. He trained all of us to be brave and generous and always ready to stop and play. He left us with more than enough joy to keep our hearts from breaking until we go where ever it is that I believe he waits.

And when he shall die,
Cut him out in little stars,
And all the world,
Shall be in love with the night.
–William Shakespeare

Grief Follows No Schedule:
It Takes As Long As It Takes

"Not the least hard thing to bear when they go from us, these quiet friends, is that they carry away with them so many years of our own lives."
John Galsworthy

My desk is a mess. Books on dog behavior, dog meditation, dog massage, tales of dogs rescued to their forever homes, and dog picture books pile everywhere.

Time cleaning can be better spent reading with a big, warm dog stretched across my lap. Did anyone ever lay gasping their last breath thinking, "I should have cleaned up?" Does

 120

history record anyone ever wheezing out a death rattle of, "Bring me the vacuum?"

My book collection reflects an abiding interest in how to cope with the agony of grieving for beloved dogs whose lives have ended. Understanding the emptiness of facing the death of a beloved pet, and our conscious and unconscious need to examine memories of dogs who have loved us, is a common theme in conversations with men and women who have been graced to know a dog as best friend and boon companion.

The Bond Will Not Break

Dog people share an unbreakable bond of understanding the myriad ways that human lives are made rich by experiencing a bond with the canine species. When you meditate on how dogs and humans become true family members, our will and our need to share our lives with another species may strike you as miraculous.

For anyone requiring proof of this unbreakable human-canine bond, we have no further to look than into the faces of humans separated from their canine family members during any life threatening disaster. During the horrors of the flooding of New Orleans, news coverage of an exhausted, frantic man swimming in circles refusing to be rescued by any boat that would not include his dog reminded me of all the people who so love their dogs that parting with them while they were alive cannot be countenanced. Whether logical, wise, or advisable, many dog

121

DEVOTED TO DOGS

lovers' worst nightmare is to be unable to protect their pet.

Several years after my best dog friend, Abroham, died, a non-dog owning person asked me, "How long do you think it takes to grieve for a dog?" This remains a question I cannot easily answer. Three years passed before the mere mention of Abe's death would not reach into my heart and rip the scab of solace right off the wound of my grief. Five full years have passed since Abe left our family, but the question of "how long does it take to grieve?" never exits my thoughts completely.

I will tell you how long it takes to grieve: it takes as long as it takes.

I no longer feel my heart literally breaking open when I think Abe's name. I can go to a dog show and watch big, powerful, liver colored spaniels stride around the show ring without my young Abe leaping to life on the screen of my mind's eye. I can allow myself to look at

Abe's doggy wheelchair that veterinarians who loved him helped me to find to assist his dear withering hind legs to walk a few weeks longer than they might have (www.K9carts.com) or (www.doggoncarts.com). I can come across a picture of him, taken during his last week, and acknowledge that his face was strained with the ravages of age.

You Will Know When It's Time
To this day, when I see a bottle of electrolyte sports drink, hesitate in the grocery aisle to thank heaven for Dr. Sheri Bakerian when she suggested that maybe Abe would drink that one week when he stopped drinking and I thought the end had really come. I can hear Dr. Frank Wagner, who had taken the best of care of him since he was a tiny pup, assure me, "You'll know when it's time", as I struggled with "will I know when I must let him go?" I see Dr. Jordan Kocen looking at Abe during what turned out to be Abe's very last acupuncture treatment, gently saying, "Abe may be waiting for you to let him know you are able to let him go." Finally, I recall the gentle kindness of the veterinarian who gave him the final gift of peace as she euthanized him; shedding tears as openly as the rest of us who held him in our arms and felt his life pass from his elderly body.

Emptiness Filled By Memories
As time passes, the pall of grieving lifts. The crushing emptiness of loss slowly releases your heart and mind from its crushing grip. Memories of all the perfect and contented times before his body wore out and his time came to leave begin

123

DEVOTED TO DOGS

to replace the fresh pain of wondering how your life will go on when your dog friend has died. You learn not to delve too deeply into wishing to see his dear face one more time. A peace from the fresh heartbreak of letting go seeps in as you lie awake, tears seeping involuntarily down the sides of your face, wondering if you will ever sleep in a room without him. You begin to accept that the dog who was your best companion lived every moment of life allotted to him.

Perhaps we are afraid to ride the waves of our grieving process for fear that to distance our hearts from the pain of grief may result in loosing memories of a great companion. Every person's journey as they move forward to celebrate their pet's life, while accepting the inevitability of death, follows a very personal path.

For me, I found great solace in remembering Abe's life with permanent memorials.

Tributes And Remembering

A few months before Abe died, I brought home an ornate concrete bench with carved lions that reminded me of Abe's great strength and majestic presence. I vividly remember going out to Pine Hollow Nursery to search for a bench because I needed somewhere to sit in the middle of the night when Abe gave me the signal we had to go out.

It can take an old boy a long, long time to gather his strength and sniff the yard until he finds the perfect spot to "go". Many nights I sat on that bench watching him sniff his yard, as I wondered, "Will this be has last night?"

After Abe died, it seemed fitting to turn the area around his bench into a memorial garden. Spotsylvania, VA stained glass artist, Karen Joos *(www.jonesstones.com)* made a perfect likeness of Abe, and has since created stepping stones of many dog faces that I have been allowed the good fortunate to love. While I sit on my Abe bench I examine Abe, Izobel, Bonnie, Quinnton, Vivien and Gabriel's faces beautifully captured in stained glass.

My Heart Will Always Be Waiting

Grieving often finds solace in quiet contemplation of the life that has ended. My Abroham bench and stepping stone garden are a daily reminder to me that grief does not go away, but memories of lives lived remain alive forever.

6

So Much Love To Give: Choosing and Preparing For Your Next Dog

"The greatness of a nation and its moral progress can be judged by the way its animals are treated."
Ghandi

Speak A Joyful Word
Of All Breeds

*"I like them all, pointers, setters,
retrievers, spaniels, what have you. Most
of the bad ones were my fault, and
most of the good ones would have
been good under any circumstances."*
Gene Hill

Two very dear, gentle and genteel ladies that I know were enjoying a long car trip, returning home from a dog activity. Name them Alice and Babette to protect their privacy.

During the monotony of their miles in the car, Babette used the car phone to say hello to a friend in their hometown.

After the phone call was completed, Babette placed the mobile phone in her purse. Some time later, the phone must have been jostled roughly. The phone, now mysteriously activated, had its re-dial button depressed.

Say Something Nice...
Or Say Nothing At All

At this point, this car phone saga takes a frightening turn that is humorous if you are not involved, but wildly mortifying if you are the person about to be captured in the act of gossip.

The phone dialed the friend who had been called earlier and this lady of the house was unavailable to answer the ring. Her answering machine kindly recorded the conversation. In fact, that answering machine recorded twenty minutes of the conversation that was going on between Babette and Alice as they traveled down the highway.

When our mother's taught us to "Never say anything behind anyone's back that we would not say to that person's face", that advice was cutting edge diplomacy; especially now, in the mobile phone age.

Mortified By Gossip

These two friends of mine are not positive of the content of their conversation as the answering machine recorded their car talk. They do have a horrible, sinking feeling that being dog women, and thinking of the friend they had just called, the conversation turned to dogs. They fear they may have spoken ill of their friend's beloved toy poodle. One of them may have wished the little fellow ill for his constant amorous attentions to her leg on a recent visit.

The very thought of having a friend hear you criticize her dog has fear imprinted me to never use a mobile phone again without making sure the last number stored by the phone, and to possibly be re-dialed by mistake, is my own home number. At least if I call home and my dogs, Quinnton, Vivien and Gabriel hear me, they will not repeat my conversation.

Bite Your Tongue If You Have To
Dog lovers, remember: never speak ill of anyone's dog. Never. Not in person. Not in absentia.

There is no sin so grave to a dog person as to hear harsh or critical words about one's own dog. Believe it. "Love me, love my dog", is a trite saying only if you do not have a dog to love.

I Always Prefer My Dog's Company

Anyone who does not like my dog, can steer clear of me and I will be so much the richer for more time to spend alone with my dog. I have yet to meet a human whose company I prefer to that of my dog. I do not think I am unusual in this strong reaction.

Need to nip a friendship in the bud? Casually say something disparaging or demeaning about that acquaintance's dog and you will never be bothered by that person's attentions again.

Guard Your Tongue

Most dog lovers think they would never say an unkind thing about others' dogs. Not true.

People unabashedly hold forth with unkind and unfair breed generalizations. "All (you fill in the breed) are aggressive. "I could never stand to be seen with a little (you fill in the breed) dog." Usually this blanket insult includes the words, "yappy", "frou-frou", "sissy" or "prissy."

In defense of all the toy and Miniature Poodles, Bichon Frises, Maltese, Yorkshire Terriers, Italian Greyhounds, Chihuahuas and all the other tiny, brave, brilliant toy breeds: anyone who thinks the toy breeds are not all dog and fine canine companions, has not had the privilege of knowing a wee mite of a dog.

Manners, Good Manners!

It is a horrible insensitivity (and terrible manners) to label, criticize and discriminate against any dog on the basis of his breed. Each breed, and each dog within that breed, deserves to be judged individually.

Not All Alike Within A Breed

While every breed certainly should have temperament, physical characteristics and skills in common, the millions of specimens within each breed will be as different as close relatives on any family tree.

Springer Spaniels should be merry creatures who wag their tales as birds fly into view. Poodles should not shed and will be very bright and curious. Border Collies will likely find something: sheep, balls, family children, to herd into a manageable flock. Most Labradors will not run away from the water in wild-eyed terror. Generally, Golden Retrievers will kiss you all over the face and be delighted to meet a new best friend.

Celebrate Individuality

Each individual dog of every breed will exhibit varying drives, aptitudes and characteristics.

As our lives change and our physical, health, economic and home needs are altered, we may find ourselves researching new breeds to fit into our evolving lifestyles.

Never Say Never

A person suffering with a bad back or other physical disability causing reduced strength and mobility may realize that a Rotweiler or Doberman pup would be physically very difficult for them to train, while a Pug or a Cavalier King Charles Spaniel is not.

A dog owner looking for protective warning barking, but moving to a tiny apartment with no yard, might find that the German Shepherd Dog or Bouvier that they wanted for a watch dog could not fit in as well as a nice, ready to bark Corgi, or Shetland Sheepdog.

The joys of dog ownership can come to our hearts in many sizes, shapes, and personalities. A huge armful of dog can make most hearts beat with companionship and security. A medium-sized fur friend can follow every step with devotion. But a tiny, furball that can be tucked in a jacket or smuggled into forbidden places in a big purse, could be the constant companion many of us need to experience.

Captivating Pug Story

"Clara", by Margot Kaufman, is a bestseller describing the life and constant fun between a woman and her domineering ,yet endearing Pug dog, Clara. A dog friend gave me this book and it sat on a table in my den for nearly a year. I was not riveted by the thought of reading about the life of someone's little Pug dog.

How misguided and ignorant my preconceived notions of Clara's story turned out to be. I

 134

laughed so hard that all my dogs woke up and ran and sat at my feet to stare at me. I could not go to bed the night I began the book. The antics of diminutive, but bursting with spirit and opinions, Clara, gave tiny dogs a whole new interest and appeal.

If you go to a local bookseller and cannot find this book, blame me. I cannot spy a copy without compulsively buying it to give to another dog lover. Thanks to "Clara", I am on the tiny dog bandwagon, albeit just in my heart at the moment.

I have not added a tiny dog to my family pack yet, but a Cavalier King Charles Spaniel is most assuredly in my future. If beauty is in the eye of the mother beholding it, I remain a Spaniel mamma. Thank heavens for a tiny spaniel breed. I have a tiny, intelligent, devoted Cavalier friend, Marley Coble, who whispers to me each time I see him, "You need a Cavalier."

As middle age, arthritis and the desire to travel everywhere with a dog, grasp me in their unrelenting clutches, I can already feel a nine pound spaniel hiding in my big purse.

The Ten
Commitments

*"Happiness never decreases
by being shared.*
Bhudda

Puppy fever.

When you have a case of puppy obsession, restless sleep grips you while little four footed velvet bundles scamper across your dreams.

You wrack your heart and brain with the question, "But which breed is for me?".

Once you have made your mind up to set sail on the miraculous journey of puppy procurement, you still can't sleep. Anticipation of holding your very own puppy, fantasies of the adoring look that is about to gaze upon you, and joyous memories of dogs who have loved you before, fill up your heart. Days cannot pass quickly

 136

enough until the pup you hope to find is warm in your lap.

Make A Very Careful Choice.

Wait. Certainly, there is nothing like a puppy for bringing happiness and years of love to a dog lover. But every puppy deserves to have an owner who is ready.

Search Your Capabilities For Commitment

Ready for the responsibility of caring for a defenseless life. Ready to commit time, money, household furnishings, worry, and entertainment as the puppy matures from pup to dog.

Puppy Rearing Requires Time

Since you will be wide awake endless hours waiting on your puppy to come, spend that time contemplating ten commitments to puppy ownership.

- *Commitment One:*
  Did you research your breed?
  Let's say you have decided on a Poodle. Do you know how long a healthy Poodle is likely to live? Do you know if Poodles have any health problems that are more likely found in one line of Poodle breeding than another? Does the Poodle you like have a family history of bad knees? Has his grandmother or mother gone blind from inherited eye problems? Do you know if one family of Poodles is known for being calm while another line has been bred to be inquisitive and busy all the hours its little eyes are open?

137

DEVOTED TO DOGS

Every breed has its own likely problems in certain families of dogs. It is very wise to know the common problems and ask the possible breeder many heath questions. Many health problems have tests that can be performed on your puppy before you buy it, or on the pup's parents to make sure they are as clear as possible from the heart ache of health concerns.

The American Kennel Club has listings for nearly every national breed club. The national breed club, in this era of internet information explosion, will have a web site that will tell you everything you ever wanted to know about Poodles (or any other breed). Breeders will usually be brutally honest about the good points and the drawbacks for health, temperament and talents of a specific breed.

Resolve to contact at least three breeders of the breed you think you cannot live without. Ask them about health and temperament problems. If they are within driving distance, ask to make an appointment to come and meet them and their dogs.

YOUR NEXT DOG

Ask the owner of a dog that you love who bred their dog. Family traits for health, talent and beauty often run very true. Reputable, experienced breeders will be impressed that you care enough to be a good owner to the pup that they have spent decades of their lives and talent to develop. If a breeder acts insulted or intimidated or bothered by your questions, run as fast as you can to the next breeder on your list.

Every dog is a great miracle. It is likely that you will love her for all her days regardless of bad knees, detached retinas, blindness, thyroid dysfunctions, hip dysplasia or any other health problem. A dog is for life. But, before you lay your hands on this living trust, take a few extra weeks to become an authority on the health and personality of the breed you think you love.

- *Commitment Two:*
  Consider your own time available to devote to a dog.
  Housebreaking may cause you a few nights of disturbed sleep. Most pups can wait to wee one hour for each month of age. Not many can wait all night to relieve themselves. They certainly cannot wait several or many hours while you go to work. Even in their little crate, they still have to leave the little crate and have someone who loves them walk them around the fenced yard saying, "Hurry up, peepee," every few hours!

DEVOTED TO DOGS

Dogs require a schedule. Examine your lifestyle and be very honest about your time available to come home at a set time, feed her on a regular schedule, and set time aside to train her. Are you able to give up many, many hours to play with her to develop her mind and her little body? A dog is not a cat. A dog must have a devoted human companion who has time to devote to her.

- *Commitment Three:*
  Buy from a breeder who would take the puppy back, if for any reason you cannot keep her. The very good sign that a breeder is devoted to the dogs she breeds ia a breeder who expects to be a part of the pup's life until death do you part.

  Your contract with the breeder may say, "if for any reason you do not keep this dog, the dog must be returned to me." Never balk when you see this demand. This sentence is the insurance the that breeder has as much invested in creating this life as you have had in researching and loving this new life.

- *Commitment Four:*
  Fence your yard.
  A dog who cannot go out and run around and answer nature's call in a fenced yard will need you to be attached by leash to her. Good intentions often disintegrate into heart break when it is rainy, cold, the dog is nearly housebroken and you think she will go straight out and come straight back. One squirrel to chase could be all it takes to have your dog

who hit by a car. The most secluded cul-de-sacs, dirt roads and hundred acre farms still have delivery trucks, trash trucks, and visiting neighbors' vehicles that can kill your dog in a second. The dog will never come back. Only a fence will save your beloved pet.

When I bought my first Springer Spaniel pup from Julie Hogan of Pride 'N Joy English Springer Spaniels in Manassas, VA, Miss Hogan said to me, "When you get your fence, I will have a puppy for you." I got my fence. The puppy that brought home from Miss Hogan spent endless hours chasing squirrels and balls safely in the fenced yard while I read great books on the deck; worry free.

- *Commitment Five:*
  Never set the dog free outside a fenced area off leash.
  Unless the dog is participating in dog sport (hunting, tracking, agility, obedience, etc.) make it a rule to keep your dog on leash. This is part of being a good citizen and guarding the safety of your own dog. You cannot control the thoughtless, ignorant people who let dogs run free to harass dogs, children, trash cans and neighborhoods. Your dog on leash is under your control. Control is a necessary part of dog ownership.

- *Commitment Six:*
  Make plans before you bring the puppy home to take her to obedience school.
  The pup will learn faster from two months to four months of age than she ever will learn

141

again. She also will accept that anything in the big world that mother says is safe is safe and friendly. Find a puppy kindergarten. A true puppy kindergarten will militantly guard the class from any dog over 16 weeks of age. Only tiny pups who learn the ropes of puppy play and learning to listen to the dog owner will be in the puppy kindergarten class. These classes can be difficult to find and they will have rigid cut off dates for age of enrollment. Make sure your tiny pup has had at least two to three of her puppy vaccines.

If you cannot enroll the pup in a true puppy  kindergarten class while she is a tot, call several experienced obedience instructors and ask if you could come, without the dog, and watch a basic training class. Ask if the instructor is certified by any professional trainer's associations: The Association of Pet Dog Trainers (*www.apdt. org*) has an informative and very helpful web site offering a nationwide listing of dog obedience instructors committed to positive, upbeat, confidence building training methods.

Obedience training will teach the two of you to work as a team. Your dog's life will be happier when she understands the rules of your home and lifestyle.

- *Commitment Seven:*
  Read everything you can find about dog health, dog training and dog parenthood.
  A dog owner must take charge of their own never ending canine education. Subscribe to several dog magazines and newsletters for breaking news and training tips. My favorite newsletter is "The Whole Dog Journal" (*www. whole-dog-journal.com*). Most breeds have their own breed magazines with news of the breed's health concerns, and lots of news about the breed.

- *Commitment Eight:*
  Read food labels.
  Commit to feeding your dog only the very best food. Consult your veterinarian. Find out what your breeder feeds. Ask the most dog fanatic dog owners what they fed their dogs. All foods are not equal. Many dog owners refuse to feed their dogs foods that do not list the first ingredient on the label as a real meat. Meat meal or meat by-products are not the same quality ingredient as a real meat (chicken, beef, lamb etc.). Many dog owners will not feed their pet any food, biscuits or

143

treats with preservatives like BHA, BHT or ethoxyquin in the list of ingredients.

Educate yourself to pick the very best nutrition available for your dog. An extensive list of meat based, preservative free pet foods can be found at *www.altvetmed.org.*

- *Commitment Nine:*
  Carry a poop scoop bag at all times.
  Resolve to be the best dog owning citizen you can be. One reason dogs are often not welcome in public, and disliked by non-dog owners is because dog owners sometimes have terrible manners in dog behavior management.

  When you leave home with your pet, tuck a plastic grocery bag in your pocket as dog poop clean up insurance. Maybe you will never need that bag. But if your dog needs you to protect the cleanliness in public reputation of all dogs, you will be prepared.

  Train your dog to be so pleasant and friendly in public that she can pass the AKC Canine Good Citizen test. Let your dog be one more ambassador of good citizenship that makes more stores, outdoor restaurants and public places proclaim, "nice dogs welcome here."

  Look over rules for the Canine Good Citizen test at the AKC's internet site: *www.akc.org.*

- *Commitment Ten:*
  Always adore your dog for being a dog.

YOUR NEXT DOG

Never expect your dog to know how to behave in any way that you have not taught her. If you ever lose patience with your dog, ask yourself, "What do I need to teach her so she will be the dog of my dreams?"

She is not a cat. She is not a little person in a fur suit. She is the best companion you may ever have on this side of paradise. She is a dog. She is the friend that dogs are made of. But you must dream your dream for her and show her your desires.

Good Dog's Bill Of Rights

*"You become responsible forever
for what you have tamed."*
Antoine de Saint-Exupery

"JUDGE NOT, lest ye be judged", wisdom for cooperative, peaceful dealings with humans. Advice equally well taken for fair and beneficial interactions with dogs.

Before we judge our dogs as unruly or misbehaved, an examination for fairness to the dog is warranted.

Dog behaviors that exasperate us can be re-trained by us, not by the dog.

Most dogs who are perceived as misbehaving are merely following where untrained doggy desires have led (or misled) them.

Dogs, who as puppies were hoping their human would be a kind, calm and willing leader, can

 146

give up hope and take on leadership roles themselves. They have read the Big Dog® T-shirt that says, "Lead, Follow, Or Get Out of the Way." Big dogs, little dogs, all breeds of canines, subscribe from birth to this 'use–it–or–lose–it' philosophy of pack–leader mentality.

On behalf of dogs, who were born good dogs, I offer you a few rules from my "Good Dog's Good Dog Owner Bill of Rights."

- *Dog Right One:*
  Owners may not now, or in the future, complain about any dog behavior that the owner has not trained the dog to either have or not have.

  One example of 'no blame without training' is the human tendency to wail and whine over dogs jumping up on them when they enter the house.

  If you dislike paws on clothes, hose, and tender body parts, ask yourself, "Have I taught this dog to 'sit' on command?"

  No? Sorry, but the fault belongs to the complaining human. Own your responsibility and teach the dog a solid, prolonged sit-stay.

  Work on 'sit' until the dog sits promptly and with understanding of the position.

  Begin with short five-second sits, on leash, with no distractions every day. Perhaps while

you have your coffee and watch the morning news. Resolve to do two practice sessions of five sits, on-leash for control and dog concentration, every day for 30 days.

Begin alone with you and the dog. Dog sits for five seconds. Add five seconds to the stay every day. Progress toward the goal that the dog can sit-stay solidly on leash for five minutes.

Next, get a helper. Practice the sit while the helper opens and closes the front door. Mastered that? Move on to a solid 'sit' when the door bell rings. Let your helper greet the dog.

- *Dog Right Two:*
  Teach Your Dog How To Greet Humans.

Dogs are born thinking jumping up is a sign of respect. They sniff the lips and faces of pack members who return to the cave after a day of hunting and exploring the world.

A dog that jumps on his owner must be taught the owner's desires. Don't blame him until you train him.

Until he is trained to sitting perfection, walk straight past him when you arrive at home. Sit down. The wild joy of flinging himself up to lick your lips as greeting will be deflated a bit if you sit down and are no longer a towering target.

Never hit out at him, push him away, or step on his toes. He may think you are playing. You may trigger his prey–chasing instinct to catch your fast-moving hand with his teeth. You may teach him all sorts of behavior responses that you will like even less than jumping up.

- *Dog Right Three:*
  Dog owners may not tell any dog to calm down or cease wild activity if that owner has not given this active, healthy dog 20 minutes of exercise and attention.

Dogs must have exercise. They will not exercise themselves. Put them outside alone and most dogs will lie near the door and hope you let them back in to be with you.

- *Dog Right Four:*
  Humans must get out of chairs and play with their dogs.

Throw the tennis ball. Play with the dog until you bore him or tire him. Stop and tell him how wonderful he is.

Take him for a walk around the neighborhood. If he is yanking your arm out of your shoulder joint, that is an entirely new training problem to confront. Find an obedience class or dog-training book. Teach the dog to walk without pulling.

Play hide-and-seek with the dog. Rev up the dog's interest in a favorite toy or ball. Teach  him to catch the toy. Place the toy in full view, while the dog does his sit-stay. Point to the toy and send him to get it. Progress to hiding the toy around the room, and then hide it in other rooms. Dogs love hide-and-seek. They have miraculous noses that they long to use.

- *Dog Right Five:*
Every dog deserves to feel good about himself.

Talk nicely to your dog. A dog understands and has reactions and feelings about human tone of voice. When we are angry or sad, dogs react to our feelings.

Dogs do not understand vast numbers of words. Tone, volume and emotion of voice quality speak volumes to a dog.

Dogs can be taught by our tone and our facial expression that they are good dogs or that they are bad dogs.

- *Dog Right Six:*
When our dogs do not meet our human expectations to be well-behaved dogs, and if we are dog lovers, it is our responsibility

to teach the dogs exactly how we would like them to behave.

To teach them, we must talk to them as we would talk to two-year-old children that we love.

Many dogs will never be more capable of problem-solving and making behavior decisions than will a small human child. To speak harshly to an untrained dog is useless and cruel. An always disappointed, angry tone of voice may teach some sensitive dogs that they cannot learn and they will give up.

When we speak to our dogs, a kind word is the foundation of the dog's receptiveness to learning our language and mastering tasks we intend to teach the dog.

I like to pretend that one day my dogs will magically wake up able to talk. This fantasy helps me be very careful how I speak into their expectant, adoring faces.

We have so much power over these defenseless lives we chose to live with us. It is one of our finest powers to be kind.

151

Careful What You Wish For

*"Even the tiniest Poodle or
Chihuahua is still a wolf at heart."*
Dorothy Hinshaw Patent

Your dog waggles up to you, watching your eyes for your mood. Will you play ball? Will you give me that last bite of cheese toast you're eating? If I run to the door, will you see me and take me out to the bathroom, or will I have to go and squat in the privacy of the dining room? How many times can I chase the cat behind the dryer before you get up from the computer and say, "Vivien, come!"

Dogs watch our every move. They understand us. They live in the moment and they make the most of the moments that come.

Dogs do not waste their days wishing. One of the reasons we love dogs so unreservedly and find their wisdom to be unspoken but able to speak volumes, is that dogs are doers, not pipe-dream weavers.

If you have had a few unrealistic dog-fulfillment wishes, you are not alone. We have all had dog wishes that had little to do with real dogs or the realities that dogs face. Here are a few dog wishes you may want to guard against:

- *Wish One:* *Wouldn't it be great to get a strong, noble Standard Schnauzer like we had when we were first married 20 or 30 years ago? (Substitute any big, strong, smart breed here.)*

Whoa there, dog lover. Many of us remember a favorite dog of our youth. Alas, many of us are physically and energetically challenged by day-to-day home and work chores, let alone able to face the rigors to exercise a young, boisterous, fast-growing, ready-to-yank-your-arm-out-of-the-socket, giant or large-breed dog.

I was loved by a huge, wild, endearingly foolish Irish Setter as a teenager. As names are very often self-fulfilling prophecies, he was named Mighty Beasley. He was mighty and he was a big, red, male beast. We spent many an afternoon racing up and down the dirt road behind my parents' barn. Now, 30 years later, I can't even race a Bearded Collie to the upstairs bedroom.

DEVOTED TO DOGS

Be careful that your first dog memories do not lead you and an unsuspecting dog down the path to disaster. Were I a medical doctor who treated mature adult patients with wrist, shoulder, neck, back or hand pain, one of my first diagnostic questions would be, "Do you have a dog?"

Beware of acquiring a dog that will grow to be very big. If he hurts himself and needs to be lifted into the car, can you lift 100 pounds?

Can you haul him into the bathtub if he tangles with a skunk on a midnight bathroom break?

Do you even want to undertake to load his big dog food bags from store to house to kitchen?

If he does not learn to walk gently on leash very quickly, will you blame yourself, not the big, happy puppy, when you feel the pain of his lunging and very normal exuberance?

With all my heart, I have longed to own a huge, white, massively corded herding dog, the Komondor. (See a Komondor at *www. maskc.org*.) As I creak to the kitchen looking for the heating pad, I face the fact that I would be no treat to a big dog as the mother he needs. Reality sets in when I picture myself attached to 100 pounds of wild, young dog.

- *Wish Two: I am going to get a Standard Poodle because Poodles do not shed. (Replace Poodle with any of the breeds that are called 'non-shedders.')*

What happens when a dog that doesn't shed changes coat with the seasons, as its new hairs are exchanged for old? In most of the so-called non-shedding breeds, the dog develops an undercoat that, if not brushed regularly, combed out and groomed properly, mats up into tangles, cords and dead hair.

Most of the breeds that shed very little are taken by their owners to a professional groomer for regular coat care. Groomers are ready, willing and very able to comb out, trim off and style these coats. But the groomers must charge for these valuable services, which require training, hours of standing, and the

substantial expense of setting up and running a professional salon.

Before you dream of a breed that won't leave hair piles on your baseboards, ask yourself a few questions: Will I be able to afford regular trips to the groomer?

Will I be the kind of dog parent who can drop her off, leave her, and pick her up hours later?

Will I take her often (from puppyhood onward) to the professional groomer, so she learns that going to the groomer is fun and just one more thing a good dog learns to enjoy?

- _Wish Three:_ Dogs are clean animals. A normal dog will not soil his surroundings.

   Nonsense. A little puppy may have a bladder the size of a big butter bean. A dog must be house-trained, emphasis on trained. There are no shortcuts. You housebreak tiny puppies, and any age shelter or other adopted dog, the same way: from scratch.

   Read and follow any good puppy-training book and do exactly what the book says, for as long as it takes. Allow the dog no freedom until it has had no unsupervised accidents for at least 90 days. "The Evans Guide for House-training Your Dog" by Job Michael Evans is one of the best guides you could find.

- _Wish Four:_ What we need is a protection breed, or protection-trained guard dog to protect our house and valuables.

   Casting no aspersions on the guarding and protection breeds: I have met gentle Pit Bulls, sweet German Shepherd Dogs, Dobermans that were soft like lambs, and Rottweilers that would like nothing better than to lick you until you giggled.

   But, there is a proverb, Chinese, I think, that translates roughly to: Never use an ax to remove a mosquito from the forehead of a friend. In other words, never bring home a dog bred for generations to be able to back up his growl with the intention to use those

157

teeth and size, if all you really need is a Cocker Spaniel.

Most of us would like a warning bark, or a hard look, given to trespassers or strangers who give us the 'willies'. Many of us do not have the dog-obedience command and training skills to manage, train and be responsible for the suspicions and guarding actions of many large protection breeds.

From buying more dog than we need, to ending up with a dog that we are actually afraid of, choosing a dog for protection requires advice from a professional. Speak at length to several breeders of protection or guarding breeds for advice before you buy more dog than you can supervise.

I have yet to see a Chihuahua who would not raise a deafening alarm when a stranger menaced her territory. Every Springer Spaniel I have owned willingly showed his or her ample 'guard-dog' teeth to any suspicious stranger who invaded my personal space without my invitation.

We humans brought the dog into our caves for protection and harmony. To sleep soundly in the safe vigilance of a good dog is one of life's great comforts. The best wish we can have for our dog is to be as committed a friend to him as he surely will be to us.

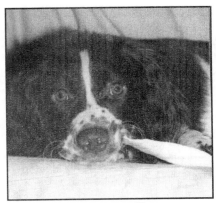

Beware Of Loved Ones Carrying Dogs As Gifts

"Acquiring a dog may be the only opportunity a human ever has to choose a relative."
Mordecai Siegal

Gifts are great. Aren't they?

If you know someone who wants a dog, help them find a dog. Help them pay for a dog, if a purebred pup is their heart's desire. Write a big check to the veterinarian of your loved one's choice to pay for the dog's necessary vaccines or neutering. If adoption will be from a shelter, visit the shelter and make arrangements to pay the adoption fees. But, never, no never, buy or adopt a dog to give to an unsuspecting friend or family member.

Dogs As Gifts: Not A Good Idea
Dogs given as gifts create problems that should
be explored before a defenseless dog lands in
a home where he was not expected and may
be neglected.

A Dog Is A Very Personal Choice
Are you sure that the gift-dog recipient wants
to and is able to look after a pet physically
and financially? It can be painful to admit that
our budgets are too tight for a dog's food and
medical needs, or that we just don't have the
physical capacity or desire to devote our time
and hearts to the needs of a vital, fragile life who
will look to us as the center of its universe.

A Dog Requires Work And Worry
If you are thinking of surprising a retired relative,
or anyone you know, with a pet, first ask yourself,
"Why does that person not have a pet?" Perhaps
they keep hoping they will travel and do not
want to leave a pet behind. Maybe they really
love their perfectly trimmed lawn and pride and
joy flower beds and do not want a dog who may
dig, may tangle in the foliage, and who certainly
will relieve himself on grass and bushes. The
dogless person may dislike dog hair. Beware
that the person may have had a beloved dog
die and their heart is not ready to open to a
new commitment. Whatever the reason that a
person does not have a dog, giving a dog to
an unsuspecting friend or relative could be a
huge mistake.

Let's get Grandmother a puppy to keep her company. (Substitute any person whom you believe needs companionship.)

Guilty? Give of Your Time.
Don't Give A Dog.

Hang on right there. Too, too many heartbroken pups and adolescent dogs wind up pining

away in rescue-organization crates or dog runs because a family member wanted to bring companionship and activity to a relative or shut-in friend.

Offering to drive them and accompany them to find a dog is a great idea. Let the desire to acquire come from the person who will own the dog.

Little puppies and older shelter dogs cannot ask the needful puppy responsibility questions, so we must ask hard questions for them.

Tell The Truth
Can You Answer These Questions?

- Can the new owner walk the pet every few hours and watch its every move?
- Does the new owner mind a few, or perhaps many, pee-pee accidents on her rugs?
- Is there a crate waiting for the new dog?
- Is there a fenced yard to protect the dog when there are bad weather days or

when the owner really does not feel up to walking the dog?

- Is the prospective dog-owner finally retired and able to travel?
- Is there a place for the dog to stay when the owner needs to leave town?
- Does this dog-parent want to spend money on dog food, medical care, grooming, obedience education and boarding?
- Does the dog-owner have the energy to romp, walk and supervise a lively dog?
- If the new owner is elderly, are there any concerns about sharp little teething teeth on fragile human skin?
- Most of all, did this person say a dog was the one thing she most wants in the whole world?

A pup needs to be planned for and wanted. A dog owner must wholeheartedly welcome the very big responsibility of another very needy life to look after.

Everyone needs exercise. A dog, however, is not expendable and ignorable like a piece of exercise equipment. A dog must run, jump, play and investigate his environment. If he lands, bored and ignored, in the home of a person who loves nothing better than long hours of reading and resting in the recliner, the dog is in trouble and the person becomes troubled. Chances are, the dog will join the ranks of the unexercised rather than making a voluntarily sedentary person leap up to exercise. Give this person a treadmill or a membership to an athletic club.

Not all children are dog-friendly. Small children and little pups are cute in pictures. In real life, the mix requires constant vigilance and vast increases of work for the parents. A dog is not a toy-like source of juvenile entertainment.

Too many of the dogs who were squeezed and enjoyed by little children as puppies now wait behind chain link fences at shelters. Too many "gift for the children" pups grow up to be sad, older dogs who wonder why the "new" wore off them so soon. There is a frightening possibility that children who see their too-old, too-much-trouble dogs disappear to shelters learn lessons that life is not very valuable, or that their parents' promises and commitments cannot be trusted. Even worse, some dogs are killed by cars when humans toss them outside and lied to the children, teaching them, "the

dog is happier outdoors." Happy, or not, the dog is probably going to be dead.

A surprise dog may suffer if no one is ready for him and, even worse, no one wants him.

The choice of a dog is as personal as the choice of any love connection. The dog who makes my heart beat with attraction may look like a rolling dust ball to you. Aunt Olga may want a tiny, three pound fluff puff of a dog, while you may think the only dog for anyone is a regal Scottish Deerhound. There are several hundred purebred dog breeds and thousands of lovely mixed breeds, all lovable, if they are matched to the person who wants to love them.

We fervently hope that our dog will grow old with us. With love, attention to the best possible diet, frequent trips to his veterinarian for checkups before medical problems arise, and vast quantities of our devotion to his needs, our dog may share our life for over a decade.

Picking out a dog for a soul mate is personal. Move heaven and earth to help anyone longing to dedicate themselves to a fine dog locate their dream dog. Just make sure the dog you help them find is their dream and not yours. Nightmares can result.

A longed-for dog is the best love match of all.

A Father Abides:
Choose The Parents Well

*"A dog has one aim in life,
to bestow his heart."*
J. R. Ackerley

Afternoons, around four thirty, he strolls over to my desk to lay his big, warm muzzle on my knee. He is announcing suppertime.

Evenings around ten, he placidly, but expectantly, takes a seat at the bottom of the stairs. We are being gently reminded that bedtime has come.

Shortly after the sun rises on the bedroom wall, a gentle paw reaches up onto the bed and pats my pillow. Who needs an alarm clock when a father–dog–in–charge will unfailingly nudge you from sleep?

165

Distinguished Dogs Have Loved Us

For decades our family has flourished under the protection, entertainment and devotion of self-possessed, serious, wise male Springer Spaniels. More than one large, solid boy has served us. Invariably, we come to think of these venerable boys as "father dogs".

Not one of our esteemed pack managers has sired pups. All were neutered early for health and over-population reasons. You do not have to beget offspring in order to excel in deed and responsibility as a fatherly role model.

Neutering has never limited the dignity, the 'maleness', nor the destiny to assume trust and leadership in our dog pack.

Our family has been blessed to know the breeders of all the male dogs who have loved us. Those breeders have been the key to creating, molding and guarding the health and temperaments of the dogs they have brought into the world.

Interview Your Breeder Well

When you pick a pup to add to your family, being able to ask questions about the health, temperament and longevity of the pup's father (and mother) opens a window of knowledge into the future of the your own pup's development.

There are many questions to ask a breeder who owns the parent of your dog.

How well-made were the father and mother's hips? Everyday, dog owners' hearts are broken

 166

when a young or middle aged dog's limp or mobility related discomfort is diagnosed as hip dysplasia.

Breeders dedicated to protecting the hips of their breeds have father and mother x–rayed and rated. Before you buy a pup, ask your veterinarian if the breed you intend to buy has a tendency toward hip dysplasia.

If the answer is "yes", do not buy a pup for whom the breeder cannot show a certificate that rates the father and the mother's hips as "good" or better. Often, as trots the parent, so trots the pup. Visit the web site of the Orthopedic Foundation For Animals (OFA) at *www.offa.org* for education and pointers to find a pup with a heritage of healthy bones.

How healthy are the parent dogs' eyes, knees, blood and skin? Ask your veterinarian about health problems common in the breed you love. Many health heartaches occur again and again in particular families of dogs.

Some breeds are subject to skin disturbances. Other breeds have high incidences of seizure activity. Many bloodlines in particular families of dogs pass on eye abnormalities that produce blindness. Often, tiny toy breeds may be prone to knee problems.

Every breed may be plagued by a health problem particular to that breed. "Medical & Genetic Aspects of Purebred Dogs" by Ross D. Clark is an eye opening book that discusses genetic problems and temperament concerns of each AKC breed. Time invested becoming knowledgeable about health concerns in your favorite breed is necessary homework for choosing a healthy pup.

How was the father dog's disposition?
Never miss an opportunity to lay your own eyes on your pup's parent. If the father dog (or mother dog) is nasty, shy, worried or aggressive, continue your search for the pup of your dreams. You want a dog to cuddle; not a danger to muzzle. Dogs learn what they live. Gentle dogs teach dogs around them to trust other dogs and other humans.

Neuter your male dog.
Your dog will be healthier and very probably live longer, if he is neutered. You will also never have to wonder if puppies sired by your dog are hungry, homeless or producing more unwanted pups who will live in misery.

I asked Fredericksburg Virginia SPCA, Executive Director, Debra L. Joseph, "How many pups could one un-neutered male dog and one un-spayed female dog cause to be born into the world?"

Joseph shared with me the following statistics from the organization, Spay USA, saying, "An unspayed female dog, her mate and all of their puppies and their puppies' puppies, if none are ever neutered or spayed add up to:
- 1 year – 16 dogs;
- 2 years – 128;
- 3 years – 512;
- 4 years – 2,048;
- 5 years – 12,288;
- 6 years – 67,000.

Thus the importance of spay and neuter."

Your neutered male companion will be healthier and he will not be emotionally, and therefore behaviorally, tormented by the urging of his male hormones. House-training, leg lifting to mark territory, unruliness, willfulness, and the flames of desire to bite and fight will be subdued. Other male dogs can recognize him for his winning personality and not for his hackle-raising aroma of 'maleness'. A dog home is incomplete without a solid, watchful father dog. If you have a male dog's steady head nearby, give him a rub and thank him for his love and devotion.

Wish him Happy Father's Day. He won't know what the words mean but he will feel your appreciation for his faithful service. Life is truly incomplete without a big boy in or near your lap.

Rescue The Perishing

"The world is a dangerous place to live, not because of the people who are evil, but because of the people who don't do anything about it."
Albert Einstein

The car is hot and I am excited. I'm sitting at a truck stop on Route 17 scrutinizing the face of every driver who looks my way as they cross the busy parking lot.

I know when I see the face I am searching for that I will know that is the one. I am looking for love.

Should my husband of 20+ years be worried? No. In fact he's right here beside me. He's here looking for love, too.

We are in fact, searching every car, truck and van; expecting to see a Springer Spaniel that needs us.

Today is our first experience volunteering for Mid Atlantic English Springer Rescue. We are one leg of a journey sponsored by MAESSR (*www. maessr.org*) to transport a rescued Springer Spaniel, Penny, to her forever home. We are the Route 17 North to Quantico, Virginia leg of the Virginia to New Jersey rescue taxi. I cannot help but wonder if passing drivers know we are a part of an underground railroad of sorts.

Penny Rides To Her Forever Home

For 30 miles, a sweet Springer girl lays her delightful head on my shoulder, panting little hot puffs of excitement. Penny warms my lap with her silky self and my heart with her joy to be in the arms of one more human to trust. She leans steadfastly onto my chest, her little liver-colored nose snuffling under my ear. I wonder is she thinking, "Mamma?"

By mile 10, I wonder if we should not run away with this lovely girl ourselves. But, no, a forever dad in New Jersey has been waiting and preparing for this rescue girl for weeks. His is the heart that awaits her entrance and that has promised to care for her all her days.

Sure enough, that very night, every single person who had driven Penny on a leg of her journey, received an e mail thank you note from Penny's new dad. With pure delight, Penny's new dad described taking her to his local pet shop for a perfect bed, her own choice of toys and oodles of delicious treats to be used for training sessions. It made me so happy to think of this

man and his dog and the years of devotion they would share.

The Best Days Are When Your Dog Arrives

Every one of us can remember days that, as we examine our lives, were days that changed our lives. These are the brief moments in normal time that stand out as momentous.

When I met Penny, I felt dog rescue transform from a term that seemed like a very good cause, to a live, tail wagging bundle of real dog. I realized my life had been altered.

Suddenly, I understood that all those volunteers who devote innumerable hours to homeless dogs, are doing so much more than saving dog lives and giving dogs and people a chance to unite. These volunteers are opening their own lives to feeling the reward of sharing in the ecstasy of storing up memories of days that were filled with wonder.

The Face Of Rescue:
Sweet, Glad and Hopeful

With enough days filled with so much delight, perhaps future unbidden days of sadness or pain can be eased by sifting through the stockpile of memories of happiness spread and happiness that spilled over to all those involved in dog rescue. After my morning with Penny, I can close my eyes at any moment and see her hopeful, eager face as she sat in my lap on her way to her permanent family.

Every breed that I have researched has a rescue league brimming with volunteers who have an ear and an eye out all the time to help dogs of the breed they love. Rescue volunteers take phone calls, visit shelters, follow up on clues of dogs in trouble, neglected or abandoned.

Rescue From The Breed You Love

Most national breed clubs have a dedicated volunteer group that works to rescue dogs of their club's breed. Many dog owners belong to the local breed club for their breed and attend meetings and gatherings to promote the welfare of their chosen breed.

To find a rescue organization for a breed that you would like to adopt to become a treasured member of your family there are several paths to take.

The Door To Rescue:
As Close As Your Computer

Your computer and the world wide web offer a world of dog rescue information. Visit the web site of the American Kennel Club (*www.akc.org*) and search for your breed. Or, perform a web search and search for the name of your breed. Most likely, the national breed club for this breed will appear, as well as several websites for that breed's rescue organizations.

Dog lovers who want to ask a live person about a rescue organization would do well to approach the next person attached to a specimen of the breed they are hoping to find and ask that person, "Do you know how I could contact the (you fill in the breed) rescue?"

The Dog You Want Is Waiting
Every week strangers approach me and rub my Springers, Quinnton and Gabriel and my Bearded Collie, Vivien and tell me how much they "would like to have a dog like that."

I direct them to the national English Springer Spaniel National Club at *www.essfta.org* or to the National Bearded Collie Club at *www. beardie.net/bcca/.* Both web sites offer detailed

information on the needs, temperament, health concerns and special skills of each breed. Links are given for finding local rescue associations with nice dogs in great need of permanent homes.

Your Vet Knows Dogs Who Need You

Don't know anyone with the breed you would like to rescue? Make an appointment and go and ask your veterinarian for a referral to the owner of the very nicest dog they know of the breed you are looking for. Chances are excellent that if your veterinarian suggests a wonderful patient, that dog will be owned by someone who will know about that breed's rescue leagues.

A dog that has been obtained with the help of a rescue league has usually lived for several months in the home of a rescue volunteer. The dog-savvy rescue volunteer has had the dog examined by a veterinarian and has spent time with the dog to make sure the dog is not aggressive to adults, children or other dogs. Rescue leagues do not place dogs that have had problems with biting, aggression or unstable temperament.

You Save The Ones You Can

Ginnie Klein, a long-time and very experienced volunteer involved in rescuing English Springer Spaniels told me, "There are some dogs that just cannot be placed. We try to give them a chance, but we also must face reality. For example, a dog who has frequent seizures and needs for extensive medical care and supervision and who is without someone willing to give all the

175

support that is needed, will probably have to be euthanized. We have placed a dog with defective eyes that came from a breeder who would not take responsibility for this dog. Now that same dog is also seriously dysplastic. The adopter spends huge amounts of emotional attachment and investment and money, because he loves the dog."

Often, An Old Dog Is The Best Dog
Klein explains, "Everyone wants young dogs.

 But we have had great success placing elderly dogs with elderly people. We emphasize that the older dog will be more calm and not require as much exercise. We tell prospective rescue owners that the older dog has already gone through the puppy stages and the 'terrible teens' and that the older dog just wants someone to love and to be with."

Rescue volunteers learn early in their volunteer efforts that rescue work can require holding to firm principles for doing everything possible to make every dog in every breed wanted, healthy and cared for all the days of its life. Klein admits, "Every dog breeder, should acknowledge that not every dog stays in the ideal home for its entire life. And until we can put a stop to all the careless breeding, we are all responsible for the results of this carelessness."

A Foster Dog Is Waiting For You
Thousands of dogs of every breed sit waiting as foster dogs. These dogs may have been given up because a family member entered a nursing home, or because the first owner enjoyed the puppy cuteness and then passed them on to a shelter or humane organization. Maybe their family moved and the dog was not seen as family enough to be taken, too.

Nice, Lovable, Ready
There can be many reasons that completely nice, lovable, ready to love dogs are in need of their forever homes. There is but one reason to seek out and bring home one of these deserving dogs. Adopt a dog because you plan to be as devoted to the dog as that dog is going to be to you.

As they used to sing at the church where my mother held my little hand while she hoped I soaked up a few feelings of compassion and responsibility, "Rescue the perishing."

The dog you rescue has more to give back than you have days to receive her gifts. Give an always–too–short life a forever home.

There's A New Dog Coming!
Will A New Pack Member Be Welcome?

*"A pup does not know words.
It just hears love, or anger."*
P. Dugdale

Dogs' social needs vary from dog to dog. Each individual dog has his own view of how much dog to dog contact he prefers, or will tolerate. One dog may wag his tail wildly in glee, as if to say, "Hello! Let me lick your face!"

YOUR NEXT DOG

Another dog may be totally indifferent to new dog acquaintances, showing little interest or desire to sniff parts or exchange doggy greetings. Worried, protective, or anti-social dogs may show their teeth and growl, "Get away. Get away now."

Humans make the decision to bring a new dog into the home pack. Before you add a new dog to your dog household, there are many dog behavior and preference points to ponder.

How does your dog react to strange dogs on walks? Does he raise his hackles, growl, or show his teeth in the "get away from me" response when catching sight of a strange dog? He may not be delighted to share you or your home with a new dog.

How does your dog react to a friendly dog who visits his home? If your dog has expressed displeasure toward a visiting dog, think carefully about adding a newcomer as a permanent member of the pack.

Are you in 'obedience command' control of the dogs you already own and love? If you can command, "Down" and your dog will stay put until you release him, this is a helpful beginning for managing a larger dog pack. If you can call, "Come" and your obedient dog will stop what ever he is doing and come to you, chances are he will follow your lead to make a new pack member another obedient member of the family.

DEVOTED TO DOGS

A good rule is: you must be in control of the dogs who live at your house now, before you add another dog to the mix of personalities.

The dogs are going to sort themselves out by dominance and canine pack standards, but unless the human has the time and the will to be the leader of the dog pack, there will be tears and trouble ahead.

Assuming that your dogs like other dogs, and are well behaved, you may be ready to add one more dog to the mix.

How do you decide on the sex, size, age, or breed of dog who joins the pack? Often, if you own just one dog, adding a dog that is opposite sex to the existing dog is the best choice. Trouble often brews between dogs of the same sex.

Generally, an older dog will accept the antics of a younger dog more readily than a dog who arrives with an already molded personality. Older dogs often will allow puppies to get away

with play and pushiness that they would never tolerate in a dog of their same age or older.

Neuter Everyone For Enhanced Pack Peace

Neutering all the dogs in the pack will frequently work miracles of tolerance and sociability. Female dogs will cause less jealousy and dispute for attention from neutered male dogs. Neutered male dogs will have less drive to assert their will upon one another. Neutered males may smell less dominant to one another, resulting in fewer scuffles for the role of chief dog.

Size Up The Pack Members

Size of the dog who joins the pack may strongly influence how well the newcomer is accepted. Often, if the dog who joins the family will mature to be either quite a bit larger or smaller than the dog or dogs already present, there is less tendency for the pack members to feel compelled to challenge one another.

Remember the wisdom of President Theodore Roosevelt: "It's not the size of the dog in the fight; it's the size of the fight in the dog."

I once knew a tiny Scottish Terrier who enjoyed and would seek out a dog fight. This scrappy girl was adopted by a family with a gentle, friendly, very well-adjusted Great Dane. When the Scottie arrived, she tried to fuss with the Great Dane. The 100+ pound Great Dane refused to entertain the silly idea that he would fight with a less than 20 pound terrier girl. Had this little Scottie girl gone to live with another little Scottie

girl, or another smallish, scrappy breed, you can be sure she would have picked fights all her days.

How do you introduce the new dog to the dog or dogs in the pack? Introduce the newcomer in a location where none of the dogs have any territorial feelings to protect. Find a park, or unused fenced area like a tennis court. Let the dogs meet. If you have more than one dog, let the new dog meet each of your dogs separately. Never set an existing pack loose to meet a new dog. Let the dogs meet one to one, with each dog on a long, 12–20' leash. A tight leash can cause a worried dog to receive a signal that all is not well. The worst thing you can do to a dog–aggressive dog is to yank on his neck and promote the syndrome that dog behaviorists refer to as "tether or barrier aggression." Yanking on a dog's neck is a signal to the dog that aggression and defense responses are required from him.

The Pleasure Of Your Acquaintance

When the dogs meet, and are friendly, let them play for a very short period of time. Gather them and stop their first play session before they become overly rambunctious or begin to play hard and test one another's submissiveness or patience.

Once all goes well with one or several meetings in completely unfamiliar territory, the time has come to give the new dog a try at the current dog or pack's home.

Food, Sleeping Place, Toys and Affection

Eating, sleeping, possessions and jealousy over the human pack leader's attention are the four areas that will decide whether the new dog is welcome in the pack. Consider these treasured dog needs and make a wise plan before you bring the new dog home.

Where will the new dog eat? Most dogs need quiet, with no competition over their food bowls. Every group will differ, but safety and good sense may dictate that each dog eats in a separate place. Place each bowl in a separate room and close the door. Give the dogs fifteen minutes to eat and then collect the bowls and let the dogs mingle. Prevention of jealousy and aggression is far superior to re-training after one of more dog learns to protect his food bowl.

Where will the new dog sleep? Many pet dogs sleep in the bed with their owners. This is acceptable if the humans want the dogs in the bed and if the dogs do not grumble with each other or with humans asking them to move or get off the bed. If the dog is in charge of the sleeping place, you can bet the dog is in charge of the house. Every dog needs a place of his own to lay down and sleep. A comfortable dog bed, either in the human bedroom, or in another room, will help the dog understand that he has his own space. The dogs may all decide to sleep on one bed in a pile. But having one dog bed per dog will give the dogs an opportunity to rest alone when they wish.

Any dog that growls at another dog or at his human when he is on the human bed, is not a dog who should sleep in the bed. Dog behaviorist Job Michael Evans, who wrote and lectured extensively on dog aggression, training and pack management advised, "A growl is a bite that hasn't connected." Evans knew that any dog who growls is voicing a statement about his needs and opinions. Growling is always a plea for training and understanding. Growling over a sleeping place is not to be ignored.

Will Your Dog Share
His Prized Possessions?

Any toy or possession that is tantalizing enough to growl to protect needs to removed. Do not wait for jealousy to promote a dog fight. If you do allow the dog to possess something so emotionally charged for him, give the toy or chew only when the dog is behind a closed door and cannot see another dog. A crate is not an acceptable chew place if the dogs can see one another. Some dogs are very territory protective when they are behind a barrier. (Canine behavior analyst William Campbell offers extensive advice on "barrier frustration aggression" in his book "Behavior Problems In Dogs".)

Will Your Dog Or Pack Share
You With A Newcomer?

You must be in charge of which dog receives your attention. Dogs who lived with and loved you first, will have strong feelings about sharing you. Pledge to spend time and undivided attention with all the dogs. Never lavish extra attention on the newcomer just because he is new or perhaps because he had a tough time in his previous home.

If you have more than one dog, do you know which one is the dog pack leader? The dogs have decided who is the leader. The human cannot dictate who the dogs follow as dog pack leader. The wise human pack leader does not interfere with the pack order if the pack is getting along smoothly. Always feed the pack leader first. Never interfere with the pack leader's gentle discipline. Give the pack leader the best place to sleep. You must not lavish more attention on a dog of your choice because it is smaller, cuter, has had a harder life, or for any other human chosen reason.

You Must Assume Responsibility
As Leader Of The Entire Pack

Establish yourself as the fair and firm human leader. Make sure all the canine pack members eat, sleep and play in peace. Sit back and let the pack settle and mingle. To live within a pack of healthy, gleeful and exuberant dogs is to experience an abandon to joy. It is better than daily life. It feels like heaven.

How Many Dogs For *Your* Pack?

"If you don't own a dog, at least one, there is not necessarily anything wrong with you, but there may be something wrong with your life."
Roger Caras

Respect your elders. Mrs. Vashti Carpenter instilled this rule in Sunday School class when I was seven years old. My mamma harped on elder respect in her daily lectures on her favorite topic: good manners.

My first Springer Spaniel, Bonnie, a dignified nine year old, taught the demand of respect for his elders to my frisky, pushy young Spaniel, Abroham, when he attempted to wedge his tiny curious nose into Bonnie's breakfast bowl while she nibbled with dignity.

Its Good To Be Queen

The puppy Abroham had been misguided by his flock of adoring humans, to believe that he was indeed King of the World. One lifted lip and sight of a shining adult 'Bonnie tooth' was enough to ingrain the lesson that as long as Bonnie was Queen (read that as alive) the King was only the boy in waiting.

Early Education Is A Fine Thing

Skills we want our adult dogs to master, we must teach them as puppies. Just as they do not know that peepee on the rug is frowned upon by humans, they must learn that they are low dog on the totem pole of power, and that old dogs rule. If they do not learn these lessons, there will be tears, fear and maybe blood, demanded by the older dog who usually will not tolerate disrespect. We human loved ones must assist the efforts the old dog teaching pack order lessons if we would enjoy harmony in the multi dog house.

Old Dogs May Be Strict Teachers

There are innumerable lessons to teach young dogs and myriad techniques to employ to keep peace in the home that houses and loves more than one dog. Harmony and peace are the rewards of managing the pack with thoughtful consistency and good dog sense.

Interfere Only If You Must

From the moment the new dog arrives, whether he is a lucky adoptee, or a wee adorable pup, the wise owner will pay twice the attention to the dog who came before the upstart. Coo and

fondle the newcomer too much, while ignoring the old guy, and you will set the stage for jealousy which can escalate to dog fights.

Good Manners:
Remember The Older Children

Good manners suggest that when you visit a friend with a newborn human you should always take little gifts to existing toddlers and older children. There is a reason for this bit of courtesy, no one wants to believe they have been pushed aside. No one. If the new pup gets a toy, the older dog gets a toy, too. If the older dog has not been in your lap today, the pup needs to be in that lap only after you take time for your old friend.

If you teach the older dog that the arrival of the new dog is a good thing, the older dog will teach the new addition important dog tasks like: where to poop, when to wee, how to play gently, when to stop playing and take a nap. A gentle, obedience–trained older dog is your best friend for making the new one fit right in.

YOUR NEXT DOG

Looking for chaos? Bring in a new pup before you obedience train and house train the older dog, your troubles will be multiplied.

Multi-Dog Household = Multiplied Owner Responsibility

For nearly 15 years I owned only one dog at a time. One day a lovely young Springer needed a home and when I fell into the hope and splendor of his brown eyes that said , "Mamma?", our home became a two dog pack.

My older dog was not pleased. Two things saved the newcomer from probable slaughter by the sister who despised him instantly.

One: I never forced him on her and I let her know she would always be queen of all she surveyed.

Two: I enrolled both of them in quality, positive and calm obedience classes at a very reputable obedience school in Richmond, VA. Working full-time and wanting to do anything but drive to Richmond two nights a week, I made myself go for the very necessary training and socialization of these two dogs. We drove in rain and dark for 12 weeks on separate nights.

Each dog benefited from undivided attention from me on their night out. Both dogs learned that I was always the boss no matter how they felt about each other. If the older dog felt like lifting her lip and beginning a charge at the usurping pipsqueak, I could yell out "sit" or "come" and the would-be attacker would obey.

DEVOTED TO DOGS

After a few months of hard work by all of us and the reward of many tiny pieces of hot dog,  both dogs recognized I was boss while they settled
their pecking order tasks. I continue to take each dog that I own to a class one night a week. Many nights, I really want to stay home. But every single time we go to class and give each other undivided attention, I think to myself as we drive home, "I am so glad we went!"

Do You Have Enough For Them All?
For every dog you add to your brood you must ask yourself :" Do I have enough......? "

- *Enough Time*
  How much time will be required, morning and night, to feed them and supervise the eating? How much time will it take to housebreak all of them and attend to their physical needs day and night? How many hours can you devote to training every single one? How much time will you spend to play with all of them and make sure they are true family members and not animals caged in the back yard, or worse, running loose entertaining themselves while they distress neighbors, neighbor dogs, and unsuspecting bikers and joggers? Dogs are pack animals and their mental health requires abundant, devoted human attention.

- *Enough Money*
Are your able to pay for necessary and emergency veterinary care? A few weeks ago one of my dogs got a touch of diarrhea. $65. Later that week, my sweet little girl dog began scratching her ear wildly in the night. Treatment: $85. Four days later, it was time for the puppy to have one of his series of puppy vaccines, heart worm preventative tablets and his nails trimmed: $95. Multiple dogs require multiple outpourings of cash to keep them well, and insure that they stay healthy.

Enough money to feed and house them. Size of the dogs and number of dogs will require more budget to feed them. Going on vacation? Your boarding bill for one dog may be low. Add a few more dogs and the boarding bill may be more than your hotel costs while you are away.

Will They All Fit In?
Keys to multi-dog harmony center around the successful management of basic bodily needs. While I have seen dog packs of up to ten sleeping in one pile and eating from one big pan, this "lets all jump in and love one another" method of dog pack management is more often a nightmare of jealousy, and pack order disruption.

A Bed Of My Own
Get a bed for each dog. Lay these beds around the room where you spend most of your time. Throw a few entertaining toys on each bed. Let the dogs choose a comfortable bed and lay down. If they all pile onto one bed and wrestle

191

nicely until they fall into a pile of sleeping angels; great. At least any little fellow who wants to stretch out with a little privacy can if he chooses.

Provide each dog with a dog crate or kennel. Teach each dog, gradually and positively, to like resting in this "den". A dog crate is not an instrument of torture or punishment. Dogs, if they have been trained properly, need and like a little privacy. Who doesn't like a nap with a few of their favorite toys around them?

A dog who has been trained to love his crate will be so much happier when he has to stay overnight in a cage at the vet, or in the run at the boarding kennel. He will also be a better traveling companion when you want to take him to hotels or outdoor events. My own dogs, during summer vacations when they could not sit in a hot car and wait, have sat in crates in the shade near a table at a restaurant with outdoor tables. Imagine you are traveling with the dogs and want to leave them quietly in their crates while you leave a hotel room to see a movie? Dogs who loves their crates will be welcome many places. If you really love your dog, the crate makes him safe and welcome many places he would not be allowed to go.

Let the dogs eat in their crates. No food bowl jealousy has to be supervised if you put the dogs in their crates to eat. Many a dog has gotten fat by sneaking over to a sister's bowl while mamma's back was turned. Puppies who need to eat more will often step back and let an older dog take her food. Maybe the oldest dog gets to continue to eat loose as a sign of respect. Maybe you do not have crates or cages. At least put each dog in a separate room and let each one eat in peace. Food coveting and competition is not the way to make finicky or slow eaters eat faster. Competition over food is always a bad training idea.

There are crates made today out of heavy duty mesh fabric (like lawn chair material) that are sturdy, collapsible, very attractive and weigh less than 10 lbs. for even the biggest giant breed.

Multi-Dog Pack Joy

After all the training, planning and the budgeting is settled and perfected, there is nothing in the whole world to equal the joy to be seen and felt living with a bunch of dogs who love one another. A group of happy dogs racing around the house is one of life's miracles. Laying on the floor with several dogs stomping on your body parts and kissing your face is as good as home life gets. Four dogs and a couple of humans who love one another piled into a big bed on a cold night is a joy to experience.

Dogs love company. Dogs flourish in packs. Humans can make this bliss happen. Dogs provide the frolic, humans provide the care and constant attention.

Managing The Whirlwind: Dogs And Toddlers

*"In his grief over the loss of a dog,
a little boy stands for the first
time on tiptoe, peering into the
rueful morrow of manhood. After
this most inconsolable of sorrows,
there is nothing live can do to
him that he will not be able
somehow to bear."*
James Thurber

My friend Jennifer has three dogs. Jennifer eats with her dogs, sleeps with her dogs and looks for her dogs when they leave the room. But Jennifer's life with dogs requires that she follow many dog safety rules.

Jennifer's Rules For Playing With Dogs

- *She is not allowed to touch a dog if the dog has a toy or a bone.
- She must not run up to dogs and pet them unless she is holding her mom or dad's hand and her parents have asked petting permission.
- She knows she must not poke any dog in the eye, ear, nor pull it's tail.
- She has learned not to approach her dogs if she has food in her hands."

There are lots more rules that Jennifer has to learn in order to play with and enjoy the company of dogs.

Parents Must Be In Charge

Jennifer is only two years old. At two, Jennifer's job is to learn to love dogs. Her parents have the job of supervising every second of every interaction that Jennifer has with her dogs at home or with dogs she meets.

Dogs Are Not Toys

Toddlers are too young to be expected to follow instructions. A big, huggable stuffed dog looks pretty much the same to a toddler as a dog whocould knock them down, and bite their fingers looking for food. Small children can get seriously injured playing with any excited wild puppy or adult dog.

Kids Are Not Popsicles

Dogs only know that nice children smell and taste good and are lick–able.

195

Parents, Not Dogs, Are Responsible

Dogs can learn that unsupervised children represent torment, teasing and trouble about to happen. Every experience between a dog and a child is totally dependent on constant supervision by an adult who must be present at all times.

Many parents of very small children have an already too full job channeling the wild energy of a toddler. Add a dog to the mix and parents can be setting the stage for mayhem and danger.

Bad Memories Linger Long

A terrible, frightening experience with a dog as a toddler can change a child's opinion of dogs forever. Before adding a dog to the family, in the belief that all kids need a dog, a wise parent must make a serious study of the pro's and cons of life with children and dogs.

Teach Children To Obey

I asked Jennifer's mom, Lisa Straus, to share her view on how she has manages a household with dogs and a toddler, and she gave me the following dog-child training advice, "Jennifer was taught from early on how to behave around dogs so when she became a toddler, it was a little easier for us. I have told her never to touch a dog when it has a bone and never pull a dog's tail. Most dogs love to jump, especially when kids are running around, so you have to be very careful that a well meaning dog does not knock the child over."

Food Can Spell Trouble

Jennifer's mom went on to explain, "Food is another issue. Children can get their fingers and hands bitten, especially if they have been holding food or they smell like food to the dog. The dog does not know there is a finger or a hand there."

Whose Toy Is This?

Dogs and children often want to play with the same toys. Toddlers can be growled at, snapped at or bitten if a toddler grabs a toy that the dog felt a need to protect as private property. Jennifer's mom said, "Teaching children to put their toys away is a good thing."

Teach No Tugging

Her advice was to also, "Keep dogs nails clipped. Even a playful swipe of a paw can cause major damage to the face of a child. 'Tug of war' is not a good game to play between toddlers and dogs since it involves use of the dog's teeth near little hands and faces."

Seeing Eye To Eye: A Worry

Adults must realize that eye–to–eye contact can be a challenge to fight or protect oneself in the dog world. Remember that toddlers and small children are just tall enough to stare eye-to-eye with many dogs. Even a gentle dog may interpret such a confrontation as an invitation to defend itself.

Delay Getting A Dog?

Parents contemplating adding a dog to the small child's family must read and research the breeds that they find appealing. Often a tiny dog is definitely not the best breed for a tiny child.

Listen To Wise Breeders' Counsel

Many reputable and long-time breeders of small dogs will not sell a pup to a family with a small child. I spoke with a local breeder of Miniature Poodles and she warned," I hate to say that dogs and toddlers do not mix, but that is sadly the result from the placements we have had of our very small dogs in the homes of small children. For nearly 20 years, we would never sell puppies to people with children under the age of six. One time we relented when a family wanted one of our pups very badly. Three months later, the puppy was returned for scratching the child."

No Hand Waving
So Screaming

When asked for her advice, this breeder warned, "Children have to be taught not to wave their hands around and scream. Frantic movements, loud squealing and running from a dog or pup can be an invitation to be bitten. Might as well hang a sign on that says, 'Bite me!' There are

more tolerant breeds to children than very tiny breeds and breeds that are excitable and fragile. I think raising either a child or a small pup is a full time job to get it right!!! The dog always gets blamed; sometimes unjustly." (This breeder is a lover of children and of dogs, just not necessarily together. I did appreciate her honesty on why she will not sell a pup to a family with very small children. I interviewed several breeders, and found this wisdom offered by many reputable breeders.)

Dog Needs To Be Acclimated To Children
Any dog that is under stress or unfamiliar with a particular child can have a less than friendly reaction.

Julie Hogan, owner of Waggin' Tail Junction in Manassas, Virginia has been training dogs and teaching obedience classes for over 20 years. For nearly that long, my dogs and I have driven up to her kennel to attend her weekly obedience classes. For many of those years, I delighted to know Julie's most gentle and perfectly trained dog, Favor.

Favor was a favorite at kindergartens and nursing homes. Julie would take her to meet preschoolers and Favor would kiss all the children and allow children to examine her every part. Favor Hogan was the queen of good will to all she met.

I called Hogan and asked for tips on mixing dogs and children. Expecting glorious stories of Favor and children, I was shocked when Hogan

stressed to me that even the saint–like, child-loving Favor could have a bad reaction under stressful circumstances.

Even A Saint Can Be Pushed To Anger

Hogan told me, "One of the best lessons I ever learned was with Favor. She had always been what I would consider a good kid's dog; used repeatedly in school demonstrations, etc. But one day, we were outside the obedience ring waiting our turn when a lady with a toddler came over and asked if her child could pet Favor. My famous words were: "Of course. She is very good with children!", followed by the child reaching under my chair to pet her and Favor coming out snapping at the child! Under stress the dog who goes to the kindergarten classes and is petted by groups of children, snapped! Never say never."

Socialize Puppies With Children

Hogan advises, "Of course, if a puppy has not been exposed to young children while still under eight weeks of age, the dog's first experiences with babies, toddlers and elementary age children may backfire and cause the dog to be fearful. Early exposure of puppies to gentle children helps. No dog can be expected to be a saint. It is unfair to put dogs in situations where both the dog and child will come out the losers due to an adult's decision that the two belong together. Supervise all dogs with small children. Be fair to both the dog and child."

Every Toddler Needs An Adult Watching

Hogan continued, "Toddlers are too young to be trainable, so the dog owner must train the dog to stay out of trouble. Use baby gates to keep the baby confined away from the dog. If the child is old enough to want to feed the dog treats, teach them to drop the food on the ground for the dog, so that the dog doesn't grab from the baby's hands. Sometimes we forget dogs can injure children by knocking them over just running past them: totally undirected "aggression" that still results in the dog being blamed."

Children And Dogs Go To School

Many dog trainers invite children to classes for the specific purpose of training the dogs in class to interact gently with children. Felicity Dog Training School, in Fairfax is a dog school that uses clicker training and positive reinforcement to teach gentle greeting between dogs and children.

201

Teresa Patton, of Felicity Dog Training School shared her technique with me saying, "I totally clicker train all of my dogs. From the time they are babies, I invite well–behaved toddlers to visit our classes. Once the dogs understand that they should sit and stay when approached by anyone, we introduce the next 'layer' of difficulty: the toddler or other distractions."

Baby Steps With Big Rewards
Patton says, "As the toddlers approach the dog, we click and treat. We do several repetitions of this until the dog understands that a toddler approaching is not a threat and they are steady. We progress to closer and closer encounters until we are able to have the toddler actually touch and pet the dog while the dog can sit and behave. This actually teaches the dog that when a toddler approaches, they are to sit and pay attention to their owner. When this happens they get rewarded."

Teach Kids To Give A Treat
Patton continued, "The final stage is having the toddler run past the dog with the dog remaining seated and well–behaved. This is coupled with a

click and treat. The sound the clicker marks the appropriate or desired behavior and is followed with the food reward. We also do lessons of 'this is how to give the dog a treat' with a closed hand also. We do this with an adult first. This prevents little hands from being bitten with teeny digits sticking out."

Are You A Dog Lover?
Chances Are You Met A Nice
Dog When You Were A Child.

Toddlers and children deserve the joy of one another's company. Ask any dog lover to tell you about their first dog and you can just settle back for an hour or so of fond remembering. I am so glad my own daddy bought me a puppy and let both of us trail around behind him learning dog ways, good manners and how to have real fun.

First, Teach Respect For
All Living Creatures

Training dogs and children to respect each other requires a very big assignment of researching child friendly breeds, preparing the dog and toddler friendly household and being able to commit long hours of undivided attention building trust and companionship between child and dog.

Supervise, Supervise, Supervise

Many days, most of the parents I know pray for a short nap while their toddler naps safely beside them. Add a puppy? Get ready for lots more work keeping the wee mites occupied, worn out and out of harm's way. Good luck to you.

7

Train the Dog: Don't Blame the Dog

"In dog training,
jerk is a noun, not a verb."
Dr. Dennis Fetco

A Pup is a Terrible Life to Waste

"I talk to him when I'm lonesome, and I'm sure he understands. When he looks at me so attentively, and gently licks my hands; then he rubs his nose on my tailored clothes, but I never say naught. For I can buy more cotton, but never a friend like that.
W. Dayton Wedgefarth

As an adult human in the United States of America, there are many pleasures you can reach right out and take for yourself.

Several banks, daily, it seems to my mail carrier and me, invite me to enjoy hundreds of thousands of dollars in charge card credit. An oiled-up muscle man on television promises that my life would be more fun if I, too, was shining with sweat and active muscles.

One more American dream says, "Everyone can have a puppy."

Just as I do not need to have too much credit, and just as I would not want to glisten with the shine of muscles rippling, not everyone should have a puppy.

Responsibility Comes With Every Pleasure.
After teaching nearly 20 years of dog obedience classes, I have seen thousands of tiny, hopeful pups staring into the faces of their human companions.

Sadly, I have observed countless tired women (and men) who have full-time paid jobs in addition to being constantly exhausted with family responsibilities that include cooking for and picking up for their human family members. These often weary women of the family pack are not jumping for joy and squealing "Yippee!" at the thought of managing and protecting the fragile life of a new pup.

House Training For The House Owner, Too.
A defenseless puppy needs careful, scheduled feeding at least twice a day. The wee canine requires lessons on where and when to pee-pee. Housebreaking does not happen merely by having a human swat him out the door with the command, "Go pee-pee."

The pup needs someone who is glad to parade around the windy, freezing yard at three in the

morning, whispering, "Hurry up, pee-pee." He needs that human ready with a little dog biscuit and gentle praise when he does sniff and circle long enough to make up his mind to "go."

Many mothers (and fathers) go to bed longing for one night of uninterrupted sleep before they begin the next nonstop day. A pup who needs a weewee companion out in the yard in the moonlight is not what the exhausted mom needs.

Too Darned Tired For A Puppy
Many a working mom or working dad has added a new pup, to bring joy to the children or to round out the family picture of togetherness. Often, these already tired adults would just like to sit on the porch and read the newspaper without anyone expecting anything to be done for, or done with, them. Sometimes life is full enough without adding a dog.

Money Does Not Equal Time
Just because I can own a dog does not mean I have time for a dog. Just because I can buy a fine dog from a top breeder, or go to a rescue league and qualify as a person who could be a dog owner, does not mean I intend to make the necessary home, yard and lifestyle changes that a dog or pup requires.

A dog needs a fenced yard. Unless you are willing to fence your yard, heartbreak and "hit by car" tragedy may very well come your way if visiting children, non-dog savvy guests or delivery people forget to mind the location of the pup and leave your door wide open for the dog to escape. This is tragic. It is not a blameless event.

No Fence? No Dog
There are many rescue leagues that have a firm rule: No Fence, No Dog. Pups are not born to be hit by cars and disposed of as if they were toys to replace. This reality is harsh, but not nearly as harsh as the life of a dog crushed beneath the tires of a car when a fenced yard very likely would have protected him. A dog is a life that needs constant protection. His life is totally in our hands from his first day in our home until the last day when he has worn his sweet body out and has to die.

No Sick Leave For Dog Sick Days
A dog needs to go to the veterinarian when he is sick, regardless of the owner's work schedule. Many dog illnesses will not wait a few days till the owner has a day off work to visit the vet.

TRAIN THE DOG

Often, moms and dads dread requesting sick leave to look after sick human children. It is a necessary dog owner reality check to know that these same hard-working moms and dads must accept the added responsibility that a pup, too, may need their time for veterinary appointments or home nursing care.

Training Is Hands-On and Time-Intensive

A dog matures to be a welcome family member only if his human adult pack has time and devotion to give him for training and behavior management. He arrives untrained. His canine drives and ideas of fun will be vastly different than those of the human pack.

Will you train him at home? Months pass. Often the "too busy for dog school" owner will dread being jumped on by the dog. The weary owner may hate to take the dog for walks, since leash dragging hurts his shoulder and wrist joints. Even though he may not admit it, he is sick to death of onlookers commenting, "Looks like that dog is walking you!"

Hopes And Promises: Discarded and Abandoned

The worst thing may happen: A little dog, who had every hope of being a perfect companion, becomes one more responsibility.

Often, sadly, a dog who was brought home for the fun of him, for the new cuteness of him, for his puppy breath, or because he was "free," finds that no one really wants him after all.

Shelters, humane societies and rescue leagues are filled to bursting with little lives that were used until the new wore off, or brought into the world to teach children the cruel and irresponsible lesson of the "miracle" of puppy birth. Birth into a world with no dog lover waiting to love you is no miracle.

Every Puppy You Bring Into The World Needs A Home Before You Breed Your Dog

If only every human who decides to allow his or her dog to breed would make a list of at least eight friends and relatives who swear they want a dog desperately until death takes him.

A reputable breeder who performs various health certifications on all puppies is often hard to find. "Planned, healthy, wanted puppies do not grow on trees," I have heard more than one breeder say. Responsible breeders tell every puppy owner who buys or receives a puppy that each puppy is always, always welcome to come back to the breeder.

Responsible breeders testify that dog breeding is not a money-making activity. Breeding fine pups requires selfless spending to keep the mom and dad healthy, to breed healthy, vaccinated, well-fed pups, and to maintain a home or kennel atmosphere that is very safe, very clean and where the dogs get first priority for care, safety and supervision.

If we bring a life into the world, that life is our responsibility. If everyone who ever allowed a

TRAIN THE DOG

puppy to be born at their home held fast to that obligation, puppies would not be used as a family entertainment, only to be discarded when their puppy breath wears off or a favorite rug is pee-pee ruined. Thousands of dog and puppy lives are snuffed out because humans used them and then discarded them when they were no longer convenient or easy to care for and about.

I have a fantasy that there is a heaven and that dogs who have known us wait for us there as angels. What if, one day, we find ourselves in a heavenly afterlife, where every dog that we have known will step forward and report on how we valued and cherished their lives? Were we gentle in word and deed when no one but our dog watched us? Did we practice kindness amid life's responsibility and hurry? Did we value every beating heart of every dog that we held in our arms as a tiny, cute puppy and also as the wild adolescent dog who ate the sofa?

DEVOTED TO DOGS

Dogs have a great deal to teach about our capacity for happiness. Dogs can assist us to realize and participate in simple joys of day-to-day living. Dogs demonstrate steadfast, honest hearts.

Promise To Cherish

Of all the things we owe our dogs for the myriad gifts they give, one is that when we bring them into our homes and hearts we will care for them their entire lives. A dog deserves to be valued every day as a living creature with feelings and a capacity for happiness, injury and loss. Dogs and all other pets are not disposable.

Hold on to your fine dog. Thank the winds of providence that your faithful dog made his fateful way into your responsible arms. Gently educate would-be and new dog owners. Pull out your checkbook and send a check to a dog rescue organization. Thousands of shelter and rescue dogs need us to care that they had the random misfortune to be born into a throwaway world.

Lucky we are to have dogs to teach us about steadfast relationships and unswerving devotion.

"Forward!", "Halt!":
Paws For Teamwork And Obedience

*"Success is a matter of luck.
Ask any failure."*
Woodrow Wilson

A dog show can be more than a beauty contest.

Brains, devotion and willingness to trust and obey are on display over in the obedience show ring.

Every dog who has loved me has marched into the dog obedience ring and demonstrated that she could walk gently on a leash at my side, stand trustingly when I allowed a stranger to greet and touch her, sit–stay and down–stay while I left her alone beside a line–up of unknown dogs, come to me quickly when I called, and take off her leash and walk freely by my side in heel position showing our unwavering bond of trust and teamwork.

A dog that can perform these skills three times, for three different AKC judges, will be awarded an obedience title from the American Kennel Club.

Best of all, a dog who can calmly demonstrate these obedience tasks will be a welcome visitor where ever she goes. Patient and committed training to develop obedience skills, will nurture a dog and owner bond to endure all your dog's life and beyond.

Recently, I had the pleasure to ask three wise AKC-licensed obedience judges questions that I have longed to ask before my dog and I entered the obedience ring. Whether you are practicing to enter an obedience trial, honing your skills for the AKC Canine Good Citizen test, hope become a therapy dog team, or are curious about dog training, here are a few pointers for training.

Question: What impresses you most when a dog and trainer enter the obedience ring?

Judge Phyllis Broderick: "I love to see a team come into a ring and immediately I can see that special bond that exists between them. Its the same bond that you see with ballroom dancers and ice skating teams; they compliment each other."

 216

Question: What is your one best piece of advice for an owner preparing to compete in obedience competition?

Judge Marilou McCloskey: "Keep moving straight ahead. Many trainers turn their head to look for their lagging dog, this slows their pace and causes the dog to lag even more."

Broderick: "Most important is that every trainer know the rules. (Available at *www.akc.org*.)"

Question: What causes the most lost points for dogs you have judged or trained?

Broderick: "Most points are lost during the heeling exercise: lagging, forging, heeling wide and lagging on about–turns."

Question: Do you think more points are lost by dog's performance or by handler error?

Judge Randy Capsel: "This is a difficult question. Many times it is a combination of both. A trainer error causes difficulty for the dog, which leads to additional points off. "

Question: What are the most common handler errors?

Judge Carol Callahan: "Adjusting pace to the dog. Not walking briskly."

McCloskey: "Tight leash, hand position, forcing the dog into position."

Question: As a judge, what is your pet peeve in your ring?

Callahan: "Handlers who arrive at ringside late and then proceed to explain they don't know the heeling pattern. Also, whiners: trainers who feel no one should be able to walk within fifty feet of their dog when they are working."

McCloskey: "I get very upset when a trainer gets angry with their dog for performing the way the trainer 'trained' the dog to perform."

Question: Is there any one behavior or specific obedience exercise that allows for more opportunity to lose the dog's attention?

McCloskey: "Coming into the obedience ring and in between exercises."

Capsel: "During the slow pace during the heeling exercise."

Question: What do you do, when a dog you are judging misbehaves or loses control?

Broderick: "Often, a team comes into the ring and the trainer has a hard time setting up the

dog to begin the heeling exercise. I know at that point, that this is not going to be a sterling performance. If the dog is out of control, I excuse them. When I have to excuse a team I feel so sorry for the trainer. I know they are embarrassed and the kindest thing a judge can do is excuse them. An out-of-control dog runs around the ring during off-lead heeling stops to look at other dogs, or I fear the dog will jump the ring barriers, dog runs out of the ring, or on the sit or down-stays a dog goes over to another dog. It is never easy to excuse a handler and their dog; but sometimes it is the safest and kindest thing to do."

Capsel: "In most cases I feel for the trainer. I am certain he or she did not anticipate or expect the behavior to be out-of-control. I attempt to reassure them this happens to us all. If the behavior is obviously not going to change or appears to be getting worse, I will ask them if they wish to be excused. While I would have excused them, regardless of whether I asked them or not, I try to make it a mutual agreement so to lessen the 'stigma' of being excused."

Question: Could you share training pointers for trainers working to get ready for obedience competition?

McCloskey: "Every dog trained can be totally different. My dog Bentley thought that dog shows were created just for his social gratification. He had to learn that when we were in the ring I meant business. I could smile and tell him "good  job", but the minute I gave him more than that he thought I wasn't serious anymore so he could 'go shopping' My other dog, Harley, is just the opposite. He lives to please me. He tries really hard and my challenge, with him, is making him understand that it is okay to make mistakes. My point is that every dog is different, even within the same breed. The time spent, in the beginning, teaching the dog to "pay attention" to you, with games, food and then consequences for not paying attention, make training the obedience exercises easier and more fun for both the dog and handler."

Broderick: "I have trained Beagles, a Golden Retriever, a Field Spaniel and four Springers. Most breeds are smart, intelligent and are willing to please. For dogs who love to eat and love to fetch and play with toys, food and toys are a definite tool for training.

"Attention training is the most important part of training. Every exercise in obedience requires attention. At first, attention should be taught with food and/or toys, keeping in mind your praise should be the primary reinforcer ; second is food or toys. Keep training light and short . Once the dog knows the exercise, add distractions. I teach my dogs in a quiet location with no distractions. Once they know the work, I add distractions and move from a quiet place to a busy place. I try to train at three or four different locations weekly.

"Do not drill your dog. Keep the sessions short. Always end on a positive note. Do four or five short sessions a day, ending with a play session."

Want to go and see an obedience trial? Visit *www. infodog.com* for show calendars and dates.

Say It Isn't So:
Dog Training Myths

"It is just like man's vanity and impertinence to call an animal dumb because it is dumb to his dull perceptions."
Mark Twain

A wild Airedale puppy grapples with the edge of the reception desk. He clutches onto the ledge; determined to get enough leverage to leap over the barrier to kiss those nice receptionists on the mouths. Scrape. Lunge. Appointment cards flying. Biscuit samples crashing to the floor.

Lay Down That Newspaper
Around the corner of the reception area, a little woman threatening with a rolled up newspaper, yells, "Ahab, I'm coming to get you!"

Ahab keeps right on leaping and flailing to kiss those nice women behind the counter. He

221

knows they want him. The enraged owner is closing the gap between Ahab and her upraised newspaper.

Enter the veterinarian. Let's call her Dr. B. The veterinarian says, "I sure hope you're getting ready to hit yourself in the head with that newspaper for bringing that puppy into this clinic without a leash!"

True story.

Hooray For The Veterinarian With The Courage To Speak!
Did Ahab's mom desist with her newspaper swatting of the dog? Heck no. She whacked him in the side of the head and shouted, "The only way to train a puppy is with a rolled up newspaper. I've always done it."

This is the rolled-up newspaper myth.

According to the American Heritage dictionary, a myth is: "a notion based more on tradition or convenience than on fact".

Myths abound surrounding dog ownership. Some are harmless. Many are total falsehoods. Dog lovers need to be award that myths can hurt the health or well being of our dogs.

Recently, I asked several dog professionals to share with me their most often heard myths. None of these myths are based in fact.

TRAIN THE DOG

Breeding the female dog is an area where weird ideas with no basis in genetic or medical fact flourish.

Margot Wagner, award winning dog trainer and receptionist at the Fredericksburg Animal Hospital, shared myths related to neutering and breeding dogs. "Dog owners often say, 'Females need to go through a first heat to calm down.' This is not true. Calming behavior has never been shown to occur due to experiencing a heat cycle."

Wagner goes on to say, "We also hear the myth, 'If a pure bred female is ever bred to a mix-breed dog, she will never have purebred pups again.' This is obviously not the case, and has no basis in genetic science."

Ginnie Klein, a long-time dog rescue volunteer told me that the breeding myth she hates to hear is, "'Having a litter will make her more loving toward any children we will have.' Totally false."

DEVOTED TO DOGS

Myths that perplex many breeders and dog professionals are related to to coat care and interpretations of colors and markings on the dog.

I brought one professional breeder, Amber Carpenter of Connemara Bearded Collies, to near fury when I asked her pet myth peeves.

Carpenter explained, "One of my peeves is people that call inquiring about Bearded Collies because 'they don't shed.' I tell them  if they want a pet that doesn't shed, buy a toad. All dogs shed. Even the hairless Chinese Cresteds shed some of that scalp hair every now and again. There is no dog that does not shed. The thing about Beardies, of course, is that they are double coated. They tend to shed their undercoat frequently and it gets caught in that outer coat before it hits the floor, thereby giving the appearance of not shedding. But, of course, they do shed."

Carpenter added, "Another myth that bugs me is that 'crating is cruel'. Dogs have a natural den instinct and feel protected and safe in a crate. It is far more cruel to allow an unsupervised puppy or untrained dog free run of the house where he can not only do damage to the house, but also do tremendous damage to himself if he gets into something dangerous. A breeder friend of mine knew a puppy owner who left her Beardie puppy 'contained' in the kitchen because 'it's so cruel' to leave him in a crate. Tragically, she came home to find a dead puppy. He'd climbed up on the counter and pulled off several items, including a plastic bag that he got his head into and suffocated."

Carpenter could not resist adding the myth, "I want a girl puppy because I want a sweet dog, and females are sweeter than males." She said. "Anyone who has known the steadfast devotion of a boy to his mom (or dad) knows that males are in no way lacking in affection or the ability to bond."

A myth for raising a good hunting dog came from author and AKC judge Carol Callahan, of Donahan Springer Spaniels, "'A sporting dog with black spots in his mouth will be hard mouthed when retrieving game.' This is a myth. Mouth color is not predictor of whether a hunting dog is likely to tear up game."

Callahan often hears the myth, "Letting a hunting dog live in the house will ruin his scenting ability". Callahan laughed at this and retorts, "Only if you have a very stinky house!!!!" Dog behavior myths try to give quick and easy ways to housebreak dogs and deal with housebreaking events. Cathi Allison, owner of Dog Dayz Boutique for Dogs and Dog Owners, hates the myth, "Dogs eat poop because something important is missing from their diet." Allison's years of training dogs and talking to dog owners has taught her that, "Dogs eat poop because they CAN!"

Allison wished that the myth, "Dogs mess in the house and/or chew up things because they are spiteful" did not exist. Allison believes that dogs react with inappropriate house soiling and destructive behaviors most often because they are suffering from separation anxiety or an undiagnosed medical problem. Punishment will only make these problems worse.

Many days, when I come home from veterinary offices, where I meet with behavior consultations, I thank my lucky stars for my dogs Vivien, Gabriel and Quinnton. I am so glad I was not born an unsuspecting, defenseless dog. Humans can do unthinking and unforgivable things to dogs out of either ignorance or laziness to find real facts and professional advice.

Each time a dog owner tells me that "the best way to housebreak a puppy is to rub his nose in the accident", it is all I can do not to leap forward and grab the speaker's nose and rub it somewhere unpleasant. Many myths may be created to give humans permission to discipline and vent their anger on untrained dogs.

Every Owner Action Produces
A Dog Behavior Reaction

When we swat a puppy in the head with a newspaper, we should not be surprised when he gets a little older and his natural prey catching instincts cause him to lunge out with his teeth and try to protect his head from harm. What is he supposed to do? He cannot reach out with a hand and stop the blow. We have triggered

his response to use his teeth as defensive weapons.

When you hear advice that sounds painful to the dog, too easy to cure a problem or just plain weird, stop and call your veterinarian's office for an opinion on the myth you have heard. Veterinary receptionists will be glad to tell you what they know. If they do not know, they are trained to ask your veterinarian for the real answer that will help your dog.

Finally, the very funniest myth shared with me came from Dr. Robert Prasse, who told me that old bulldog wisdom warns, "Better not let a bull dog bite you because if he does, he will not let go till it thunders."

DEVOTED TO DOGS

Some myths are so strange they are hilarious. Some may really harm your unsuspecting, defenseless dog. Don't grease him up in used motor oil to cure his skin (another myth), don't breed her to make her sweet, don't worry that she will attract lightning during an electrical storm.

Love her and take her to the veterinarian any time you have a question.

If You Love 'em, Leash 'em

"If it wasn't for dogs, some people would never go for a walk."
Unknown

Where is your dog's leash right this minute? A dog without a leash handy is a dog headed for trouble.

A dog needs an owner with a relentless commitment to love him, train him, and consider his needs all the days that that owner may be blessed to have him.

Are you an owner with a sense of fun? Do you see dog enjoyment and dog training opportunities where non-dog lovers might see fuss and bother? A dog behavior problem is a training opportunity for you and your dog.

DEVOTED TO DOGS

When I hear the dreaded phrase, "I'm at the end of my rope," I think, "Probably what you need right now is a leash."

What Kind Of Leash?

For training, restraining and parading around town, a 6-foot leather leash no more than a half inch wide, is the best tool for a well-behaved dog.

While the very popular reel-in/reel-out, extendable long leash may be a helpful tool for exercising a dog that will not come reliably in park or field, use of the long, retractable leash teaches the dog unwanted, dreadful lessons about dragging the owner in the dog's wake on his walk, about lunging out at strange dogs and people before the owner gives permission, and promotes the dog being in control of the owner. Dog classes, dog shows and dog sport camps often proclaim, "No Dogs On Extendable Leashes Allowed."

Buy several 6' leather, half-inch leashes and keep them near your hand and your heart.

Grandkids Fear KoKo

KoKo is an exuberant, healthy, curious large breed puppy. KoKo's owner is grandmother to three human children ages 18 months, 3 years, and 5 years. Grandma wonders why one daughter-in-law never visits. One grandchild pulls KoKo's ears and begins to cry saying, "KoKo nipped me." KoKo leaps on the children. No one enjoys a visit to Granny's house.

Solution: Granny must attach KoKo to the leash. Next, Granny must sit on the leash. KoKo gets just enough leash to sit or lie at Granny's feet. All responsibility to manage KoKo and the children belongs to the adults. Adults must be in the room at all times with KoKo.

Scarlett Is A Loud Mouth

Mother excuses herself from the phone and tells her caller that she has to leave the phone to teach her dog that barking does not get her attention.

Dog mother gets Scarlett's leash, which is nearby. Dog mother may need to keep the 6' leather leash tied around her waist for constant access. Scarlett is placed on leash. Dog mother returns phone call. Owner sits down on leash and ignores Scarlett. It is perfectly acceptable to give Scarlett a toy, safe chew object, or a rubber toy stuffed with peanut butter.

If the dog mother can enlist several helpful friends to telephone, Scarlett would learn faster with repeated leash control lessons, for as many days as possible.

When the phone rings, before she answers the phone, the dog mother places Scarlett on the leash as a barking preventive teaching technique.

Dog mother may pet Scarlett only if Scarlett is silent.

Fritz Will Knock You Senseless

You have already guessed, right? Before Uncle Faulkner touches the doorbell, Fritz is on the leash. Surely a Southern gentleman like dear genteel Uncle Faulkner has telephoned first and you are expecting him.

Can't control Fritz while you hug Uncle Faulkner hello? Tie Fritz to the chair leg where you intend to sit, or to a strong table leg near your chair. When the hugging ceases, leave Fritz on leash and sit on his leash.

I have a soft leather leash tied to a leg of my heavy coffee table for this very purpose. Even a dog trainer's dogs can be too much for some visitors. Anytime my dog cannot settle and lie quietly, I attach him to the coffee-table leash. When not in use, I stuff it under the coffee table and try not to forget and vacuum the leash. Vacuuming is a rare activity at my house, so the leash is safe and the dogs are ready to be reminded gently by their tether to lie down and let the humans mingle.

(This dog problem solution also works for the case of: Guests Won't Come: Caddy Rips Their Clothes and Hose Off).

Unless you have unlimited millions to purchase vast amounts of liability insurance and settle injury lawsuits, it is best to restrain your dog before Pluto decides the plumber is bending over too close to his coveted bag of dog kibble.

Some dogs hate service people, uniforms and all new smells invading their territory. Again, leash control to the rescue. As a favorite teacher of mine warns: "prepare and prevent, or repair and repent."

A leash keeps a territory–protective dog safe. It lets him know that his owner has the situation under control.

Won't Come = Keep On That Leash

I worked with a woman who was reprimanded repeatedly for being late to work. She never admitted to our boss that she was often late because her young, frisky dog, Willie, ran her all over her neighborhood every morning as she begged him for "one last wee wee."

Use of a leash was all this frantic, wheedling dog caller needed. Dogs who walk on leash do not run away. They can listen and respond as you whisper, "hurry up, pee pee." A dog biscuit in the other hand as you command this will invariable teach your dog to be the fastest wee in the East.

Leash Teaches Control

Restaurants that allow nice dogs, on leash, to lie quietly beside a dog lover's table are tiny spots of heaven on Earth to dog and humans who love them. All dogs lucky enough to find themselves watching humans eat in public should be seen, not heard, and certainly not felt by strangers.

DEVOTED TO DOGS

Make sure your dog sets a shining example of perfect manners. Down the dog. Sit on the short leash. Even if Saffy has not mastered down-stay, she must lie down. A short leash allows her no alternative posture.

Many dog owners hate dog cages. A dog with no cage is often a dog that is never truly housebroken. How will he learn to "go" on command and to control his output urges if he never has to learn to "hold it"?

When, or if, a cage is not available, the leash will also safeguard the rug or furniture from urges to eliminate at will. Leash the dog when he is in the house. Attach the leash to your chair or other solid object. Six feet of leash will give your dog roll over, curl up, walk around room. No more freedom is needed, nor wisely given, if the dog has not had a minimum of 90 days without a single "accident" in the house. Leash use will train the owner to recognize when the dog needs to go out. The leash will give the dog insurance that he is taken out whenever he sniffs, circles or is restless.

One leash attached to one bath-reluctant pup will corral the pup and give the shampooer two free hands to gently and quickly wash the dog. We all have to take baths. Sadly, resignedly, there is no escape.

Love your dog. Use your leash. Drape leashes over doorknobs. Secrete them under car seats. Get up off your chair. Take control. Rub him. Love him. Leash him.

Reining In An Obedient Dog:
Horse Trainers Train Dogs, Too

*"Some of my best leading men
have been dogs and horses."*
Elizabeth Taylor

Her strong, capable hands neatly gathered the leather leash, leaving no leash flapping in the dog's peripheral vision. She listened intently to the obedience teacher's instructions.

Down on her knees, quietly, she stroked down the little white dog's shoulders and back. Left hand behind his knees, she quietly said, "sit". Her right hand clasped his collar between his little ears. She guided the dog into a precise, straight sit.

The woman did not nag her dog. She gave her command one time: sit. Her confident hands guided the tiny, squirmy Jack Russell Terrier bottom into the sit position. Giving him a rewarding pat on his proud, out thrust chest, she whispered for his ears only, "What a good dog you are." Observing her calm, confident, precise training technique, I thought to myself "I bet this woman is a horse trainer."

Horse Trainers Rein In Unruly Dogs
Horse trainers have told me that nagging, yelling, or ignoring a misbehaving horse will result in the horse learning nothing and perhaps causing physical danger for the human trainer. Horse trainers bring excellent training skills to dog obedience lessons.

Do You Have Quiet Hands?
Horse trainers strive to master "quiet hands". The best dog trainers learn that gentle, controlled leash handling has a quieting effect on dogs.

Too Much Talking = Dog Tunes You Out
Often, the more the trainer talks, the less the dog listens. The more influenced the trainer becomes on outside stimulation, the less the dog learns to pay attention to the trainer. When a dog demonstrates a behavior problem, the owner must analyze human behaviors surrounding the dog in order to understand why the dog is misbehaving, anxious, destructive, or demanding more attention than the owner

feels able to give. Calm the owner and you will usually calm the dog. Dogs are like sponges who soak up and react to our every emotion. Horse trainers frequently speak of human emotions traveling down the rein to the horse. This concept works in dog training, too.

Always: Watch Your Dog

Horse trainers usually have good manners and good sense when mingling with strangers and unknown dogs. Horse trainers do not let their horses gallop wildly into the faces of other horses, nor do they allow their dogs to lunge into the muzzles of other dogs. All creatures require varying degrees of space for physical comfort and to feel that those around them respect their need for space. Many dog fights would never happen if all dog walkers learned that dogs can be very offended when suddenly kissed or prodded by an unknown dog displaying pushy lack of basic manners.

Riding teachers school young riders in the necessity of grooming a horse before and after the horse is worked. Horse trainers realize that brushing, combing and caring for a dog calms him, insures he has no lumps, bumps, nor lameness, and builds a bond that makes the dog more easily trained. Get your hands and a quality brush onto the body of your dog everyday. Watch his eyes watching your eyes as he gratefully accepts the undivided attention. Feel his body relax under your hands. Pack leadership is earned. One of the ways the pack leader instills respect is to look after the needs, mental and physical, of the pack members, from head to toe.

Recently, I asked several horse trainers to describe the lessons horses have taught them that have helped them to be better dog trainers.

Deborah Collins of Spotsylvania, VA, who has ridden horses for pleasure and in all levels of riding competition, told me, "I have owned a Jack Russell Terrier, a German Shepherd Dog, and a Golden Retriever while owning and riding horses. My Jack Russell Terrier, Spike, was the best of the horse dogs. While riding at the farm, the entire pack of dogs would follow me. Spike, being the smallest, would race behind but could not keep up with a cantering horse. He would cut across the field. You could see him tunneling in the high grass. He would stop and start, leaping straight up, pivoting in the air a few degrees each time. He would spot me and take off as fast as he could to catch up. Spike was kicked by one of my horses and suffered an injury. He sported a somewhat horseshoe shaped scar on his side. My horse trained him to respect the rear end and to never chase again. He was an awesome dog and I still think about how much fun he had in his life."

I asked dressage competition trainer, Ann de Matteo to describe the lessons she has been taught about dog training from her years of

horse training. She explained, "Horses are big and unpredictable. Even though dogs are small and not as unpredictable, if you treat them a little like they were bigger and dumber, you won't go wrong. For example, you teach a horse early on not to get in your space, for safety's sake. That works well for dogs, too. Horses don't learn like dogs do. They don't understand the concept of trying to please the handler! With horses, you set the horse up so the easiest choice he can make is the right one. I think setting a dog up so he can't fail is a really good training tool."

Set Up For Success

The technique of setting a dog up to do an exercise correctly over and over again is a concept dog trainers learn as 'pattern training'. Just like horse trainers, the dog trainer works to let the dog perform a task correctly so many times that the task becomes second nature. This is a great positive method for training dogs.

Praise! Praise! Praise!

When asked, "What is the most helpful tip you can give to dog trainers?", de Matteo urged, "Praise, praise, praise." She concluded her advice, telling me, "Horses command respect from their handlers, by virtue of their size. Give your dog the same respect." Ann de Matteo's great love for training horses and dogs in her leisure time carries over into her professional life. She and her husband, Chip, and their perfectly behaved Cardigan Corgi, Danny, design and craft horse and dog jewelry which can be admired at their website at *www.hand-hammer.com.*

Your dog may not be a little horse, but you can rein him in with a few tips from the horse trainers. Praise, tireless repetition and attention to his mental and physical needs will prepare your dog to master "sit", "down", and the most important command of all, "come".

Horses are wonderful creatures, but you need a well trained dog to curl up in your lap for company and delight. A horse cannot sleep at the foot of the bed and protect you from frights in the night.

If You Train Them, They Will Come

"Do not call to a dog with a whip in your hand."
Zululand Proverb

Ah, to come. perchance to come quickly, with a wagging tail. That is the dream of dog owners whose dogs have learned to run away.

"What is the one single obedience command you most want to teach your dog?", I ask every student who comes to my obedience class. At least seven of every ten dog trainers will admit, "I want him to come when called."

No wonder an owner's fervent hope is that their dog will come. While there are many dog safety and dog obedience issues that make us want our dogs to come, I think the primary reason we want our dogs to come is that we need to know that we are their masters.

Being Ignored Hurts Our Feelings

We want evidence that the dog will not only obey us by coming, but that by coming to us when called, our dog says, "Thanks for calling me. I really would rather be with you than do whatever it was I was doing before you called me."

A dog that will not come to us hurts our feelings. A dog that will not come is proof to us that we have neglected to build a bond of master and trusting companion. When a dog does not come, we know intuitively that we have somehow failed the dog.

Dog ownership is not an egalitarian relationship between you and your dog. If you let the dog make the decisions about where he goes, whether or not he comes, what he eats, where he sleeps, you will turn him into a dog who makes his own rules, and comes when he pleases. You do your dog no favors by neglecting to be his leader.

Your Dog *Will* Learn To Come

It is not too late to retrain a dog who will not come when called. You can train him to be a dog that stops what he is doing and runs straight to you when you say the magic words, "Rover! Come!

"Come Checklist and Recall Rules"

- *No Freedom Until You Know He Knows 'Come.'*
  Even if it does your heart good to watch him run freely in the woods, the dog park, the beach, or even the big back yard, if your

 242

TRAIN THE DOG

dog does not come promptly when you call, he absolutely must not be allowed 'off-leash freedom'.

Each time you call him off-leash and he gives you that over the shoulder "kiss my foot" look and continues about his sniffing, frolicking business, you reinforce his opinion that come is an option, not a 'must do' command.

- *Reel Him In*
  Until he comes reliably, in a fenced area, an owner must stop being a lazy exercise person and allowing the dog to exercise himself off lead. Attach a 20'–30' long cotton line to his collar. Let him run free on his long line. Every few minutes, hold up a treasured toy or a hunk of treat and yell, in your most kind and happy voice, "Rover! Come!"

If he comes, praise him wildly, gleefully, like he is the most brilliant dog on Earth and give him the reward.

If he does not come, immediately begin to reel him in on his long line, saying, "What a good come! What a good dog! Good to come!" Once you have reeled him in, pet him profusely, give him a small reward and let him go free on the long line again. Practice this at least every ten minutes while you are in the open space.

- *Never Give The 'Come' Command If You Cannot Go And Get Him*
  When you give the 'come' command, with the dog off-leash (in the house, or in a fenced back yard, etc.) you must walk to the dog and physically lead him by collar or leash, if he does not come promptly.

  Until the non-coming dog masters 'come', you would be wise to keep a short, soft leash in your pocket at all times. When you call and he does not come, you must not go to him wearing a stormy face, nor yelling and stomping your foot. Calmly, walk straight to him. Put on the leash. Walk him wherever it was you wanted him to go.

  The "show me" method of training is all about the trainer taking charge of the dog's learning. Show your dog without emotion, nor negative reinforcement, that he will do as you ask or you will enforce the command.

TRAIN THE DOG

During your re-training period, you think
to yourself, "From now on, he will not learn
to run away. If he does not come when
called, it is entirely my fault for not being in
charge."

- *'Come' Must Be Pleasant*
Never again will you call the dog to you
in order to yell at him for any kind of
misbehavior. Imagine you find the biggest
puddle of peepee on your clean bedspread.
Nothing helpful will be learned by the dog
if you yell "come!" and proceed to show him
what he has done.

If you call him in your hateful voice and
he does come, you will have just set your
training program back disastrously. Calling
a dog to you to speak harshly to him
teaches him that 'come' is a stupid thing to
do. This same "don't call me if you're going
to hurt me" logic applies to anything the

245

dog may prefer to avoid: toe nail clipping, ear washing, anal sac squeezing, anything your dog may be less than thrilled to have performed on his canine self.

Yes, of course, a good dog owner must perform tasks the dog may not enjoy. Just don't use the magic 'come' command. Go to the dog.

- *Lavish Rewards For Coming*
  Tackle any unpleasant procedure armed with the dog's favorite treats. Be generous with the treats and praise while you do whatever it is you know he would prefer not having done to him.

  If you are not quick and capable of any of these dreaded tasks, quit tormenting your dog and pay a professional to provide the service. How many dogs hate having their toe nails trimmed because the owner is slow, cannot see where nail ends and quick begins, and the dog has learned that pain and bleeding is about to befall him? Dogs are not stupid.

- *Food May Be The Cure For 'Come'*
  Most dogs like to eat. Leash the dog. Show him a delicious morsel of something to eat. Wave the treat at his nose while you run backwards saying, "Rover! Come!"

- *Unleash Your Silly Side*
  Give him the treat and lavish praise upon him the moment he arrives at your feet. If

TRAIN THE DOG

you are physically fit enough to roll around on the floor, squealing with delight, "good come! good come!", the dog will like that, too.

Make your dog believe that you go wild with joy any time he comes when his name is spoken. Retrain the dog to think that his name is a magical sounding word to you and for him.

Sadly, many untrained dogs have been taught that their name is a word that signals mean talk and disdain is on the way. No wonder so many dogs do anything but come when they hear their name.

- *Feed Him By Hand If You Must*
  My Bearded Collie, Vivien, now comes to me faster than a speeding bullet. But as a young girl, 'come' meant nothing to her. I understood that turning a deaf ear to Mother was not a good sign in a tiny puppy. Puppies, usually, are born with a natural following desire. Puppies quickly learn to come, if no untrained human messes up this

247

natural tendency. But Vivi would plant her little fuzzy paws and stare, unfazed, at me when I called in my sweetest voice.

- *For Every Morsel She Must Come*
How did I nip this bent of self-will in the bud? For weeks, I fed her every morsel of her dry food meals from my hand.

My other dogs would eat eagerly in their crates while Miss Vivien sat in my lap and was given every piece of dry food piece by piece, from my hand. No human food, mind you. I wanted to teach her to look to me for dog food, not to train her to be a picky eater!

Week two of this hand food training program, I would walk around the house with her bowl of dry food in my hand, while saying in my sweetest, happy voice, "Vivien, Come!" The ten week old prancing Vivien would scamper behind me and I would turn and whisper delightedly, "Good to come!", and give Vivien a little handful of food.

Three weeks of this "come-to-eat" training program and Vivien changed from an aloof puppy to a puppy who would stop all pursuits to find her mamma when called.

Master Come: Start Today
Come is the one command a dog requires to be safe, to be allowed freedom to explore doggy pursuits, and to build his bond to come to your side any time you tell him he must.

 248

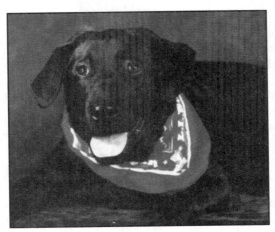

Is Your Dog a Canine Good Citizen?

"His name is not wild dog anymore,
but the first friend, because
he will be our friend for
always and always and always."
Rudyard Kipling

The American Kennel Club (AKC) is on the hunt for good citizens. Canine Good Citizens, that is.

All well-behaved dogs and their devoted owners are invited to participate the AKC Canine Good Citizen Program. Your dog could be the next proud dog to pass the test and begin signing his name, "Rover, CGC."

Does your dog have to be purebred to take the test?

No. As long as his veterinary chart labels him, "canine" he will be as proud a citizen canine as any who have gone before him.

Does he have to be registered with the American Kennel Club?

No. He will need to show proof from his veterinarian that he has had his rabies vaccine, and has had his vaccinations for all communicable diseases. Owners must show their dedication to his grooming needs by presenting the handsome dog at the test clean, brushed and polished for a special outing.

Evaluators for the test will ask the dog to demonstrate that he is respectful of strangers and of unknown dogs. If he jumps on strangers or lunges in dislike, or even with too much friendliness, he will have to keep practicing his social meeting and greeting skills before he will pass the CGC test.

The Good Citizen candidate must walk calmly, without pulling on his leash through a crowd of dogs and people. He must not react by pulling on his leash in alarm if a loud noise occurs near him. No skittering, cringing or leaping behind the owner's leg is allowed in order to pass the test. He must be able to walk nicely without lunging or tripping his owner as the owner makes sharp turns and about-turns. A dog who walks regularly with his owner in his neighborhood or on downtown excursions will have no problem walking nicely on his leash.

TRAIN THE DOG

A stranger must be able to approach, greet and pet him. He must submit for grooming by a stranger without great interest or worry. The evaluator will brush him. She will pick up and look at his feet.

The same friendly stranger will approach to shake hands with the dog's owner. The calm dog must not jump on the stranger, pull away, show shyness or aggression, be overly friendly. A nice stand with a wagging tail is best.

A Canine Good Citizen will trust humans enough to allow a friendly stranger to hold him on least for three full minutes while the owner is out of sight. The dog must not whine, bark, nor jump on the person holding the leash.

The test evaluator will ask to see the dog perform a 'sit–stay' and a 'down–stay' on command. While the dog holds the position on a very long leash, the owner will walk away, turn and return to the dog.

Finally, the dog will perform the task many dog  trainers consider the most important command that a dog must master. He will 'come when called'. The owner, with a friendly, upbeat voice, will say, "Michael! Come!". The dog will hop up immediately and come straight to the owner. No detours. No wheedling. No begging. No mean threatening voice. Just, "Michael! Come!".

Many Commands, But No Treats

Owners may give commands repeatedly, but may not use food on the test.

Why Pass The CGC Test?

Owners and their dogs hope to pass the test for many reasons. When asked why she wanted her dog to pass the CGC test, Cathi Allison of Fredericksburg admitted, "Since Pumpkin is an American Pit Bull Terrier, many people assume the worst of her. I wanted her to have a clear proof that she is a wonderful dog. I also wanted her to become a Registered Therapy Dog, and passing the CGC test is the prerequisite."

"The first step to preparing for taking the CGC test is to enroll in a basic obedience class,"was the opinion of local dog trainer, Sylvia Neely. Basic classes teach the dog to pay attention to the owner and to master the basic commands of sit, down and come.

Ranger, a very smart and outgoing Labrador Retriever, calmly passed the test in spite of youth and high energy. His owner, Amy Thorpe, advised, "Wear your dog out with lots of exercise before you go for the test. The dogs are so excited when they arrive at the test site and see lots of dogs to greet and investigate that they have a hard time paying attention to you. Run your dog around at home before you go for the test. Ranger was pooped when we took the test and he really paid attention to me during the test."

Dog trainers who have given the tests to many hopeful dogs agree that obedience training and socialization are the keys to passing the test.

Sue Peetoom tests dogs who hope to become therapy dogs and offers this advice for preparing for the test, "Socialize a lot. Once your dog knows the basics in controlled situations, take your dog to meet and greet other people and dogs, all the while practicing the different test exercises so the dog is used to listening to you in areas full of activity." When asked, "What do you feel is the most difficult area of the test to pass?", Peetoom said, "Walking on a loose leash is the hardest. Many dogs are pulling with a tight leash; not walking next to their owners."

Sue Lough, who has trained and tested many area canine good citizen candidates, including her own brilliant Golden Retriever, Cassie, CGC,

reported that it was hard to decide which of the 10 test behaviors were the most important for a well-behaved dog to master. Lough explained, "I am torn between 'come when called' and 'sit-stay' being most important. I have seen first-hand the value of both these commands to the safety of loose dogs in my neighborhood. Getting a dog to come to you, or to sit on command and stay until you get to them just may save a dog's life. "Lough's own dog Cassie is frequently pressed into service to be the perfectly calm heeling dog who heels past dogs taking the test.

Every dog owner who makes the commitment to begin today teaching their dog the good dog behaviors of the Canine Good Citizen program will be rewarded with a companion that is a joy for life. A CGC dog can be proud that is well trained and that he and his owner are a team.

A Canine Good Citizen dog is an ambassador for all the dogs that want to go out into the world and be welcome. For every CGC certificate the American Kennel Club issues, there is one more dog and owner who can know they have shown their devotion to one another that will last all the days of their time together.

Start practicing. Your dog wants to be a bona-fide good citizen.

8

Behavior Problems: Understanding, Managing And Re-training

"There's facts about dogs and there's opinions about them. The dogs have the facts, and the humans have the opinions. If you want facts about dogs, always get them straight from the dog. If you want opinions, get them from humans."
J. Allen Boone

It Takes A Slow Hand
To Reassure A Dog

"The greatest prayer is patience."
Buddha

When my mother met my husband-to-be, she summed him up later saying, "He comports himself like a gentleman."

If asked, how would your dog say you comport yourself? Are you calm and gentle? Are you deliberate and reasonable? When he does something you do not like, do you analyze "why" he did this, before you speak harshly to him? When was the last time you sat quietly on the floor with him, doing nothing, just being with him?

257

Every Breath You Take
Your Dog Observes
Dogs are emotional sponges. Dogs reflect our moods and our temperaments. Show me a nervous, rushing, frenzied dog owner and I bet you will see a dog that reflects his human's unrest in his own canine behavior.

When the humans he watches are unhappy, look out for a dog that will behave in an unhappy or stressed way. With every breath we take, with every movement we make, we send a signal to the dog that loves us.

There are many specific times when dog parents must be watchful of our own emotions, actions and reactions.

When You're Down And Troubled
Wise dog owners must become great actors. Imagine that you arrive home to find a grave emergency. No matter how excited or distraught you may be, your dog is watching.

Fears Imprinted
When my own Gabriel was 5 months old, he was promoted to staying in my bathroom behind a baby gate. His housebreaking skills were coming along nicely, but he was not ready to circulate and investigate the house alone.

I had been out to dinner. Straight to the bathroom I went, to put Gabriel on a leash and lead him outside to relieve himself.

BEHAVIOUR PROBLEMSS

Behind the baby gate, I was greeted by young Gabriel, who appeared to be covered in bright red blood from the tip of his nose, all over his lovely square springer muzzle, smeared down his neck fur and under his chest.

The sight of Gabriel stopped my heart. I had to find out where he was bleeding. My dog-calmness skills went down the drain. I grabbed him up, surely reeking my distress, my eyes wide and terrified. I carried him to the bathtub. With the shower sprayer and warm water, I began to hose him off, afraid to see why he was covered in blood.

The moment the warm water hit his fur, and I got close enough to really see him, down on my knees by the tub, my heart relaxed and I nearly fainted with the sudden relief of understanding the cause of the brilliant red puppy. Gabriel had found a plastic bag containing oodles of lipstick tubes. Being a puppy, he had investigated the lipstick with his curious nose, had chewed a few, rolled in many, and must have played with them in ways I cannot even guess as he entertained himself alone in the bathroom.

Memories Linger
Happy ending? Yes. And no. Even though Gabriel was not injured, as I had feared, my frantic, hurried, panicked reaction did cause him harm.

I am sure that I showered his young personality with so much fear that to this day, Gabriel is 4 years old, he is less than thrilled when I lift him into the bathtub to have a bath. He does not struggle. He freezes into a rock-solid springer statue and stoically submits to all necessary lathering, conditioning and rinsing. There is a worried look in his eyes and he stares questioningly into my face during the bath process.

Lessons Learned
I would give anything to be able to go back to the night that I know my own fear imprinted his puppy personality. When we bathe, I make sure to take a few delicious dog treats and offer them to him as I lather and rinse him. I never give him a bath if I am in a hurry or feeling less than eager to do the job slowly and gently. I learned, too, that Gabriel is emotionally very soft and easily worried. Insight into Gabriel's personality was a good thing. Striving to be calm and

merry for Gabriel makes me a better dog mother.

Worried Dogs Act Out

Many dogs are worried or act out their anxiety with unwanted chewing, digging, destructiveness and other "active" behaviors. All dogs, but especially reactive dogs, need calm home life and more stress management in their lives.

Slam-Bam: Scare The Dog

Suppose your dog has a veterinary appointment at 4 p.m. You have to take off work early to go and get the dog and drive back to town. Situations like this are prime occasions for rushing, worry about forgetting checkbooks, keys, purses, the dog's leash, and so forth. Make a list the day before of everything you and the dog need for the appointment. Put everything in the car the morning before the appointment.

If the dog needs brushing before you allow him to be seen in public, either do that the night before in a leisurely way or let the dog go as is. Rushing at him with the brush, or

261

the nail clippers, minutes before you have to throw him into the car will only set the dog up to be stressed by the whole experience.

Make sure his crate or dog seat belt is in the car, ready for his trip. Take fabulous dog cookies, hot-dog pieces, or bits of cheese with you to the veterinarian. Reward the dog with treats for riding calmly, for walking on a loose lead into the vet's office, and for patiently letting the doctor examine and treat him. Stand at the head end of the dog and give him the treats.

Do everything you can to make every car ride and outing calm and enjoyable. Dogs remember every experience and draw their own conclusions. Try to imagine how the dog may view events and procedures.

Stay Prepared
The same attention to calm and preparation applies to all your dog's activities. Going to obedience class? Keep all your supplies in a specific carrier or bag that will be ready to go. Rushing and dragging the dog to school sets him up to take longer to settle into his class and be attentive to the skills he is learning.

Exit Serenely
When you leave for work, make sure the dog does not witness last-minute key search frenzy, or wild house straightening. Some dogs pick up their owner's stress and will chew the last objects that the owner touched.

Newspapers, shoes or throw pillows that were frantically picked up by a departing owner may find their way into the teeth of a stressed dog. Humans may have a tendency to eat and smoke and drink when stressed. Dogs are left with only their teeth as oral stress-relievers. If you have a dog who often chews your belongings, examine your stress level and question if your worries are also a worry to your dog.

Its Okay To Please Your Dog
Sit down with your dog and consider ways to offer him activities that he enjoys and that you both find calming. Maybe he likes to lie beside you on the bed while you read a good book? There are many excellent dog massage videos and DVDs that will teach you to gently massage your dog. He will love having your hands on him. Find a local dog massage therapist to teach you gentle moves to relax your dog. Take him for a long walk in a park. Be with him. Let him

know you brought him home because he is
your favorite companion.

Need something to hum to your perfect dog
companion while you gently brush, massage
or just be with him? Conway Twitty's love
song, "Slow Hand," may be just the melody
you need:

> *Darling, don't say a word*
> *You're tired of fast moves*
> *You got a slow groove*
> *You want [a dog owner] with a slow hand*
> *You want [a dog owner] with an easy touch*
> *You want somebody who will spend some*
> *time*
> *Not come and go in a heated rush*
> *[Dog's name], believe me I understand*
> *When it comes to love you want a slow hand.*

To assist your singing this to your canine
companion, I have changed a few human
endearments to suit a canine listener. Your
dog will never know the song was not written
especially for him.

Toys in the Toilet:
A Dog's Going to Do What
a Dog's Bred to Do

"I wonder what goes through
his mind when he sees up
peeing in his water bowl."
Penny Ward Moser

"**D**o those dogs hunt?", asked Mr. Pierpont the plumber. That depends on whether or not the lid to the toilet is up or down.

Here in the woodsy suburbs of Spotsylvania, Virginia, Izobel Margot and her little brother Quinnton Benjamin Pig spend their days hunting for Mr. Porcupine, the stuffed toy, and yanking the big chewy Gummabone© out of one another's freckle faced jaws.

Every breed has a job to do. Never forget that. Like it or not, dogs are going to do whatever job hundreds of years of genetics have programmed them to do.

Cooped Up, Ignored and Bored Courts Dog Behavior Disaster

Coop them up in the house, limit their exercise, go to work and wish them well on the sofa. Keep this up and, sooner or later, their natural working abilities will surface. When inbred drives are demonstrated, owners can be in for a big surprise.

Imagine my surprise when Mr. Peirpont, after diligent probing and determined plunging, called me in to the bathroom to see why the toilet suddenly would not flush. A great big nylon dog bone. Not the first toy to be found in the toilet, but the first to be deposited and flushed.

My English Springer spaniels, lacking pheasants to flush and retrieve (no pun intended) have had to innovate and find indoor prey and convenient bodies of water. Show them anything to retrieve, especially if it squeaks, and they will carry it proudly down the hall to the guest bathroom and stuff in in the toilet. Water retrievers.

The Lid Is Up? The Pond Is Open.

For years I have begged my husband not to put the lid down on the toilet because they love to drink from the toilet. So what if occasionally a human visitor to the toilet finds a floating porcupine, a fleece chew man, or a submerged chew bone?

Any retriever hard at work fetching and carrying, occasionally must stop for a drink from the toilet. Put out ten dog bowls of water and every dog I have ever had will continue to prefer toilet water. Izobel's godmother, Margot McBrayer Wagner, recently said to me, "Izobel's preference for drinking from the toilet bowl is like looking for your own favorite coffee cup every morning."

Now, I am begging my husband to put the toilet lid down to avoid future plumbing emergencies. A big water bowl waits beside every toilet in the house as I try to teach a watering hole substitute to the spaniels.

Lest anyone believe Izobel and Quinnton are the only dogs in town to invent entertaining activities specific to their genetic drives, let me share a few dogs at work stories from dogs who have come to see me for dog behavior advice. Dog's names have been changed to protect the innocent.

Terrier Games: Take Your Digging Where You Can

A Jack Russell Terrier, we can call him Digger, ate a hole larger than his wee self from the top of the leather sofa cushion, all the way through the cushion and out the bottom of the sofa. He was looking for the piece of chicken that his human father had dropped onto the sofa while watching a baseball game. The chicken was gone, but the yummy scent was not. Owners of this Jack Russell realized that tantalizing food scents on the living room furniture was as much to blame as the digging and fabulous scenting abilities of the Jack Russell.

Herding Dog Blues: Pace The Fence, Sheep May Come

A brilliant Border Collie, Dwayne, had worn the pads off his busy feet from herding up and down his gravel filled, very large dog run. It did not matter how deep the gravel. Every day he would stalk and run up and down the gravel until it was piled aside and a dirt track had been worn into the rocks. He was doing his job. He was herding invisible sheep along the fence line.

 268

BEHAVIOUR PROBLEMS

Guard Dog Lament: Don't Tie Me Up To Calm Me Down

George, the German Shepherd, came to see me when he went from friendly tail-wagging to lunging with teeth bared at every passerby. A natural guard dog, bred with generations of training to protect and serve, he had been tied on a long rope to the side of his family's garage.

 Every time a stranger passed, he would fling himself forward to investigate and be jerked hard and painfully backward when he hit the end of the rope.

A few weeks into this "who hurt my neck?" training and George was trained himself that the jerking on his neck was caused by the evil stranger passing his territory. It didn't take long for George to develop territory protection aggression. He was much relieved when his family brought him into the house with toys stuffed with treats and peanut butter and left the television on while they worked long days and he was bored, ignored and alone.

Why shouldn't a nice boy like George guard his house from inside while his pack was away? He was totally housebroken, he didn't chew and he could protect his house much better from the inside.

DEVOTED TO DOGS

Yasmin: Tiny Terrier With Plenty To Say

Barking, barking; never stopping for a breath, was the sin committed by Yasmin the Yorkshire Terrier. She barked at every noise. Unfortunately for Yasmin, she lived downtown on a busy, historic street and saw every tourist, and every delivery truck from her living room window. She had torn the back off a sofa, shredded innumerable drapes and torn up untold mini blinds. The front door had been repainted so many times the paint store workers knew Yasmin's name.

Natural terrier alertness, hair-trigger reactions to sights and sounds, and high intelligence made her life miserable.

Her owners took steps to make the world less noisy and visible to Yasmin. They left the television loudly playing the animal channel when they left for work. They rearranged the living room so that Yasmin could not sleep on the sofa and be able to leap into the front window. They installed mock stain glass windows that covered the view and were indestructible. They disconnected the doorbell. Best of all, before they went to work every day, a family member made time to take Yasmin for a 30 minute walk and wear her high energy down before she was left alone, bored and looking for stimulation.

BEHAVIOUR PROBLEMS

Ask Yourself, "Why?"
The next time your dog does anything you wish she would not do, ask yourself these questions:
- How much hard exercise has she had today (and everyday)?
- What was this breed actually bred to do?
- Does she get to do anything to relieve those drives and energy needs?
- What can the humans around here do to channel her natural abilities into something we can all enjoy?

Active Companions
Not Neglected Loafers
Our dogs were bred to be with us as companions and willing workers.

All dogs must have mental stimulation. Dogs must have work. Without work and human supervised activities your dog will invent work you may not want to have done.

Remember, don't blame the dog. Train the dog

Chew on This:
Don't Blame the Dog,
Train the Dog

*"When the chips are not exactly down,
but just scattered about, you discover
who your real friends are."*
Richard Burton

Another workday; finally over. Home at last. But wait. Where is Buddy?

No Buddy in the living room, but the evidence screams that he was here earlier. Shredded newspaper; ankle deep, spread from rug to sofa. A tall leather boot, toe gnawed off, peeks out from the paper pile. Fringe on the carpet: chewed off with scissor sharp puppy teeth.

 272

BEHAVIOUR PROBLEMS

Horror In The Hallway

Walk on down the hall. One sherpa fleece bedroom slipper: chewed toeless. Leather belt: gnawed in half. Box of tissues now a gummy wad of soggy mess. New Johnny Depp DVD, tooth gnashed and cracked. Dirt! Where did that pile of black dirt come from? Dragged from the big potted fern you nursed through the Winter. Fern devoured. Dirt trail leads to the bedroom.

Mayhem In The Bedroom

Cast your angry eyes up on the big bed. You always wanted a bird dog? Welcome to Buddy's first big kill. Expensive feather filled comforter has gone the way of puppy teeth.

Are you mad? Are you going to let this little creature with knives for teeth destroy your happy home? Things need to change around here, don't they?

Blame Yourself

Blame and anger will teach your little pup nothing. But to blame is human, so sit yourself down in a comfortable chair and blame yourself for as long as you feel the need. While you castigate yourself for leaving this dear, untrained, playful, curious, very active puppy alone, unsupervised, and on the loose to entertain himself, let us go over my 'Don't Blame the Dog, Train The Dog' rules of puppy chewing management.

The Truth About Chewing

Puppies and dogs are going to chew. You will not stop the dog's natural need and urge to chew. Dogs chew for many reasons. Puppies chew

while teething. Many pups chew and teethe for at least two years. Punishing the dog will only add emotional stress to the dog. A stressed dog will chew more, not less. Would you yell at a human child for crying and putting things in her mouth while teething? No. Yelling at or punishing a young dog who is suffering through the stress of teething is equally inhumane and a waste of energy.

Dogs Have Oral Fixations

Have you ever wrestled with a bad habit? Ever over-eat when stressed, bored, agitated, or unhappy? Notice that the more you think about not over-eating or doing any other bad habit, the more likely you end up drinking, smoking, over-eating, shopping, etc.? Chewing can become a stress relieving behavior for dogs of any age. Many dogs relate to the world with their mouths. The dog cannot raid the refrigerator, take himself out for a walk. He cannot select an appropriate chew toy if no human has provided appropriate chews for him to find. Blame the human. Don't blame the dog.

Stress Sets Off The Need To Chew

Make a list of everything you can think of that could be stressful for your dog. What are the stressors in his environment? Door bells ringing. Noises outside: school bus arriving and children squealing. Squirrels scampering outside his window; begging to be chased, Mail carrier invading his territory and daring to come into his yard. Sirens, sonic booms, thunder. Leave the radio or television at low volume to mask outdoor noises.

Just Plain Bored

Dogs are not wind up toys that jump to life to entertain us when we are present. Dogs are domesticated animals who must run, play, investigate the world around them. A bored dog will make his own entertainment. His mouth is his best world investigation tool. Pent up energy and loneliness are invitations down the destructive chewing path.

Chew Ignorant

A dog must be trained to chew things that the humans want him to chew. Appropriate chewing is a learned skill. What have you taught him to chew? How much time have you spent on chew lessons with the dog?

Does His Mouth Hurt?

An older dog who has never chewed anything inappropriate will sometimes chew a rug, chair leg or other forbidden object. Let his veterinarian check him over. He may have a broken tooth, or other medical stressor causing him to chew.

Basic Chew Training Tips

Every behavior problem deserves a thorough analysis of why, when, how the behavior began, developed, and became a habit. Destructive chewing is a serious behavior problem that requires gentle retraining and understanding rather than punishment and blame.

Educate Yourself About Canine Chewing Do's and Don'ts

For an in-depth look at how to develop a re-training plan for the problem chewer, dog writers and behaviorists Dr. Karen Overall, Dr. Ian Dunbar, and William Campbell offer excellent advice. Educate yourself to re-educate your dog to chew his own possessions rather than your treasures.

- *When Unsupervised: Confine the dog.*
  A large crate, dog exercise pen, or a baby gate confining Buddy to a small, chew-proof room is an absolute must until Buddy masters appropriate chewing behaviors.

BEHAVIOUR PROBLEMS

- *Spend Time With The Dog*
  Play with him, walk him, entertain his little
  doggy brain and paws before you take off
  and leave him alone and bored. Fulfill his
  exercise and entertainment needs.

- *Accumulate a Large Pile of Chew Toys*
  Building your dog's chew arsenal is
  personal to your dog. Try hard nylon bones,
  soft nylon bones, plush toys, squeaky toys,
  rope toys, and large, safe balls. Chew toys
  that can be filled with chew enticers like
  peanut butter, small hard dog biscuits are
  great for dogs who will work for hours
  trying to dislodge the treats.

  Rawhides may be an option, if the rawhides
  are safe and your veterinarian approves of
  rawhide use. Some dogs will devour huge
  hunks of rawhide in minutes, making edible
  chews a poor choice for long term chew
  entertainment.

  Beware of rawhide and animal product
  chews that are not made in the United
  States. If the rawhide, cow hoof, or pig
  ear is made anywhere, or imported from
  anywhere other than the United States,
  leave it at the store. Take a look at the
  fine print the next time you find a bargain.
  Chances are these chews were made
  in a country where the processing and
  sanitation of the cow or pig who was killed
  and processed for his hide or parts cost
  less because health and safety standards
  were poor.

- *Approved Chewing: You
  Must Teach the Dog*
  Get down on the floor. Be wildly excited to play with the chew toys that you want the dog to love chew. Toss them. Smear them with something enticing: peanut butter, melted high smelling cheese, bacon grease, chicken fat. Out doors or on an easily cleanable floor, enact a chew toy tasting, tossing good time.

  I once simmered a dozen hard nylon bones in a big pot of chicken for a few hours. Next, I let the nylon bones sit in the refrigerator in the chicken pot over night. This was for a puppy, who, prior to the chicken simmered chew toys, only wanted to chew chair legs. Dog bone simmering and marinating was an effort, but well worth it. This dog joyfully carried these bones around until the day she died, nearly sixteen years later. With dog training, you reap in dog behavior perfection what you sow with time and training of the dog.

- *Pick Up, Straighten Up. Tighten
  Up Your Housekeeping*
  Until your dog is trained to chew only his own approved chew items, you must take on a " pick it up or don't get mad when he chews it" mind–set. If his busy teething teeth find something on the floor, chances are he thinks you left it there for him.

278

BEHAVIOUR PROBLEMS

- *Never Give The Dog Old Shoes, Socks, or Household Discards*
  Your dog cannot discern your old bedroom shoe from your best leather loafer. A shoe by any other name is a chew toy. As you hand any chew item to Buddy, ask yourself, Do I want him to chew everything he finds that looks or feels or tastes like this?"

- *Fill Your Pockets With Chew Toys*
  Every time you interact with Buddy, bring forth an approved chew from your pocket and praise him for his interest. If you find him with his mouth on an unapproved chew (a magazine, a shoe, your purse) remove the item from his mouth and bring a good chew from your pocket. Put the approved chew object in his mouth and praise him lavishly.

- *Keep A Sense of Humor*
  No matter what happens on the road to chew perfection, keep negative feelings to yourself. This dog loves you. Teach him how to be the dog you want him to be. His life, happiness and good behavior will be molded by your very capable hands.

279

When They Gotta Go, You Gotta Go, Too

"The trouble with a very happy puppy is that it leaks."
Charlotte Gray

How long does it take to house train a dog? Attention-intensive methods are quick and lasting. Slack, sit-on-your-bottom and ignore-the-dog methods may take a life time.

Why take the long and wee-stained carpet road to teaching the dog where to go? Examining what not to do to house train your dog may lead away from peepee pitfalls and onto the happy highway of dry carpets and sleeping through the night.

Sure Failure Step One: Bring the dog home without procuring basic house training equipment and supplies. You do not have a dog kennel or crate that is sized for the dog.

 280

BEHAVIOUR PROBLEMS

The kennel should be long enough for the dog to lie down comfortably, even with his legs stretched forward, tall enough that his head does not touch the roof, and wide enough that he can turn around. The purpose of the containment device is to discourage the dog from urinating and defecating where he sleeps.

Veteran house trainers will flatly stare into your face and say, "No crate? No house training." Human babies watch the world from play pens, car seats, and bassinets. Young canines, too, benefit from small, supervised areas of containment.

The 'exercise pen' is another a house training miracle tool when the time comes that the puppy can 'hold it' for a few hours but must not be left on the loose, alone in the home. An exercise pen has folding wire panels, is about four feet tall, makes a great dog play pen and will fold flat when not in use. Try an internet search for 'exercise pen'. See many types, sizes, colors and prices of this miracle dog management tool.

Sure Failure Step Two: You do not have time to watch the pup every moment that he is awake and on the loose sniffing and investigating his new surroundings.

Until his bladder matures and enlarges, and various urinary and rectal sphincters mature and master control, a dog does not know how to 'hold it'. Assume that a young pup can wait to go to the bathroom one hour per month of age. Have a pup who is three months old?

Remind yourself that he cannot 'hold it' more than three hours. Even that length of time may push the wee wee envelope.

Some dog owners rave, complain and whine  about dogs who have been so badly behaved as to relieve themselves while the owner was away at work, or shopping, or sleeping. If I allowed myself to blurt out what I actually think, I long to ask, "So, tell me, did you urinate even once today while you were away at work?"

Think about this: You are probably a grown human, between 100 and 200 pounds, with 20+ years out of diapers. If you, a big toilet trained human, did not have to 'hold it' for more than six hours, why would you expect that a young, physically immature and untrained animal will not have to answer a liquid or solid call of nature?

Puppies Have To Pee
We need to get real about the habits and needs of canines. They are going to go to the bathroom. They have to be taught precisely when and how we want them to relieve these very necessary bodily functions.

Sure Failure Step Three: You do not have the desire to go in and out into the yard, at all times of day and night, in rain, hot, freezing, or otherwise unbearable weather.

Your dog wants nothing more than to be with you, his hero human. Swat his warm little bottom out the door and go back and sit in your easy chair. Give him time to 'go'. Find him waiting behind the door, wagging his little tail, delighted his human has come to bring him back into the glow of the family circle inside. He plays at your feet for a few minutes. He circles, sniffs, and looks at you. His sniffing and circling goes unnoticed. The puppy squats and urinates right in front of you, probably looking up into your face.

Bad puppy? No. Human House Trainer Must Work Harder

Did you go outside with him to see if he used the bathroom? No. Did you put him on a little leash attached to your chair for supervision when he came inside? No. Did you see the sniffing and circling signs? No. You all but asked him to anoint the rug. At the very least, if you were not going to watch and interact with him, he should have been put into his kennel until you could keep an eye out for possible wee wee signs.

For Success: Go On Outside With Him

Keep a coat for yourself, hat, gloves, and umbrella, as needed, by the door you want the pup to learn to go out. Hang bells on the door. Ring them softly each time you and the pup exit. The dog will learn to ring the bells as a "need to go" sound to alert you. Conditioning that the bells mean "outside" may take a few weeks or

a few months, but with repetition, the dog will make the connection.

Set a timer if you need to be reminded take the pup outside.
- Take the pup out every two hours, minimum, when you are at home.
- Go with him.
- Softly repeat the same house training command over and over. "Hurry up, peepee," is a favorite of many dog lovers.
- Going with the dog is not a choice. Rain, snow, blow, wee hours of the night: if the dog goes out, so do you.
- The moment the dog relieves himself, go to him and give a "going outside" reward cookie. Coo, "Good peepee!" as you deliver the reward.

When Will He 'Go' Alone?

Are you asking, "When, oh when, may I stop going outside on every bathroom trip?"

The answer: When you have had six months of no accidents in the house. Even then, a few times a week, you must go out, just to praise the dog and deliver the random reinforcement "good to go" cookie.

Sure Failure Step Four: No clean-up supplies have been organized before the dog's arrival Before the dog arrives, prepare a tote bag or bucket with your "accident clean-up" tools and products.

Outfitting the clean-up bucket:
(Listed here in the order that the products are used on an accident):
- Large supply of old rags, towels, or paper towels, that will be pressed into the urine to soak it up.
- Club soda or seltzer water, poured onto the remnants of the just soaked up urine (or thrown away solid product).
- Soak up the club soda. Stand on the folded piece of old towel. Do this wearing shoes or you will have a damp foot or sock.
- Pour urine odor neutralizer liquid on the spot. The brand I like is "Nature's Miracle." Buy at any dog specialty store. Urine neutralization is the most important step. This product will eradicate the organic smells that call the dog back to the spot.
- Spray the now very clean spot lightly with any perfume or cologne. Dogs are very smell sensitive. They return to spots that smell like something they left behind to mark their spot. The less the spot smells like anything related to bodily functions, the better.

The entire clean up process will take less than three minutes. Look on the bright side: puppy clean up will be good exercise. Down on your knees bending, scrubbing, reaching, sniffing. Look on the clean up bucket as an exercise tool. Forget the "Thigh Master" and "Ab Cruncher". Following behind and cleaning up for a little canine family member will keep you exercised nicely.

Sure Failure Step Five: Bring the new dog home without reading at least one good dog care and training book.

Reading is fundamental for dog owner education. Buy or borrow a dog care book that explains house training and the needs and possible behavior problems that develop with uneducated dogs. Two great books are "Mother Knows Best: The Natural Way to Train Your Dog" by Carol Lea Benjamin and "The Evans Guide for House Training Your Dog" by Job Michael Evans.

Once you know how not to house train the dog, you are ready for the short and simple rule of how to house train the dog.

The House Training Golden Rule

Take your dog out every time he: eats, wakes up, plays hard, sniffs the floor, circles the floor, before bed time, before you leave the house, before you put him in his kennel or exercise pen, and every time he goes politely to the door and looks back expectantly at you.

There may be other times and signs that your dog will teach you as you become a team. The sooner he understands the process, the sooner you will both be able to sleep though the night.

Ask Not On Whom the Dog Jumps, He Jumps On You

"Who kicks a dog kicks his own soul towards hell."
Will Judy

How can I stop my dog from jumping on me when I come in the door? Resolve to devote a few minutes every time you come home to teach your dog that a sit will be rewarded as the best greeting behavior.

Why Does Your Dog Jump Up?
Bongo is trying to sniff your face and investigate what you have had to eat and where you have been. Your dog's returning pack member greeting behavior has been offered by dogs for thousands of years. Did your mother teach you to always stop when you enter a room and greet everyone present? Good manners. Your

dog is offering you his version of good doggy manners: canine greeting behavior. He is not a bad dog. He is an untrained dog.

No-Jump Training Program "Don'ts"
There is no magic cure for Bongo's exuberant jump-up welcome. Don't waste your money on gimmicks that will not produce desired results. Humane, consistent, positive work with the dog are key to teaching what you want him to do.

Promise that you will not do these things:
- _Do not wham the dog in the chest with your knee._
  You may hurt the dog enough to impress upon him that he gets hurt when he jumps up. You may also teach the dog that coming to you is a very bad thing. A dog that is afraid of you and will not come to you says more about an owner's bad temperament than it does about the learning capacity of the dog.

- _Do not step on the dog's toes._
  Hurting the dog may bring about a change in the dog's desire to get close enough to jump on you, but punishment will not teach the dog not to jump on people other than you. He will probably still jump gleefully on tiny children and small or frail humans. If these people are knocked down and possibly injured, the dog will be blamed even though the owner of the dog is always to blame for not controlling the dog.

Punishment techniques teach the dog very little about not jumping up. Take time daily, for as many days as necessary, to teach your dog to sit for greeting.

No-Jump Training Program Must-Do's

The true no-jump fix will occur when your dog learns to automatically sit the moment a human arrives in his company. This learning will take time. How long? As long as it takes you to teach the dog a sit-stay, followed by teaching the dog to sit as his greeting behavior.

- *Keep a supply of delicious dog treats in your pockets.*
  Enter your house armed with rewards. The moment you open the door, show your dog a cookie and lure him into a sit. He will

jump on you the first few times your try this. He has not realized that sit will produce a better reward (food) than the glee he has taught himself to feel when he jumps on a returning pack member. Keep a firm grip on the cookie. Hold the cookie almost touching his nose. Slowly lure him backwards as you say, "Sit!". The moment his bottom touches the floor, praise him lavishly. Smile brightly and say, "Good sit!". Feed him the cookie. As long as he remains sitting, rub him from head to toe. Show him that sitting to greet you makes you very pleased. Use your cookie and your praise to produce a sit every time you come through

290

the door. Train all family members and guests to require him to sit to be petted.

- *Keep a short, sturdy leash near the entry door, and use it to control your dog.*
  The leash is a tool that many dog owners forget to use when training behavior management skills. Keep a leash near the door, ready to snap onto the dog as you enter.

  If delivery people or unexpected guests arrive and Bongo stakes out the door before you can get there to control him, snap the leash on before you open the door. Every time you prevent the dog from the doggy gratification of jumping on a human, you are teaching him not to jump.

- *Ignore jumping up.*
  Let us imagine that a day comes when you do not have a cookie, and you forgot to keep  the leash near the door. Bongo reverts back to his natural jumping up greeting behavior. Turn your back on the dog. Or, turn sideways and deflect his leap toward his focus: your face. Walk away from your leaping dog. Shun him. Pay him absolutely no attention until he calms down. Get your treat. Snap on his leash. Work on several sits. With practice, your dog will grasp the message: "I sit when I greet a human."

Do Your Own Homework

Obtain professional training for yourself. Whether you enroll in a local basic obedience class, or buy yourself a dog training book or video, invest in self-education for teaching positive, humane, result-producing dog training.

Four exceptional books are:
- "Dr. Dunbar's Good Little Dog Book", by Ian Dunbar, PhD, BVetMed, MRCVS (*www. jamesandkenneth.com*). Dr. Dunbar's writing is witty, wise and fun to read. Can't find time to settle down with a dog training book? Dunbar offers a terrific series of four dog training videos, "Training the Companion Dog". Tape three focuses on "preventing jumping up and walking on leash".

- "The New Better Behavior in Dogs: A Guide to Solving All Your Dog Problems" by William E. Campbell. With plain talk and kindness, Campbell's training methods are easy to follow and make sense to the dog owner. The positive reinforcement training methods teach dog owners to lead without force, and train dogs to be calm, well-adjusted canine family members.

- "Twenty One Days to a Trained Dog" (Fireside Books) by Dick Maller will teach you, step-by-step, how to praise, reward and teach commands to your dog every time the dog offers you a "sit", a "down", or a "come. Maller's method puts a name on naturally occurring body positions that you want the dog to repeat on command.

- "Getting Started: Clicker Training for Dogs" by Karen Pryor is a book that I wish every breeder, every rescue or shelter placement person could afford to give to each person who goes home with an untrained dog. Pryor's positive reinforcement training methods make sense, are easy to perform, and help the dog to like to learn. Pryor's book includes chapters explaining, "Why every interaction with your dog is a training opportunity, why mistakes are best ignored and why punishment doesn't work."

Quick Fixes: No-Jump Foundation Training
Sometimes your granny is coming and you must stop Bongo from breaking her hip. Problem is, you do not have time to train the no-jump method before granny crosses your threshold.

The Out Of Sight Prevention Method
When you know company is coming, put the dog in another room with door closed until company settles and sits. Bring out big bowl of popcorn and ask all guests to ask your dog to sit and give one piece of popcorn, with praise when the dog approaches and sits. If your dog is so untrained that he is going to jump on the sitting guests, this is the opportunity for you to snap on that leash that you should have nearby at all times.

This 'put away and then bring out on leash' method' works only if you see an unexpected guest heading toward your door. Any would-be visitor who arrives unexpectedly is just as rude as your dog who is wont to knock them down with a wild greeting. As a genteel host, if you decide to reward the drop-in quest by opening your door, you must smile stiffly while you corral your could-be errant dog.

"Pizza pan on toe nails" method

My dog Izobel and I took a puppy kindergarten class taught by Julie Hogan at Waggin' Tails Junction Kennel in Manassas, Virginia. Frazzled dog owners asked Hogan, "How can I stop my dog from jumping up?" Hogan taught us the "pizza pan method".

Buy several cheap pizza pans. Any flat metal pan will do. Keep one pan in your car, one outside all entry doors. Before you greet your jumping dog, get the pan ready to deflect the scrape of jumping toe nails. Hold the pan at the exact level where the jumping dog's paws will touch you. When the dog jumps up his toenails will rake the pan.

Most dogs do not like metal under their toes. You are not trying to hit ,swat ,or hurt the dog. You are simply trying to keep the dog's toe nails off your body. As the dog jumps, and you hold the pan at paw touch height, command, "sit!" in a firm, but not punishing voice. Get your always ready cookie out of your pocket. When the dog sits, feed the cookie while the dog is in sit position. Praise enthusiastically, saying, "Good, sit!!!"

All of the dogs that I have met who were trained with this stopgap anti-jump technique have thrilled their owners with positive results. Within a few weeks of pan training, the trainer can hold out just the flat palm of their hand toward the dog, instead of the metal pan, as they command, "Sit!"

Make time for upbeat practicing and gleeful playtime

Promise yourself and your dog that you will stop wasting with merely wishing he would not jump up. Begin today with his sit for petting and praise greeting. Resolve to read at least one helpful dog training book. Take your dog for a long walk. Vow that you will never again chastise your dog for misbehavior unless you can swear that you have trained him and that you have spent exercise time with him. Ask yourself, "Has this dog had at least thirty minutes of exercise and mental stimulation today?" If not, you probably have a bored dog who needs more attention and playtime.

Train him. Don't blame him.

Thunder and Lightning: It's Frightening

"Oh the saddest of sights in a world of sin is the little lost pup with his tail tucked in."
Arthur Guiterman

Oh, me! Oh, my! A tale of terror.

Stop Petting Your Frightened Dog
Absolutely no cooing, stroking, whiney voice reassurance and fondling. No clutching the dog to your chest cuddling. No commiserating.

Divert Your Dog's Attention From The Storm.
- Turn up the stereo.
- Close the windows.
- Bounce the ball.
- Play hide and seek with scrumptious treats.

 296

BEHAVIOUR PROBLEMS

**Entertain your storm-worried dog.
Do anything except rub, whine
or agree that the sky is falling.**
Whether your dog is worried about thunder, petrified of lightning or frenzied during driving rain, before the next storm descends is the time to practice jolly activities. Teach your dog to love a ball, a game, or a word so much that the mention of that activity or object will always make his tail begin to wag.

What does your dog love?
John Uther Pendragon, a Springer Spaniel of mine, was very storm-phobic when I adopted him as an adolescent. The first storm cloud that blew over sent John under our bed. He shook so violently that I would wake up sure I was in a cheap motel with the "magic fingers" at work under the mattress.

Luckily for John, and for me, John loved to chase a tennis ball. His love for his ball was more intense than his fear of thunder. If I would throw the ball, John could forget his fears. Many nights, John and I played ball while thunderstorms raged.

Loud music also helped take the edge off John's horror of thunder. I have turned the volume on the stereo so high that the windows shook with Led Zeppelin.

Analyze your music collection to find selections with room-shaking bass and loud upbeat singers. Drown out the thunder. A pounding

beat will set the tone for playtime as you divert the storm-anxious dog.

Some fearful dogs prefer to be left alone. Dog owners have told me that their dogs had a favorite place to go and wait out the booming light show.

Beware Of All Loud Noises and Celebrations

A friend recently told me, "The first dog I had growing up hated thunder and Fourth of July fireworks. She was driven to curl up in the bathtub during a storm. If she could not get in the tub, she would wedge all 50 pounds of herself behind the toilet. Quite a feat. We found it was better to give her a hiding place than it was to bring her on the bed or sofa to provide comfort. She seemed to the best judge of which spot felt safest."

One dog that I know is determined to make a nest under the bathroom sink. If a storm rumbled in while his master was at work, this Labrador

Retriever would be found having opened the sink vanity doors, clawed out all bottles and jars underneath to curl in the tiny cabinet.

This dog's very smart daddy knew to work with his dog's need for fear relief. He cleaned out the cabinet, took off the doors, and added a big fleece sleeping pad. During storm season he leaves upbeat music playing on a radio in the bathroom.

Every Phobic Dog Is Different

The most unusual storm anxiety relief procedure I have heard of is the dog who is petrified, whining, racing from room to room until her mom takes her into the garage, invites her into the car and drives her around. Dog and mom slowly cruise the neighborhood until the tempest has passed.

Each thunder-fearful dog will have different fear reactions that will need to be calmed by a behavior-modification plan personalized to each dog.

Veterinarian Elizabeth Ubehlor, who owns a storm-phobic dog, explained, "As far as lightning goes, for my dog Bandit, as he loses his hearing and eyesight, he gets much less worked up over thunderstorms. He seemed to be most secure in his younger days if he could be with us in a room with few windows and with the television playing. I send home sedatives and tranquilizers from time to time for dogs with storm phobias. Unfortunately, the medications don't take effect soon enough. I have known

dogs to jump through screen doors and window in absolute panic during a storm."

Leading canine behavior modification experts, including Karen Overall, VMD, William Campbell, Victoria Voith, DVM, and Benjamin Hart, all teach that the worst thing the owner of a frightened dog can do is to scoop him up, pet, stroke, or coo at him in a whining high-pitched voice. These comfort attempts may reinforce the fear reactions and actually train the dog to be more fearful. The very worst thing the dog can think is, "Oh no! Mom is scared and crying, too!"

Re-Train At A Speed Comfortable To The Dog
Behavior authorities agree that dogs can be taught with very small lessons to focus more an owner's upbeat reactions and less and less on the sights or sounds they found frightening.

BEHAVIOUR PROBLEMS

Counter-conditioning is a technique that trains the dog to react in a positive way to a stimulus other than the thunder and lightning. Many behaviorists teach the dog to sit on command, gradually rewarding the dog for sitting longer and longer periods. All the while, the owner rewards the dog with abundant praise and delicious treats. Playing ball, finding hidden toys, retrieving the Frisbee are all counter-conditioning training activities.

Saffy, a West Highland terrier, has had counter-conditioning training. Her mom, Sandra Fischer, explains, "I have been able to calm Saffy down  by teaching her that I am not frightened of loud noises. On the Fourth of July when firecrackers went off, first I taught her the word 'firecracker.' I would get very excited and happy to hear them. 'Oh, Saffy! That's a firecracker! Yeay!!!' This game seemed to help, so I tried it with thunderstorms, and it helped there, too. I've seen that the worst thing to do is coddle her and pet her when she is afraid. This just reinforces that they should be afraid."

Desensitizing techniques teach the dog in tiny steps to be less fearful by learning to tolerate very low levels of storm noise.
A recording of thunder and rain noise is played very softly as the dog learns to listen with no fear reaction. It is very critical that the owner who uses storm noise to desensitize the fearful dog

research and understand this method. Working with a behavior-modification counselor to be taught the steps and signs of fear would be very helpful. It is important that the owner not overburden the dog's ability to cope with anxiety. This process must go slowly and carefully or the well-meaning owner may make the noise-fearful dog even more afraid.

Dogs who are storm and noise fearful need understanding and careful supervision. A dog who becomes destructive or difficult to manage while severely frightened is not misbehaving.

Fear May Trigger Destructiveness
I met with a family whose Samoyed had completely shredded the leather interior of their car while the dog was left in the car and the family sat a few blocks away enjoying a fireworks

show. This dog did not have a behavior problem with destruction. This dog had been left alone to be tortured by fireworks noise, in a confined space, while undergoing terrible panic.

Noise-sensitive dogs require supervision and understanding care if fireworks, loud roadwork, traffic noises distress them.

Be Alert: Independence Day and New Year's Day

July 4th and January 1st are red-letter distress days at many animal shelters when frantic owners search for frightened dogs who have escaped home and yard wild with fear of fireworks noises. Many dogs will run for miles in noise-driven panic and find themselves lost and searching for their human families.

Puppies from 8 to 20 weeks of age can be especially frightened by anything unknown to them. Puppies and older dogs should never be taken to fireworks celebrations, loud concerts or any place that could frighten the dog.

Be brave and let your dog see that you are fearless and always ready to play. Actions will speak louder than fears.

Start your wild fun therapy today.

The Angel Barks
(Part One)

"Whenever I hear a dog continually barking, my reaction is one of relief-that it's not my dog making all that racket and inciting the neighbors to call the police."
John McCarthy

Vivien is a talker. She has opinions. She offers commentary on everything that enters her world.

She talks to squirrels outside her living room window. She is sure that the humans need to know if a squirrel is stealing sunflower seeds from the bird feeder. She announces the UPS truck is at the top of the driveway. She resents that the doorbell has the audacity to announce anyone on her doorstep.

 304

BEHAVIOUR PROBLEMS

Vivien, my Bearded Collie, speaks her pleasure if she hears any of 'her' words: "Outside," "PeePee," "Cookie," "Lucy," or "Sam-Bastid" (her own personal cats), and "Suppee-doo" (aka, supper, for those of you who do not speak dog at dinner-time). Many other words appeal to Viv's desire to comment. Perhaps the Beardie has a wee smidgen of parrot or other talking winged creature in her bloodline. Her mother's name is Connemara's Quoth The Raven, so it may be so.

Barking Is It's Own Reward

Dog lovers with overworked eardrums and sleep-deprived, complaining neighbors call me frequently to sit down for a "What to do about barking?" behavior consultation. I tell my barker clients that I am happy to tell them all I know about vocal dogs and the reasons dogs may be barking, but I offer no guarantees that the behavior will be easy to change.

The next time you are scanning dog magazines at the newsstand, look for articles on unwanted barking. I wager that if you look at four dog magazines, you will find at least one that addresses nuisance barking.

If this behavior were easy to change, there wouldn't be such an army of dog writers rehashing barking's "do's and don'ts", issue after issue.

Why Does Your Dog Bark?

As with all dog behaviors you wish to change, you must first know "why" before you can ask 'how' to retrain.

- *Some Are Born To Bark*

  Many breeds are programmed by their genetic code to bark, bark loudly, bark consistently, and bark until attention is paid to their barking.

  Herding breeds need to bark to fulfill their mission in life. Barking is bred in the bone. If you absolutely cannot abide barking, you are asking the dog to be a breed other than what she is, to expect complete silence from a herding breed.

  All of the collies, Bearded, Border, Bobtail, Shetland, "Lassie"–type and Australian (the list goes on), may bark to move their sheep or cows or children and cats in order to do their job.

- *Suspicious Barking*
  Dogs from the Working Group will also use barking to alert their owners of trouble, suspicion or unusual happenings in their territory. Most of the shepherds, German, Australian and others, need to bark to fulfill their destiny. Even sedate, watchful Rottweilers and Dobermans will bark when suspicion calls them to bark the alarm.

Nothing Improves A Game of Chase As Much As Barking Your Head Off

Many terrier breeds bark, sometimes incessantly, when they spy other animals that they consider to be game. Squirrels, cats, groundhogs and rabbits in their territory will usually stimulate a wild barking spree.

Dogs bred to hunt, Beagles, spaniels and Poodles, to name a few, are driven to bark to alert their hunter that they have seen the quarry.

Accept It: Dogs Do Bark

Most dogs were bred to bark. Or whine. Or bay. Or squeal with delight at the sight of the object of hundreds of years of prey and chase drive. Even the Basenji, the so-called "bark-less" dog, will vocalize when stimulated.

Before you take action to stop a barker, have you investigated the cause of the barking? Some barking dogs will stop barking if the human pack leader will get up and go to see why the

dog is barking. Is that too much to ask? Don't you want your boss to notice and acknowledge your work? Barking is dog's work. Check out the cause. Call the dog to your side. Tell her 'down.' If she does not leave the barking stimulus, put her on a leash and enforce a very long down. It's harder to bark when you are in a down position.

Dogs who are booted out into the yard to entertain themselves will do just that. Barking is high on the dog entertainment hit parade of leisure activities. Bring the dog back inside. She is a pack animal. Outside, bored, restless, looking for companionship, she is going to bark.

Bring The Dog Back Inside With Her Pack
The outside barker is easier to rehabilitate. Bring her inside. If she is outside because of other bad indoor habits, then, those complaints must be addressed. Remember the scene in

BEHAVIOUR PROBLEMS

"101 Dalmatians" when Pongo and Perdita went outside to bark their news on the evening bark circuit? That is what your dog will do if she is left outside, unable to interact with you. Bring her in.

Every breed has been programmed for thousands of years to perform a task. It is doubtful that most families have a flock of sheep, or that many of us take our dogs into the forest to help us hunt for our dinner. We may not need the dog to perform her job. Our suburban, often sedentary, lifestyles are irrelevant and usually counter-intuitive to the dog's needs. She still needs to do the job she was bred to do.

Wear Your Barker Out With Exercise
Give every dog at least 10 minutes of play, obedience training, or a long walk, before you leave her for work. Do the same when you return from work. More human-dog play interaction is necessary before bed. She is not a stuffed ornament purchased to look good beside the fireplace. Stimulate your dog's brain or body, lest behavior trouble, often arriving in the form of "nuisance barking," will be brewing.

Seek Out And Eradicate
Stimulations To Bark
Cover up the windows. Leave a moderately loud radio playing when you leave home. Tape up the doorbell if you know the noise sets the wee barker to booming that her territory has been invaded. Out-think the dog, if you can, or better, think like a dog of your breed. Make a list of everything she might see or hear while you

309

are away. Cover stimulating sights, and mute invading noises.

Don't Be Supervised By Barking

Never, but never, let the dog bark you into doing her bidding. My Uncle Bob Ferrell had a Chihuahua named Bitsy who would run to the breakfast nook and bark at the little box of mailman– and cat–shaped biscuits that Uncle Bob and Aunt Anne kept in a glass–front cabinet. Uncle Bob would leap up from the sofa to retrieve a biscuit for Bitsy. All the little children in the family, who adored Uncle Bob and Bitsy, would troop to the kitchen, and, with great joy, applaud Bitsy's parlor trick. Before Uncle Bob gave Bitsy the cookie, he would ask her to sit, and she would. The Ferrells have always been a family that appreciates dog antics. It is a good thing that barking did not bother my Uncle Bob. He had trained Bitsy to bark, and trained her well.

Training Your Barker To Hush

If you would like to train for less barking, rather than more, the dog's bark should never successfully induce you to follow her command. Tiny dogs often are trained to bark when their human's respond to their insistent barking by picking them up when they bark or display other unwanted behavior (like growling at the veterinarian or small children).

Bark? Get Your Way.
We Call That Training.

When dogs get what they want by barking, namely, your attention or getting to do something they choose to do, they learn to have their desires granted by barking or misbehaving. These dogs become experts at training their human companions.

Shun Your Rude Barker

If you want to retrain a dog behavior, withdraw your attention every time the dog performs that unwanted act.

Barking is a major dog-owner complaint.

Read On.

Vivien and I will disclose the training techniques that Vivien suggests for retraining the urge to bark in the next chapter. A little Beardie girl requires training to accept that little girls can be seen and not heard.

The Bark Goes On:
Vivien's Bark-Retraining Therapy Program

"Do not respond to a barking dog."
Jewish Proverb

Prancing around her domain, Vivien keeps an eye out for bird, beast or lawn ornament that has had the nerve to disturb her territory. Let one stray dog pass her fence, or one out-of-place trash can be left in an unfamiliar place, and Miss Vivien has something to say. She will attempt to herd the offending interloper. Barking will be utilized to ensure that the world knows Vivien is on the job. I have no doubt that barking is a joyful act for Vivien.

My Bearded Collie Vivien and I stay up late. The best time of the day for us is between 1 and 3 in the morning when I can really read my book in silence. Late-night reading causes one potential barking opportunity: Just before I go to bed, the dogs require one final lap around the fenced yard for a bathroom visit.

Exit Barking: Vivien Announces She Has Arrived

Miss Vivien believes that she must not exit any doorway without barking several ear-splitting woofs. Maybe she is alerting her imaginary sheep that she is coming to their aid. Maybe she is telling the two springer boys, Gabriel and Quinnton, that they are too darn slow getting out the door and down the steps.

It is my nightly chore to shepherd Vivien out during the wee hours, and preempt her will to bark before she sets off the barking of every dog in the neighborhood, who would have stayed asleep if not for a night-owl, insomniac neighbor.

Goal: Lessen The Frequency And Duration Of Barking Outbursts

When Vivien barks, there is a reason, or stimulus, as the canine behaviorists would say. While the overwhelming need to bark may not be obvious to me, I promise you that Vivien knows why barking is needed to alert the dull humans.

From the point of view of the herding dog, who is very intelligent and aware of all that moves in her surroundings, Vivien is doing her job. My job is to retrain her to understand that, as the dog mom, I am the one in charge. I am here to teach that Vivien can bark a time or two and that is enough. My bark needs to be the final bark on any subject.

Barking is a natural dog behavior. Have you ever tried to go one whole day without speaking a word? Even if we humans could master a vow of silence, we would certainly retain the desire to communicate.

Dogs communicate with vocalizations, and many of the sounds they use to communicate are barks. Discover the reason for the "talking" and you will find ways to reduce their need to say whatever it is they are offering in "dog speak."

Forget Finding A Magic Cure

It is natural for a dog owner to want a quick fix or magic cure for barking. Magic is not going to happen. If the dog has learned to "talk" too much, it will take time, analysis and work with the dog on retraining to lessen the dog's proclivity to speak her mind.

Dog books may suggest quick no-bark remedies: the "throw can" with pennies, the squirt of water in the face while barking, and several other shock treatments that I am not going to be a part of promoting. I have more time to love and retrain my dog than I have the will to frighten my dog into submission.

While some fast aversion therapies work for a few dogs, a few times, they teach the dog nothing about a new desired behavior. Maybe they teach him that when you pick up the can or the squirt bottle that something bad is about to happen. Why teach your dog that you are going to hurt him?

Management Methods: Not Cures
In an emergency "dog-must-not-bark" situation, I have successfully used a citronella spray no-bark collar to pre-empt Vivien from barking. Vivien wore this collar when we had to stay in a hotel that would definitely evict a barker. The collar's unpleasant squirt under her sensitive nose when she emitted one woof kept her quiet. I do not believe the citronella squirt collar would have continued to thwart her barking if used for many days, nor in an unsupervised environment.

Peanut Butter Closes The Mouth Temporarily
When Vivien was a tiny pup, I took her to a wise and delightful clicker-training teacher, Kathy Hughes, at Mountain View Dog Training (*www. mountainviewdogs.com*) in Amissville, Virginia. Hughes knew that she could not talk to the humans over the yapping, yowling, barking

315

noise of tiny pups. Her gentle and very humane advice to moms and dads who had barkers was, "Bring a jar of peanut butter to class. Put a dab on the roof of the pup's mouth."

What a cure! While the pup licked clean his palate, students could hear our teacher. Since the pups were now quiet, we could softly coo, "Good puppy! Good to be quiet." Learning the peanut-butter trick for silence had kept many a loud, reactive dog from needing to be expelled from dog class. Sometimes a gentle, positive, motivational quick fix may not cure the problem, but it may give a frustrated dog parent a starting point for training.

Barking Stimulus: Squirrels At The Window

No-bark training technique: Human watches for squirrels. If you can spy the squirrel invader before the dog begins to bark, that is extra points for you. Maybe (likely) the dog sees the squirrel first and commences to communicate

loudly in dog-speak to the territory-invading creature. The key to training this no-bark exercise is that the dog knows how to sit and that you have a delicious dog cookie reward in your hand. Ask the about-to-bark or already-barking dog to "sit." Make sure the dog does sit on your command. We want her to be rewarded for stopping barking and for doing what you said to do: sit. Let her sit for three to five seconds. Hold the cookie up to your eye level. Say, "Good to sit, good Vivien" in your best soft-praising voice. Give her the cookie. Repeat the "sit for cookie" process five times right then.

No-Bark Mastery A Hard Nut To Crack
No-bark training will not happen quickly. You may have to watch the squirrel window, along with the dog, for months. If you practice often enough, you may train the dog that when she sees the squirrel, to take a seat and look to you, as if to say, "Where is that cookie?"

Dog Training Requires Exactly That: Dog Training.
All of us wish it was "dog talking," "dog magic ESP," or "totally safe dog drug that cures unwanted behavior." It is not. It is time spent with the dog, talking to her, showing her where and when to position her body at your command, and rewarding her when she learns the behavior you want.

Do Not Hurt The Dog
Aversion therapies that cause shock or pain to the dog may change a behavior in some dogs, but the owner runs the risk of teaching the

dog a new unwanted behavior that they never intended. I would rather have a dog that barked than a dog that was afraid of me, or that did not trust her environment to be safe.

Barking Stimulus: Mamma On The Phone
Vivien will bark as loudly as she possibly can until Mamma has to pay attention to Vivien.

If your dog barks at you for attention, it is key that you never, no never, give her one speck of your attention while her boisterous jaws are in motion. If you are in a room with a door, and using a cordless phone, glide yourself over to the door. Before the dog can follow you, abruptly close the door in her face. Do not slam the door in her face to scare or hurt her. Let her see that she has gotten exactly the opposite of what she was demanding: your attention. Take the very thing for which she is barking away from her.

From the other side of the door, the very second the dog stops vocalizing, spring out of the door and ask her to sit. When she sits (quietly), give her a tiny cookie and praise her. Enlist a dog-friendly person to call you several times in a row every afternoon for two weeks to let you practice this withdrawal–of–attention therapy. No helper? Pretend you are talking on the phone.

Does the dog know why you went away while she was barking? Does the dog know why you came back when she was silent? Probably not. Pure repetition and rewarding her for the behavior you desire will lessen the frequency of behavior you do not want. With time and repetition, you will teach her to offer the behavior that pleases you and earns her cookie reward.

Do Your Homework: Reading Soothes The Barking Beast

You could spend lots of money for a behavior consultation with a specialist and ask all your behavior questions. But first, you might solve your problem by reading and following the training instructions from a few fun books and videos that would teach you step by step, on the comfort of your sofa, how to train your dog to do your bidding.

My favorite training and problem re-training books are "Behavior Problems In Dogs", by William Campbell; "Mother Knows Best" by Carol Benjamin (www.*dogwise.com*), "Clinical Behavioral Medicine for Small Animals" by Karen L. Overall and two fabulous videos, "Sirius Puppy Training" by Dr. Ian Dunbar (www.*training-dogs. com/sirius-puppy-training.html*), and "The How of Bow-Wow" by Virginia Broitman and Sherri Lippman (www.*takeabowwow.com*).

The Rule of Same: Like Reflects Like

Never yell at the barking dog. You sound like you are barking, too. The dog is pleased to see her training program for you is working. A quiet home atmosphere calms the would-be easily stimulated dog. Train the dog. It's the only way.

Good luck retraining your barker.

Digging: Dirty Little Secret

"The cure for boredom is curiosity. There is no cure for curiosity."
Dorothy Parker

Dogs like to dig. A dog snuffling busily in dirt is a happy dog. Add a little rain, a lot of scratching with paws, claws and teeth and the digging dog is transported to excavation nirvana.

Digging Is Destiny

If the digging dog is a terrier, he is performing the work that destiny calls him to perfect. If he is a hunting dog, he knows the scent below his nose will reveal a bird or dog delight that his human will be thrilled to have brought home for dinner. Hounds live to find a scent and follow it wherever it goes, be that up a tree, through the hedge, or into the earth. Any dog that is hot may be digging a cool pit; looking for refreshing relief from Virginia's Summer swelter.

Whatever his heritage, size or shape, a dog who digs is a normal, inquisitive dog. He is a fully functioning canine. Digging ability is one of the reasons humans put dogs to work in their hunting and vermin extermination pursuits.

You Dig. Your Dog Imitates.

Owners may not like holes in the lawn, but that

 is an owner problem, not an unnatural behavior for the dog. If digging in yards, or flower beds drives dog owners crazy it is time to examine solutions that will save the flowers and divert the dog to another acceptable activity.

Be warned: many dog behavior specialists and veterinarians will tell you that stopping the dog's desire to dig is not an easy task.

Prevention is always best with every dog or human behavior problem.

Never let the dog watch you dig anywhere in your yard or garden. If you plan to spend the afternoon on bent knee putting in little perennials, or spreading the new mulch, or troweling in the petunias; put your dog in the house. Give her a nice toy and leave her in a

321

room where she cannot watch out the window. If necessary, put her in her dog crate until you return to set her free and entertain her.

Dogs, horses, monkeys, birds and humans often learn by imitating each other. If your dog watches you dig in the dirt, she may return to the spot to imitate your work. Your hands, while working on plants and dirt leave the marvelous aroma of you all over the yard. Smells are thousands of times more apparent and interesting to your dog than they ever will be to you.

The scent your gardening leaves behind could be inviting enough to give the dog who has never done any digging the cue to begin. Take no chances. Do not give the dog new ideas. Put him far from the sight or sounds of your work in the dirt.

After you work in the garden, and the new shrubs or tender plants are beginning to take root, it is a good idea to go with the dog into the yard for a few days just to supervise her activity and prevent digging.

If you do not have a fenced yard, the dog should be on leash and supervised any time she is in the yard.

Why Does The Dog Dig?

Before solving any dog behavior problem, an owner must try to understand why the dog is doing whatever it is that we wish she would stop doing.

 322

BEHAVIOUR PROBLEMS

Dogs dig for several reasons. First, dogs are good at digging. Second, we must ask: is there something she smells, sees or wants to find that is driving her to dig?

Examine The Yard And The Digging Area

Any type of animal life sharing the yard with the dog can make many dogs wildly focused, obsessed, with digging for the animal or digging where the scent is left behind. Squirrels, moles, voles, chipmunks, skunks and groundhogs are favorite lawn residents that can cause the family dog to begin ground patrol and lawn upheaval.

My own dear Springer, Izobel Margot, was a pristine Southern belle until the afternoon she discovered snakes in a flower bed by our deck. I tried every digging behavior deterrent I had ever read.

Nothing discouraged Izobel's focused frenzy as she stalked, stomped and clawed at the flower bed.

One sultry July afternoon, she caught the prey. A medium sized copperhead snake. Even after emergency veterinary care, and having had her sweet, gorgeous head swollen to look like a monstrous football, Izobel returned home ready to dig.

Re-training Your Digger

Dog behavior books suggest many methods to stop canine digging.

DEVOTED TO DOGS

- *Aversive Smells*
Covering a preferred digging area with strong smells that do not appeal to dogs will sometimes end Rover's digging spree. Vast quantities of baby powder, cheap horrid perfume, after-shave cologne, black pepper, spraying with a strong antiperspirant spray, or commercial anti-dig sprays or powder may take the thrill out of the digging spot. These smelly techniques work best if the digging area is small and the dog has not been going to that spot to dig for very long.

- *Barriers To Claws*
A piece of screen wire or small mesh wire like chicken wire, buried under a layer of dirt where the dog likes to dig will discourage some diggers. As with any behavior modification technique, the owner must watch the dog carefully and see if the dog stops digging in this area and make sure the dog does not injure his nails if he persists in digging over the wire.

- *Water In The Holes*
I have read the advice that filling holes dug with water may make the area unappealing to a digging dog. My own spaniels just gave each other the," Yippee! Mom made us some mud!" look of delight and dug all the harder.

- *Excrement In The Holes*
A friend of mine owns Peyton, a fluffy, gigantic Bernese Mountain Dog, who is perfect except for digging a few huge holes each Spring. My friend read a stinky solution in a dog magazine

 324

and was thrilled. The article instructed the dog owner to collect a big bag of dog poop  and put the poop into the hole the dog had dug. Dog sniffs hole, says, " That does not smell like the smell I was digging to find." Dog stops digging. My friend swears her frenzied digger gave up digging with this solution. Its free. Its worth a try. All of us know we should poop scoop the yard regularly anyway.

- *Startle The Digger*
  Many, cheap balloons (twenty or more) tied to the bottom of a rhododendron, a mountain laurel and two little boxwoods in Izobel's snake garden caused her briefly to give up digging at the bases of these trees.

  Four days later the balloons drooped. The earth moving princess resumed her snake work. Dog books suggest that the balloons will pop in the dog's face and this will scare the dog out of the area. Worth a try.

- *The Digging Pit*
  Dr. Ian Dunbar, veterinary behaviorist and author of several best selling dog books and puppy behavior videos (*www. jamesandkenneth.com*), suggests that the owner of the digging dog build the dog a

325

"digging pit". This digging pit would be exactly like a child's sand box. The owner must interact with the digging dog by letting the dog watch while many dog toys and chew objects are buried in the pit. The owner encourages the dog to dig up the toys and teaches the dog that digging is okay to dig as long as the dog digs in his own digging area. I have met behavior specialists who report this technique is excellent. A nice summer activity for the owner of a digging dog.

- *Manage The Digger*
As long as we have dogs, and I assume we dog lovers cannot, will not, imagine living without them; we will be faced by dogs being dogs. Digging is a difficult, but not impossible, canine behavior to work with or work around.

Before we scold and blame the dog, we must blame and examine ourselves as dog owners. We need to master behavior management.

Have we given the dog thirty minutes every day of hard, physical exercise like throwing the ball, the Frisbee, or running around the yard with her? How many days has it been since we got out of the recliner and took her for a twilight walk and let her stop and sniff the roses and the road kill? Has she been in the car and inhaled the passing breeze and perhaps the occasional French fry?

BEHAVIOUR PROBLEMS

A bored dog will certainly be more inclined to go outside and pursue dog sports like digging.

Have we abandoned the dog outside for long hours to be bored, useless and looking for her own entertainment? If the dog is neglected and not allowed in the house fro companionship and stimulation all sorts of behavior problems are likely to begin.

Dogs Will Find Stimulating Activities: Make Sure You Supervise Their Choices.

Dogs are very social creatures. Left outside alone, digging is a likely entertainment. A dog who did not try to dig out of the fence looking for stimulation, companionship and activity

would not be a very smart or a very normal social canine.

Find a sport for your dog. Begin regular walking, swimming, hiking or nature observation with him. If you like the company of other people and dogs, check out the sports of agility, flyball, terrier races, hound lure coursing, sheep or duck herding trials, Frisbee contests, field trials for hunting breeds, or competitive obedience work for all breeds.

Take Your Dog To School

Promise yourself to begin spending time training your dog right now to pass the ten tasks on the American Kennel Club's Canine Good Citizen test. Even mixed breeds are welcome to take this test and receive an official canine Good Citizen award.

The next time the dog digs and you wish he would not, ask yourself, "What have I done this week to teach this dog a fun activity that will bring him praise and build his self esteem?

Don't blame the dog. Train the dog.

Give Peace a Chance:
Fight Club Commandments

*"While a dog gnaws a bone,
companions would be none."*
Latin Proverb

The dogs that love us do not always love one another. Dogs will fight.

Humans hate this. No one wants their dogs to show one another their teeth. A punctured snoot or a tattered ear is a heartbreaking sight to the dog owner.

At my own house, I have held my breath for a fight or two to settle down. I have listened to years of breathless, anxious dog owners describe dog fights.

Dogs are not particularly worried about a brief skirmish. They blurt out a few grumbles and flash what I call 'the ugly face', replete with teeth. Odds are good one of the fussy siblings will back down, and real gnashing of cuspids won't happen.

Sometimes not. Dogs lock on to each other while their owner watches in horrified dismay. Seconds pass like hours.

No Magic Cures

There are no quick fixes for ending 'fight club' in your dog household. Here are a few peace-keeping commandments that will help you manage 'fight club' if it does break out in your pack:

Unless you were an only child, you probably recall a time when you wanted to offer bodily harm to a brother or sister. Dogs have sibling scores to settle, just like human family members. Lay down your burden of denial that you have the only dogs that ever pierced one another's noses. Taking a cold, analytical look at dog-fight truth will set you on the path to making a behavior change plan for your dogs.

Slow And Easy Supervision

No matter what else you do: remain calm. When dog fights break out, some wise, gentle, normally sedate humans begin to squeal, yell, kick and hyperventilate. Human wildness and anxiety will make the dog fight worse.

A behavior diary is a magic tool for putting the pieces of the 'why dogs fight' puzzle together. Record before- and after-fight observations. Where were you when the fight broke out? Do

BEHAVIOUR PROBLEMS

you remember hearing any growling or showing of teeth in the minutes or hours before the actual fight? What did you or other family members do the moment you heard the first growl? Who growled first? Was there a toy or any food item present with the dogs when the fight broke out? Did anything exciting to the dogs happen close to the time of the fight (doorbell, squirrel sighting, etc.)? Do you have a feeling that one dog was the "winner" or the "loser"?

Describe how each human acted toward each of the dogs who were in the fight once the fight was over. Write down every detail you can remember. Do this every time the dogs have a grumble. A pattern will most likely develop that will help you help make a behavior modification plan.

Teach Basic Commands For Control
There is no hope at all of stopping future fights if your dogs have not learned the most basic commands of 'come' and 'sit'. With delicious treats, train each dog separately until each dog will comply immediately to your commands.

William E. Campbell's "Behavior Problems in Dogs" is a book you need to own if you have dogs that growl, skirmish or fight. Campbell teaches many behavior-modification techniques to retrain dogs that fight. Many of his articles can be read at his Web site, *www.webtrail.com/petbehavior.*

Campbell's Jolly Routine
One of Campbell's techniques that I have seen work miracles with intra-pack aggression is "the jolly routine." Teach each dog, when he is not feeling threatened and getting along with his other pack members, to respond to a sound or phrase with great anticipation and joy. Using treats and praise and joyful repetition, practice your "jolly" trigger until you are sure the dog will wag his tail when you give the jolly cue.

Fast Owner Response To All Growling
Years ago, I loved a dog who was very jealous over sharing me with another dog in the family. This female would raise her lovely head, stare hard at my younger male dog, show one big tooth and offer a low growl. If I did not act immediately when her fight signals were given, this otherwise perfectly behaved female would launch herself across the room and wipe up

the carpet and walls with her unsuspecting brother.

My Fighter Loved Rattling Car Keys

After attending a seminar with Campbell, I taught her to respond with tail wagging and running to the back door of the house to sit, every time I jangled the car keys and announced in the most gleeful voice, "Wanna go to ride?" Her jolly response would preempt the fight.

Coveted Items Must Go

Many dogs are jealous of any possession, treat, toy or human lap that they perceive as a choice place to be or thing to possess. If your dogs have toys or treats that they growl over, logic and experience dictate that these dogs cannot have these jealousy-ridden items.

Be Calm After The Fight

After a fight, good-hearted human dog moms and dads will often take the side of the dog that received the worst injuries or who seems to be the underdog. This "rewarding the victim" may make the dominant dog who won the fight react by having to offer more discipline to the underdog.

Teach The Dog How To Rest Quietly
Every dog needs a peaceful rest area. After a fight, both dogs could be sent to their beds and the beds should be in separated locations. Gently and firmly send them to their place, and tell them "down." A dog that will not follow your command to stay put needs training.

Consider The Role Humans Play In The Fight/Jealousy Dynamic
Do you treat one dog in the family far better than another? Realize that the favorite surely knows she is the queen. You must never reward her lording her favor over the other dog. Many dog fights happen because the owner inadvertently promotes one dog to pack leader when the other dog family members have not accepted the preferred dog as the leader.

BEHAVIOUR PROBLEMS

Be Warned: Reach In. Get Bitten.

Every dog-aggression professional that I have ever heard laid down this dog-fight law: "If you reach into a dog fight, you are going to be bitten."

One measure to prevent fights before they begin is to have fight-prone dogs drag their leashes around the house when you are present to supervise. At the slightest hint of a fight on the horizon, pick up one of the leashes and call the dog in a normal voice. Put him through his jolly routine and his sit practice.

The best advice for dogs who have not yet learned to fight, bite or settle claims with teeth is prevention. The more your dogs look to you for direction, the less they will attempt to rule one another.

Happy training. Teach the jolly routine today.

Back to School:
Home Alone Can Spell Trouble for Your Dog

"The greatest fear dogs know is the fear that you will not come back when you go out the door without them."
Stanley Coren

A groaning, gear-grinding screech and an orange blur getting bigger as it rounds the curve confirms Biscuit's worst fear that school is starting up again.

There's that despised school bus that takes her children, but never offers to take her. No one realizes that being by her children's side is her job. Fall comes. Off they straggle, back to school and Biscuit feels lonely and useless.

Biscuit dreads the days ahead, alone in the boring house. What fun she had all summer

 336

with her children home and with the parents organizing kid/dog fun activities .

Biscuit had important jobs to do for the family. She had to walk her boy twice a day on her leash. She let both kids have fun brushing her. Sometimes they would squeal, "Tick!", with delight and take the prize to the mom for her tick removal skills.

Where Did My Family Go?

When they ate lunch, Biscuit demonstrated tidiness and vigilance and never let a crumb fall. Only Biscuit knows how much time she spent all summer cleaning up after the kids.

Afternoons, she enjoyed lounging around listening to her teenaged brother talk about CD's and girls. A dog hears all the secrets and hopes of a family. Biscuit takes great pride in her ability to keep secrets and to share whatever her humans are feeling.

Running herself ragged, playing soccer with the little sister was a job Biscuit took seriously. When mom mowed grass, Biscuit took every step mom took; only Biscuit paced back and forth behind the patio doors. Mom is a worrier. Afraid Biscuit would be hit by flying sticks or rocks. Even worse, Biscuit might get her dainty white feel stained grass green. Whatever the family did, Biscuit watched over them with selfless devotion.

The height of dog delight came last week when everyone Biscuit loves wedged themselves and most of what they own into the van and arrived three hours later in dog heaven.

The beach. Swimming. Biscuit delighted her hot family members with generous river water dog shake showers. She waded, neck deep in the cool water. The family ran from jellyfish, but not brave Biscuit, thanks to lovely dog fur protection.

No Invitation For Biscuit
On The School Bus

When shopping bags bursting with notebooks and backpacks began to pile up on the dining room table, Biscuit knew Summer dog camaraderie was about to be ruined by the return of that school bus. Suddenly, everyone had calendars,, plans and talked of teachers.

To make Biscuit feel worse, her human mom is a fourth grade teacher. Off she will go. too. A house full of fun will turn, overnight, into empty rooms that smell like the family Biscuit loves.

BEHAVIOUR PROBLEMS

This shoe smells like mom. Oops. Somehow Biscuit has chewed the toe a little while she carried it lovingly from room to room wondering when will mom be home.

Hey! There's the mail lady. Wham! Crunch. Biscuit fell off the back of the sofa trying to get to the window to say hello. The mini-blinds behind the sofa caught in Biscuit's toes and have crashed over the sofa onto the coffee table. Uh,oh. Mom's favorite photo album was knocked into the big cup of coffee that Dad rushed off and left behind on the floor.

All this crashing and breaking has stressed Biscuit into a barking frenzy. Oops. Wee-wee happens in the excitement and there's no one coming home for eight more hours to take Biscuit outside.

Alone Makes Day Long
For Pup Left Behind
It is only nine in the morning and already Biscuit remembers that being left at home alone is a nightmare.

Sadly, down every street, up every road, there will be happy, well-behaved lonely dogs like Biscuit trying to cope with new routines and isolation now that the relaxed routines of summer end.

Home Alone Check List:
The following checklist for safety and well-being is offered for all the dog's like Biscuit who

find themselves left behind with time on their paws.

* *Nature calls:* Be sure to take her outside for bathroom needs both when she first wakes up and again before you leave her. Go with her. Fenced yard or not. See what she does. Reward her with praise and a cookie. Many a sick dog got very sick because no one knew the dog had loose stools, worm segments, or problems urinating when the problem first began. A dog mother or father must monitor what comes out as well as what goes into the dog they love.

* *Schedule:* Get up in time to take Biscuit for a short walk on leash or if you have a fenced yard, taker her out for a short period of calm play. A dog should never exercise or play hard for one hour before she eats or for two hours after she eats. What she needs before you leave is your attention and a little playtime.

* *Breakfast:* Put her breakfast down no more than thirty minutes and take it up before you leave. Nibbling all day can encourage the urge to go to the bathroom all day. Make sure you carefully wash her water bowl and leave clean, fresh water every day.

* *Out of harm's way:* If there are rooms that should be off limits to Biscuit; close the doors. Avoiding temptation is a secret to good behavior.

* *Be calm yourself.* Don't rush around like a worried, maniac yourself. Put keys, book bags,

purses, anything you need to take away near the door. Families with crazed, wild leavings teach already lonely dogs to be crazed and wild, too. The next time you even think about telling Biscuit she is not perfect, stop and make a list of your own mishaps and worries first. Then, rub Biscuit all over and realize that she thinks you are perfect.

- *Entertainment:* Scatter a few favorite toys. Offer her a hollow, rubber toy filled with treats and a little peanut butter. Try a nylon, or flexible rubber bone. Latex (but never vinyl) squeaky toys will entertain dogs who like squeakies for hours. Try to avoid hard bones, thick rawhides, brittle cow hooves or anything that could wear down teeth or cause an intestinal blockage. Many toys that are safe when you are there to supervise can be dangerous when she is alone.

- *Think ahead:* Put away anything that the dog might investigate, chew, walk on, drag around or disturb. Many dog crimes are really owner oversights. Most dogs are as good at problem solving and judgment as a two year old child. Bear this in mind and protect the dog from temptation and trouble.

- *Noise and stimulation:* Find a stimulating channel on television and leave it playing for the dog. Noise will reduce the dog's attention to sounds outside the house. Nice , loud classical music on the radio could help the canine thunder storm worrier hear less frightening environmental nose.

- *Outside:* How often has your dog been able  to go outside to the bathroom during the summer vacation season? She cannot suddenly adjust her bladder skills from going every four hours to waiting to go every ten hours. Ask yourself: Do I wait ten or twelve hours and never go to the rest room while I am away from home? Extend this consideration to your dog. Arrange for a friend, neighbor or a house sitter to come to your house and let Biscuit stretch her legs and use the bathroom.

  If this is not possible, paper training the dog is an option. There are step by step books to teach you and the dog the best way to accomplish this.

  Confining the dog to a crate is an excellent way to teach housebreaking skills, but the crate is a teaching tool, not a bladder guard. No dog should be confined to a crate more than six to eight hours.

- *Routine:* Stick to a schedule. Dogs have amazingly accurate inner clocks. If Biscuit waits to wee until 5:30 every day with never an accident, don't blame Biscuit if a puddle awaits you at seven.

BEHAVIOUR PROBLEMS

- *Visit the Veterinarian:* A Fall check up could be just what the doctor ordered. Especially if Biscuit is feeling great. It is important for her veterinarian to see her bouncing and feeling fine as well as when she is feeling not so perky. Having a record of her normal results from blood work and a complete check up is good insurance as she ages. Take a urine and stool sample and let her know its fun to go see the doctor.

- *School:* Enroll Biscuit in a training class that focuses on fun. Biscuit will look forward to going to her own school.

Deserve Your Dog's Trust

Your dog's miraculous trust in you is the reason she waits patiently for your return. You have the whole world to explore and experience. To Biscuit, you are the world.

As you consider your plans and responsibilities of going back to work and back to school, please let your priorities include: Back to Biscuit.

9

Your Dog's Body: To Care For And Protect

"I care not for any man's religion whose dog and cat are not the better for it."
Abroham Lincoln

When In Doubt:
Go To The Vet

"A righteous man has regard for the life of his beast."
Proverbs 12:10

I avoid taking my dogs for routine veterinary care on Mondays.

Mondays are often days when veterinarians fight all day to save dogs who have gotten very sick over the weekend. Many veterinarians go home Monday night exhausted from saving lives of dogs who presented themselves Monday morning already at death's door.

A dog who was not very perky and "maybe a little sick" on Friday, may be so unlucky as to have to endure the "let's wait and see if he is not OK tomorrow" health watch.

Saturday arrives and the dog may act a little more like himself. But Saturday night comes and he hasn't eaten for two days, and maybe he has vomited a little, or has a touch of diarrhea, and he seems further under the weather.

Weekend Watch: Not A Good Idea
By Saturday night, the dog's regular veterinarian is closed until Monday. Many owners, understandably, hope to avoid the additional cost for care at an emergency veterinary clinic. Or, an owner can have such complete confidence in their own veterinarian that they hate the thought of taking their dog to see a stranger.

Many sick dogs continue on the "lets see if he is not better tomorrow" health watch.

Monday: Dog Is Really Sick
Monday comes. The owner is faced with a dog who is definitely sick. Not eating. Diarrhea much worse. Maybe he lays around and just doesn't notice the squirrels that he was hurling himself onto the window to nab just last week. Whatever he is doing or not doing, at this stage the owner is worried and making plans to be in the veterinarians office on Monday.

Go Early or Regret Later
When in doubt: go to the veterinarian. Don't wait and see. Take your little fur angel to be looked over by his doctor at the very first sign he is not himself.

Give the dog's doctor an opportunity to cure a small bout of diarrhea before it gets worse. Find out for sure why he vomited this morning.

Don't Play Doctor At Home
Let the doctor have the opportunity early on to check all the dog's vital signs. Make sure that a life-threatening medical crisis is not on the horizon.

Waiting Costs More
Save the dog from feeling worse and having to undergo additional tests, treatments and waiting to feel better once he is really feeling bad.

Silent Symptoms Can Be Deadly
Remember that your dog cannot talk about his symptoms. A little white foamy vomit may be his body's cry for medical care right now.

What if he is restless and asks over and over to go out and try to use the bathroom because he is in the beginning stages of the dangerous,

often deadly crisis of 'bloat' (gastric dilation or volvulus)?

Has he, unknown to his owner, been bitten by an insect, spider or snake, or sniffed or lapped up a deadly toxin or poison that can shut down his kidneys, or his respiratory system? His symptoms may not get visibly worse as he sickens more and more as his vital systems fail.

Veterinarians are amazing practitioners of science, healing and assurance for the dogs that need them. Every dog we love deserves to have his doctor see him any time he is not acting like his healthy self.

Good News Is Good News

So what if the doctor checks him over and pronounces him fine? The cost of an office visit is never wasted. Every time your veterinarian examines your dog while he is healthy, the better the veterinarian comes to know your dog and be prepared to treat him when he is really sick.

I am always thrilled when blood work and tests produce negative results. Normal results recorded in your dog's permanent file will give the doctor a better idea of what is not normal for your dog if the frightening day comes that he is really sick and his tests do not fall within normal limits.

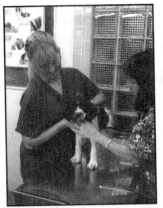

Early Treatment: The Best Treatment
Ask any vet. Many slightly sick dogs who could have had medical care on Friday at the beginning of a bout of illness, often require less medical treatment and testing than they may need if the veterinarian is required to go to emergency measures to treat the dog when he arrives in serious medical crisis several days later.

Know Your Dog's Moods And Habits
Learn to know when your dog is not feeling like his normal wild and/ or happy self. Owners know more about their own dog's habits, attitudes appetites and activity levels than anyone else in the dog's life. A full report of owner observations are valuable to the veterinarian who is treating the dog.

"How's He Feeling?" Checklist
- *"When did he eat last?"* If he likes to eat and he misses a meal, or certainly two, this is a sign he may not be well.

351

- *"How much water did he drink in the past day? More than usual? Less than usual?"* Dogs need a constant supply of fresh, clean, changed at least daily, drinking water. Any changes in drinking habits should be discussed with the dog's doctor.

- *"Have his toilet habits changed?"* Keep an eye out for how often the dog goes to the bathroom, and what his output is when he goes. For some dog owners, this task of watching output may be a slightly to very yucky responsibility of dog ownership. But how will you know what is going on inside your dog if you have no idea what is coming out of your dog? Sorry. Dogs need us to know these things.

- *"Think there's a change in your dog's output in any way?"* Take a sample to the veterinarian. Simple tests on your dog's toilet products can tell your vet vast amounts of information. Practice catching a urine sample now, before you think you need one. Your veterinarian will tell you how to do this. I wait for the dog to squat or to lift his leg; wait for a stream of urine to begin, and then silently, gently slide a pizza pan or cookie sheet under the flow. Hold the pan carefully. Don't touch the dog, if you are able. Practice your urine catching periodically just to acclimate the dog to these peculiar proceedings.

- *"What is his temperature?"* You need a rectal thermometer to find this magic number. The modern digital ones are faster to use. That

352

will no doubt please you and the dog. Don't forget the lubricant. Remember that a dog's normal temperature is higher than a human's 98.6.

His body heat will most likely be between 100 and 102.5 degrees. Average canine rectal temperature is 101.3 degrees. Write the temperature down and report it to your veterinarian. If you are not practiced in taking dog temperatures, get a friend or family member to talk to and steady the head end while you keep an eye and hand on the thermometer. Not something you want to do at all? All the more reason to go to the veterinarian as soon as you have any inkling your dog may be sick.

- *"Has his breathing pattern changed? Panting? Wheezing?"* Any change in breathing should be seen by your veterinarian right away.

- *"Did he wake you up whining or asking to go out or just by being active during the night?"* If this a dog who usually sleeps through the night, sleeplessness and restlessness must mean something. Maybe it means Grendel smells that Grizelda next door is in heat. But maybe it means he can't sleep because he feels bad. Let one who went to veterinary school to be qualified to decide why he is not acting like himself.

- *"Accidents in the house?"* If a dog who is normally well housebroken surprises you with puddle or pile, give the dog credit for being as

353

unable to avoid this bodily function occurring on the carpet as any other creature who can't turn a doorknob or ask to go outside would be given. Let the vet decide why the dog lost control.

- *"Your dog just doesn't act like himself?"* The times my dogs have been most sick, were the times they did almost nothing that I could write down as unusual symptoms. Hours of staring into the face of the dog you love will prepare you to know without question if your dog looks sick or in pain or frightened. Every dog lover can recall a sick dog's battle with an illness that left us saying, "I just knew she was not herself."

Trust Your Judgment
Your vet will not think you are a hypochondriac. You are not inconveniencing your vet to take in a dog with a slight odd symptom that worries you. Your vet will be so proud and delighted that you are an educated, caring, observant partner in your pet's health care. Sit down with your dog and repeat your vet's office phone number until you have it memorized. Let this number be your gateway to curing little problems before they require serious medical intervention.

May you never have to pace the floor on a Monday morning around 3 am counting the minutes until your veterinarian's hospital opens. Kiss your dog on the head right now and promise her you are at her service to get veterinary care any time she needs it. There is nothing she would not do for you.

First Aid:
Be Prepared

"Before anything else, preparation is the key to success."
Alexander Graham Bell

"When in doubt, go to the vet!", is my dog care motto.

A sudden injury, life threatening situation or accident befalls your dog. First aid is needed right this minute. What do you do?

Immediate Care Needed!
Being hit by a car, falling from a height, or getting stepped on are three common injury situations that require the pet owner's immediate care.

Open wounds that are bleeding, whether inflicted by a dog fight, a wild animal bite, a laceration from a sharp object, like barbed wire or a metal fence, or gunshot wounds, all require owner bandaging and intervention before the veterinarian takes charge. An overheated dog needs immediate cooling to possibly save his life.

Mastering first aid techniques and assembling a canine first aid kit today could save your best friend's life tomorrow when seconds drag by like hours.

Dr. Molly Herdic's devotion to her own three dogs, Teela, Paco and Daisy, and her deep concern for dogs who place their health in her hands, set her to explaining first aid situations and listing supplies when I asked her advice on dog first aid.

What Does The Veterinarian Say?

Question: *What are the emergency signs that call for immediate veterinary attention?*

Answer: See your veterinarian immediately for any trouble breathing, all bleeding, any problem walking or keeping balance, or for any dog that repeatedly tries to urinate and cannot urinate.

Q: *Summer adds the threat of overheating to dog owners list of emergency worries. What should an owner do if a pet is found overheated?*

A: Take the dog's rectal temperature. Average dog temperature is one hundred and two degrees. Place the dog in a cool, but not cold, bath. Gently pour cool, but not cold, water over the top of the dog's neck until temperature drops. Take the dog to the veterinarian immediately.

YOUR DOG'S BODY

Q: *If a dog is hit by a car, what are the first aid steps to take?*

A: Place a tourniquet on any bleeding limb. Cover dog with a blanket. Go directly to a veterinarian.

Q: *Is there a best way to deal with a dog fight and resulting injuries?*

A: Do not attempt to break up a dog fight unless two people are present who are capable of each grasping a dog's tail and pulling the two apart. Separate the dogs. Check for wounds. See your veterinarian.

Q: *What are the signs that a vomiting dog needs medical intervention?*

A: If a dog has vomited food or water for more than twelve to twenty four hours, veterinary attention is needed. Usual causes of vomiting are inflammation of the stomach lining caused by something the dog ate, poisons, a foreign body (ball, toy, food wrappers, etc.) or from bacterial or viral infection. Emergency signs are lethargy and dry mouth. A veterinarian needs to diagnose the cause of the vomiting.

357

DEVOTED TO DOGS

Q: *Should an owner induce vomiting if they believe the dog has eaten a poisonous substance, plant or a foreign object?*

A: Never induce vomiting if you suspect a dog has swallowed any sharp object like chicken bones. A veterinarian must determine if inducing vomiting will pose a danger to the dog.

For some dangerous substances, such as eating large amounts of chocolate, when the owner is sure the substance was ingested in the past hour, inducing vomiting for immediate first aid may be suggested by the veterinarian. Call the veterinarian and ask how much hydrogen peroxide is needed to induce vomiting. Take the dog immediately to the doctor's office for further diagnosis and treatment. Be able to describe any vomited substance to the veterinarian.

Q: *How does an owner know if a dog is in pain?*

Some dogs will cry out or yelp. Crying and yelping are often signs of spinal pain. A pet in pain will often stop eating. A dog in pain may limp.

- Stoic or Dramatic? Different Dogs Reaction To Pain
  My dog Quinnton once broke his tail. He had been playing hard in the back yard, chasing his sister beneath the branches of very low hanging tree limbs. When he came inside for his supper, all I knew was that he did not act like his usual merry self.

- Restless Pacing
  He was restless and would not sit or lay down.
  He stood beside the bed most of the night
  staring at me. I would wake and he would be
  standing there looking into my face. I knew
  something had to be wrong. Off we rushed
  to the emergency clinic in the middle of the
  night. After a complete exam of every inch
  of his body, the only sound he made was to
  whimper softly when the doctor touched his
  tail.

- Strong Silent Type
  Some dogs are very well behaved and quiet
  even when in great pain or seriously ill. I
  learned from Quinnton's stoic, but peculiar,
  night of standing by my head for hours that
  when a dog acts unusual in any way, a trip to
  the veterinarian is never wasted.

Q: _What supplies go into a dog first aid_
kit?

A: Include a tourniquet, several rolls of gauze (2",
3" and 4"), 1" porous tape, gauze pads, muzzle to
fit your dog since an injured dog may bite from

359

anxiety or pain, eye irrigation rinse, tweezers for tick or foreign object removal, antibiotic cream,  blanket for transporting an injured dog, and a thermometer. Ask your veterinarian for advice on the size Benadryl™ capsule suitable to the size of your dog for emergency treatment of an insect bite or allergic reaction.

Be sure to keep your first aid kit in the car when your dog is in the car. Keep a copy of your vaccine record in your first aid kit. Pack fresh water from home. Replace this water if it has been stored in the car for several weeks. Dogs need fresh, clean water at all times.

Q: *Are human over the counter drugs safe for dogs?*

A: Some human drugs must never, under any circumstance, be given to a dog. Tylenol (acetaminophen), Advil (ibuprofen), or any drug that contains either of these medications should never be given to a dog. Ask your veterinarian for advice before you give any drug to your dog. Some drugs that are formulated to help humans may be poisonous to dogs.

Parties: Keep An Eye On Your Dog
Parties for humans can be dangerous settings for dogs. Place foods, drinks and garbage in elevated, closed, completely contained receptacles.

Alcohol is very dangerous to dogs. Dogs should be supervised carefully in human party settings to make sure they never lap up any alcoholic beverage.

Prepare Your First Aid Kit Now

Make your shopping list for your dog's first aid kit and place all the supplies in a bag or carrying case. I keep mine near the garage door. I also make my dog ride in a dog crate. Even a small whack by another vehicle could throw a dog from the seat and cause painful injury to your dog. If you will not put a crate in the car, please buy the dog a dog seat belt and fasten him down in a rear seat for protection.

Where's Your First Aid Book?

Pull out a lawn chair. Let your dog relax on a nice comfy dog bed beside your chair. Spend an afternoon reading the first aid book to the dog. He will enjoy the attention. He loves your voice. Thrill his little dog heart with your company while you educate yourself to rise to the emergency occasion that we hope never arises.

Like carrying an umbrella everywhere to ward off rain, maybe carrying your first aid kit from hither to yon will make sure you never need it.

The Angel Gabriel's Early Christmas Gift
(Surgical Aftercare For The Dog You Love)

"Truth, like surgery, may hurt. But it cures."
Han Suyin

The Angel Gabriel received castration as his early Christmas present. I doubt he requested, "lop off my boy parts", in his letter to Santa.

Did he guess his romping puppy life was about to collide with the speed bump of responsible pet ownership the morning before surgery when he was not on the guest list for breakfast ?

Gabriel and I went for a short walk while the dog father stirred up breakfast for his sister and brother. Our veterinarian was very clear

 362

that Gabriel must have absolutely nothing to eat after eight the evening before surgery. Pet owners agonize to see their pets miss a meal. Just because it makes us feel comforted to see our pets eat, does not mean eating is always best for the pet's health. Better to follow doctor's orders and not the leanings of our nurturing hearts.

After surgery, with medical staff watching over him, Gabriel spent time at the hospital waking up. He needed quiet time to rest and heal. My job, while I counted the hours until his release, was to prepare for his homecoming.

Crate Rest Means Just That

A big boy now, and nicely house trained, Gabriel's dog crate had been stored in the garage. His surgeon, Dr. Frank Wagner of the Fredericksburg Animal Hospital, wanted all romping, bouncing and interacting with his dog brother and sister limited for a few days after castration. Gabriel's collapsible wire dog cage was dragged from garage to the foot of my bed the afternoon before Gabriel arrived home. His favorite fleece dog bed was tucked inside the crate. I clipped a stainless steel pail of clean water to the door. Dogs returning from surgery often go straight to their water bowl for a drink.

Finally, the animal hospital receptionist, Wendy Schwartz, called and said, "Come and get your big boy."

At the hospital, Gabriel pranced out wagging his merry Springer tail. He looked just as handsome

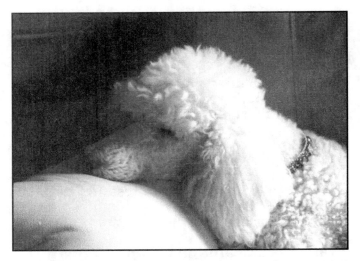

and was just as thrilled with life as when I had left him the day before.

On-Leash Walking
Gabriel's leash was in my hand, ready, when we got home. Dr. Wagner said, "walk only on leash for seven days." A young dog like Gabriel with a big fenced yard could easily bound from the house and chase a squirrel or rabbit. Recovery required calm bathroom breaks to safeguard newly placed stitches.

Take A Peek At The Stitches
Each morning after surgery, I asked Gabriel to do a "down". Next, I gently rolled him over on his side to take a look at his stitches. Using a hot dog to keep Gabriel's attention on his nose end, only a few seconds were needed to see if the suture area was clean, dry and pink. Dr. Wagner explained that any, "redness, discharge,

or swelling" meant I must call the hospital and bring Gabriel back for a recheck. Knowing me well enough to know I would love to administer some ointment or home doctoring, Dr. Wagner made sure I understood that I needed to let the surgery area heal on its own and not practice home medicine. He said, "If you have any concerns or questions at all, bring Gabriel back to me."

Precisely Follow Doctor's Orders

When a dog comes home from surgery it is important to share all the post surgery care rules with the entire human family. Moms and dads may realize the dog has to remain on leash, rest in his crate and not run and play, but children may not. A few minutes of breaking aftercare rules can be very harmful and painful for the post surgery dog.

I knew that Gabriel was a laid back, not very interested in licking, chewing or investigating his parts kind of guy. I felt quite safe that in a crate Gabriel would nap and watch the household go by him. As a get well treat, I tossed a whole raw carrot in his crate as entertainment and chew toy.

Never Take Calmness For Granted

Not all dogs are calm. I once owned a Scottie, Muffin, that removed her sutures twice in twenty four hours after being spayed . Her veterinarian, Dr. Chip Byrd of Blue Ridge Animal Hospital, advised that Muffin wear a fancy white cone shaped collar for one full week after her surgery. Muffin was driven to investigate and chew any irritant on her body. For anti-chew insurance, I swaddled her little black torso in a child's tee shirt. Many safety pins securing the tee shirt and coming home to check on her chew, lick, escape artist antics at lunch time brought her safely to suture removal eight days after surgery.

Every dog has his own personality. If you have a strong feeling regarding how your dog will react to any situation, it is best to take precautions for after surgery success.

Plan The Recovery
Surgical aftercare goes most smoothly with planning. Make sure your dog's vaccines are current. If your doctor would like to see blood work results before your dog has surgery, make sure you plan for that expense when you budget for the surgical procedure. Be sure that your pet has no worms, fleas, ticks or other parasites before he enters the hospital.

Go Forth Clean To Surgery
Realizing that Gabriel would not have a bath for at least a week after his surgery, I gave him a bath the day before I turned him in for his castration. Soaped up and wagging his tail, he had a few little biscuits while the whitening shampoo worked its magic. I did not tell him he was going off for neutering.

Owners: Be Upbeat!
Many pet owners speak with pitiful voices to pets during times of stress. Owners believe they sound reassuring. Cooing and cajoling voices

may sound frightening to the pets who only understand tone of voice.

The morning that Gabriel and I rode to town for his rendezvous with the scalpel, I talked to him of all the fun we were going to have in the weeks ahead.

Dogs are very sensitive to our moods, our fears, our feelings. One thing we can always do for them is pretend a brave face even if we feel sad, worried or fearful. A car ride to relinquish your reproductive parts feels no different than a car trip for French fries.

Neutering Is A Good Thing To Do

Gabriel is resting sweetly on my feet as I type this. He does not know that he has taken a stand for neutering. He does not know that he is never going to be responsible for siring one tiny pup who might not find a home or who might displace another little pup from finding a home. He does not know that other boy dogs may look more kindly upon him in public now that he smells less macho. I hope that his neutering will insure his good manners to remain courteously housebroken and not feel the need to anoint upright bushes, trees and furniture.

My beloved boy's boy parts will never lead him into trouble. Santa will bring him something very special for being a brave, good boy this year. He is, after all, the Angel Gabriel.

Peanut Butter Makes The Medicine Go Down

"It don't care whether I'm good enough.
It don't care whether I snore or not. It
don't care which God I pray to. There
are only three things in this world with
that kind of unconditional acceptance.
Dogs, donuts, and money."
Danny DeVito

Dogs and human companions will follow you anywhere if you offer the right reward.

Since dogs are the most esteemed and delightful companions, I intend no slight when I compare humans to dogs. Most of us would be pleased to share our lives with a partner who adores our every action, jumps up and comes immediately when called for dinner, and who waits cheerfully in the car for long hours while a loved one shops.

Everybody's Granny taught, "You catch more flies with honey than you do with vinegar." Honey as a dog reward is difficult to offer and messy to deliver. Peanut butter, however, will catch, distract, entertain and hold enraptured almost any dog.

Love That Peanut Butter
Toes, Toothbrush, Tablets

The uses and dog joys of peanut butter are endless. My dog, Bonnie, would submit to toenail trimming but would hang her head and look as though I betrayed her trust with every squeeze of the clipper blade. Our relationship and her toenail health was saved by peanut butter.

I would smear a deep, generous patch of peanut butter on the glass patio door. Applied to the glass at precisely Bonnie lick level, she would stand distracted while I trimmed all sixteen nails. The glass patio door gave me optimal daylight, helping me see through her white nails and never nick the pink quick. Bonnie happily slurped clean the glass, paying little attention to me. The earlier in the dog's life you begin this positive reinforcement peanut butter training, before negative associations are made with nail clipping, the better.

Training your dog to look forward to daily use of her toothbrush will be easier if you begin rubbing her teeth daily with a tiny bit of peanut butter. In a few days you can graduate to peanut

butter on the toothbrush, and then on to doggy toothpaste.

Maybe you have an appointment to have your dog microchip'ed for identification and protection should she ever be lost? Take a little peanut butter to hold for distraction while your veterinarian inserts the rice sized chip.

Lick This: Put Those Sharp Puppy Teeth Away

Owners of busy puppies and older dogs rave about successful management of destructive chewing, nuisance barking, separation boredom and time outs from constant owner attention by using peanut butter and dog biscuits to fill a hard, hollow, rubber dog toy. The "Kong" toy is a perfect vehicle for stuffing with edible goodies.

Dog trainers, veterinarians and dog lovers have many uses for peanut butter. Whether for home obedience, luring canine models and actors, or for teaching tasks in dog sports like agility and competition obedience, peanut butter is pressed into service.

Walk This Way With Peanut Butter

Tracey Johnston, an obedience trainer, told me, "I use peanut butter for teaching heeling. Put it on a wooden spoon and start walking. The dog licks the peanut butter while you command, "Heel.""

Johnston continued, "At obedience class, we use peanut butter to stop barking dogs. Smear it on the roof of the mouth before the dog actually starts barking. Put a small cracker over the top of the peanut butter. This keeps them busy so they don't have a chance to think about what they normally bark at."

Leslie Wagner from the Peanut Advisory Board (*www.peanutbutterlovers.com*) shared television trick teaching techniques, "Many 'talking' television animals are moving their mouths because the trainer has put peanut butter in their mouths. I've seen a dentist's patient reminder card photo of a squirrel brushing his teeth. The photographer put peanut butter on the tooth brush to entice the squirrel over to pick up the brush and hold the peanut butter to his mouth."

Phyllis Broderick, a Springer Spaniel mom and obedience and agility enthusiast, uses peanut butter to get dogs to do all kinds of things willingly. Broderick trained her dog to star on television commercials for "Meaty Bone Dog Biscuits". Broderick divulged her training secret,

"There was an empty shiny bowl and Cassie's job for the commercial was to lick her chops, like she had just finished eating. I put peanut butter between her teeth and gums. Cassie would lick and lick; sticking out her really long tongue. "Cassie was so good at this that she later went on to be photographed on the box for "Liver Treats" dog biscuits.

Broderick teaches dogs to walk at her side in heel position using peanut butter. She explained ,"I took a long pointer and put duct tape on the end. Then, I dipped it into a jar of peanut butter and held it up high at my side, so Cassie would look up and lick the peanut butter. I have also used peanut butter on the pointer stick to teach her exactly where to touch as she races across agility obstacles."

Peanut Butter Pills For Gatsby

The most popular use for the nut butter delicacy is "to make pills go down more easily", I was told by Jan Vallone, mother of three lovable Beardies, Chloe, Sara and Gatsby. Vallone explained, "Peanut butter on the roof of the mouth causes lots of licking and swallowing. Gulp. The pill goes down."

Veterinarians Share Peanut Better Secrets

Veterinarian Pam Fandrich employs peanut butter techniques for dogs who visit her clinic. Fandrich explained, "We use peanut butter to distract our canine friends from the noxious procedures we must perform. I smear peanut butter on the examining room tables to let the pups lick it off while I give an injection. I use it to lure large dogs onto our floor scale. I put it on the end of a tongue depressor to make a "peanut butter popsicle". I also put it in an empty syringe case and hold that for the dog. It is harder to get to that way and lasts longer."

But Don't Over-do It!

Dr. Elizabeth Ubelhor offered advice along with a bit of dietary caution saying, "I use peanut butter mostly to give medication. I often make a tiny peanut butter sandwich because some dogs love the taste, but not the viscosity. I tell my clients that a little goes a long way because I have seen some dogs get pancreatitis from too much peanut butter, or anything with a lot of fat. I have also used peanut butter to remove chewing gum, tar, adhesives from fur in a pinch. The dogs sure seem to enjoy the clean up!"

Since peanut butter is as high in fat and calories as it is in dog appeal, save your peanut butter magic for times when you really need to capture your dog's attention. Be sure to reduce her dinner portions on days that you use food rewards.

Gentle Procedures = Positive Learning

How compliant, willing and companionable are the dogs who share our lives. If only every problem could be solved and all humans in our lives could be convinced to do our bidding with a mere teaspoon of peanut butter.

Begging the pardon of Mary Poppins, a spoonful of peanut butter really will make the medicine go down.

Give That Dog
A Toothbrush

"Nature has given us two ears,
two eyes and but one tongue;
the end that we should hear
and see more than we speak."
Socrates

Doggy breath! How many pet owners dread the aging of a pet and hate to see 'puppy breath' replaced by the eventual bad breath of older dogs?

If you are turning your face away from your dog's offerings of kisses, the time has come to think about canine dental disease, and how to prevent the problem.

Today, dogs live much longer and healthier lives thanks to advanced, caring techniques

 374

of modern veterinarians. Pet dentistry is a necessary and life enhancing service offered to our companion animals. Anesthetics are much safer, with dogs waking quickly and in fine spirits. Ultrasonic cleaning devices provide faster and improved cleaning of tartar from the teeth. A broad spectrum of modern antibiotics treat the gums and many organ systems affected by dental disease. 85% of pets over the age of 4 suffer from periodontal disease. Untreated, the dangerous condition gets worse and the pet's health declines.

Dirty Teeth Hurt The Whole Dog

Diseases of the teeth, gums and mouth are far more serious than the mere symptom of doggy breath. The dog feels pain, can lose teeth, often forms pockets of infections around teeth and gums, and worst of all, sheds bacteria from the infected gums into the bloodstream. This steady shower of germs into the blood can affect many vital organs. Dr. Terri Horton, "This bacteria can spread throughout the body and affect the heart, lungs, kidneys and nasal passages".

Many owners, fortunate enough to own and be loved by a really old dog will make many trips to their veterinarian asking, "Is there anything to be done to prolong the life of our beloved four footed family member?" According to current veterinary advice, the answer is a resounding, "Yes!" Taking care of your dog's teeth today, no matter how young or how old, will keep him healthier and feeling better longer.

375

Clean Teeth: Heart Health Protection

Dental health educators at the Cornell University College of Veterinary Medicine say that in aging dogs the most common age-related cardiac disease is congestive heart failure resulting from problems with heart valves, traced to bacterial infections resulting from fight wounds, other trauma or periodontal (gum) disease. These infections can create scar tissue on the heart valves, which alters the shape, inhibiting proper function.

Does Your Dog's Mouth Hurt?

Adding to the dog and owners problems is the danger that behavior related problems may result from poor dental health. A dog that

has problems with her teeth may be in pain, and may not eat, chew or digest her food to the full benefit of her body. While her nutrition suffers and general health is negatively affected, other bad habits may develop when the owner of the difficult to feed dog may resort to special tidbits: chicken, human foods, sticky canned foods, in a desperate effort to get the dog to eat. Soon the dog has been taught by the owner to be a finicky eater, while the dog continues to suffer; getting sicker all the time due to poor dental health.

Dogs in pain may learn to growl at their owners, or unsuspecting children, when they have areas around their mouths and heads touched or petted. Many dogs have been labeled "aggressive" because they had a toothache. Dogs who have to growl to fend owners away from their mouths learn another bad lesson: if you growl owners will go away and you get your way. How confusing to the dog who is in pain to learn to shun the company of humans who are the ones who will need to touch her to treat her medical problem.

Dry Kibble, Toothbrush, Veterinary Advice

When asked what should an owner do to prevent the problems caused by dirty teeth, Dr. Horton suggested a three part prevention treatment plan. "Feed a dry food as the bulk of your pet's diet. The act of chewing hard pieces helps prevent tartar accumulation. Brush your dog's teeth daily." Visit your veterinarian for a complete check-up that includes an oral examination.

Once the brushing program is begun be sure to use a very soft toothbrush designed for pet's mouths and a pet toothpaste. These pastes are flavored with chicken, beef or peanut butter and many owners find the pet accepts brushing readily and enjoys the close contact, the extra attention and the delicious toothpaste.

Ease Into Brushing

Begin your brushing program slowly. Never charge into the dog's mouth as though she has

377

enjoyed having her teeth brushed for years. Like any new behavior you wish to teach your dog, the lessons should be in gradual steps, with positive rewards. Tiny, delicious treats will pave the way to the dog accepting and learning the new skill. Your veterinarian will have excellent brochures giving you step by step advice on beginning to brush and teaching the dog to enjoy the new daily routine. Most good pet care books will include a section on how to brush your pet's teeth.

Until you begin your daily brushing program, or if you just cannot make the time to brush, Dr.Sheri Bakerian offers the following advice, "Special chew toys made for application with doggy toothpaste will help the dog who likes to chew to clean her teeth and will apply enzymes formulated to attack plaque build up and doggy mouth odors. These same beneficial enzymes are available on American made quality rawhide

chews available at your veterinarian. Rope toys act like dental floss to buff off the tooth surfaces and massage gums."

Dr. Bakerian adds that if all else fails, "At least spray your pets teeth and gums with one of the specially formulated dental health enzyme sprays available at your veterinarian." She suggests you "Keep the spray beside your own toothbrush and at least once a day, when you brush your own teeth, give your dog's mouth a spray."

Take A Peek At His Teeth

When you take a peek into your pet's mouth there are signs that a trip to your veterinarian is necessary as soon as possible. Look for bleeding gums, swollen gums, loose, broken or missing teeth, or a pet that acts like its mouth is in pain. Bad breath that goes on for weeks is a true sign of a mouth that needs attention.

Adios, Dog Breath!

Remember: 'doggy breath' should not be ignored. Start your pet's dental health prevention program this week. Whether she is young or old, she wants fresh breath as much as the humans who love her.

When Your Dog Needs To Go On A Diet

"The dog's kennel is not the place to keep a sausage."
Danish Proverb

My dog, Quinnton, and I have reluctantly begun a weight reduction diet. We drove into town and joined an internationally known weight control group. I dragged myself into the building , held my breath, and let the lovely thin lady at the scales weigh me.

Quinnton waited in the car. Poor little guy, with such a happy appetite, unsuspecting that french fries and potato chips just went out the window.

We joined the group with the famous British Duchess leading the pack of would-be thinner people. Now, as we prepare our high fiber, low

380

fat meals, we wonder just what is the duchess dining on across the Atlantic? Wonder if she has a dog? Wonder if her dog got fatter and enjoyed offerings of the same delicious morsels that rounded the curves of the royal spokes person?

Little Spaniel Loves To Eat

Quinnton is a medium sized, six year old, not very active Springer Spaniel. He would rather lie on his mother's big bed surveying his squirrel infested driveway than be shown the leash and offered a walk. A while back, Quinnton hurt his knee and had a ligament replaced. Cage rest for six weeks turned into glorious, languorous lounging on the bed for a longer time than his guilty mother wants to tell.

Why Walk When You Could Be Snacking?

Once Quinnton's knee healed and he was able to take walks, the best walk in his opinion was into the garage, to be hoisted into the van and driven off to town for French fries.

Will There Be French Fries In Heaven?

Quinnton is not planning to cross the much spoken of Rainbow Bridge where devoted dogs go after life to wait for their owners' arrival. He will be trotting up to the eternal, perpetually generous drive through window where wisps of glorious fried food smells settle into his twitching nostrils and make him smile a dog delighted smile. Anyone who has not seen a dog smile has not communed soulfully enough with a dog.

DEVOTED TO DOGS

When employees at the bank drive-up window forget to shoot a dog biscuit out to Quinnton,  he jerks his dear little freckled snoot abruptly in my direction and asks me "Mother, is this really our bank?" If a bank is not solvent enough to offer biscuits to canine depositors, it is time to worry about the bank's finances. Immediately, we drive to the closest potato bearing drive though and we celebrate the potato together. I'm Irish; he's hungry. Potatoes call out to us.

Admitting We Are Helpless
When Faced With Potatoes
We hate to admit it, but me must: our eating habits need adjustment. If I can commit to eat more healthy foods, surely Quinnton, who watches and hopes to participate in every bite I take, will benefit.

The Vet Intones Diet Advice
Quinnton's veterinarian recently had a talk with the brown spaniel about the need to locate his lost waist line. His veterinarian has generously invited Quinnton to return any time we pass the veterinary hospital and be plopped onto the scales to check his reducing progress. Quinnton and I are in this together. We got chubby together. We will learn to eat carrots

and take long walks with smiles on our faces; together. One must never leap upon the weight loss bandwagon unadvisedly. To be safe and to make sure you find the most beneficial plan, you must begin with a health professional's approval. Both our doctors think shedding a few inches would prolong our health and happiness. Sadly, we were not told by a health professional that we are the perfect weight for our age and bone structure. No one said, "You have big bones; you are too thin; go out and have a nut sundae."

Diet Advice Abounds

The would be slimming individual needs wise advice. Quinnton has spent hours with his head propped on my tummy while we lay upon the bed and read about nutrition and healthy approaches to weight loss. Advice given for chubby dogs appears compatible to suggestions for humans aspiring to look good in skimpy clothing by Summer.

Fewer calories, plus more exercise, equals less fat on the dog or the owner. Seems there is no way around this rule of fat breakdown. Where's that leash? Walking will let us eat a little more. We are all for that.

Weight has to come off slowly or the dieter will suffer. Quinnton did not get tubby over night. It is fool hardy and dangerous to try and get skinny on a speed plan, either.

Go Slowly Into Your Healthy New Weight

To abruptly reduce a dog's calorie intake is very dangerous. Owners must seek veterinary

advice to find a gradual, nutritious plan that insures the dog continues to nourish his bones and tissues with adequate levels of proteins, fats, carbohydrates, minerals and other nutrients. To be extra sure that Quinnton's metabolic systems were in great shape, our veterinarian took a small blood sample and checked Quinnton's thyroid function, his blood sugar levels and every other function that could be tested by analyzing his blood.

A veterinarian may suggest a prescription weight loss food for dogs. Our veterinarian suggested Quinnton reduce his intake of dry food slightly and that we add a low calorie vegetable to the dry food to make sure Quinney did not feel empty and suffer longing for more food in the bowl.

A Green Bean Experience

Green beans were suggested to us to stretch the dry ration. Quinnton turned up his brown nose to the beans. He tossed them, individually, and gleefully around the kitchen floor. Our cats, Sam and Lucy, found the beans and batted them into the living room. My husband unsuspectingly stomped the beans and then I ended up on hands and knees scraping green gunk from the crevices in the hardwood floor. Much more exercise than I was looking for on my own weight loss plan.

Canned carrots appealed to Quinnton. He prefers his dinner to be served around four in the afternoon. Conveniently for both of us , this is the time I find myself searching the pantry. On our diet regime, Quinnton has half a can of carrots stirred into his reduced ration of dry food. I eat the other half can with a little soy sauce. We watch each other mournfully, wishing the diet fairy would turn these carrots to mashed potatoes.

Results Are Our Reward
After two weeks of practicing this new eating behavior, both of us saw a little dip in the numbers on the scale.

Junk food has been taken from us. No more last bites of doughnuts for Quinnton. No more licking dinner plates. Even if we have no garbage disposal and Quinnton's pre wash skills were so appreciated by the cook, those half eaten cheese raviolis, puddles of gravy and smidgens of blackberry pie were not really a way to show love to a little dog who needs to preserve his joints and stay with his mother for a pain free old dog age.

We are drinking more water. Dogs should have lots of fresh water, with their bowls washed diligently every day. Germs grow in those bowls. Quinnton enjoys watching the bowl be refilled and runs over to drink anytime a fresh bowl lands. How much trouble is it to delight a little dog boy with clean water? Not much.

Changing Cherished Habits

Instead of meeting dog lover friends for pasta and potato lunches with tables out doors, we are now meeting at coffee houses with tables on the sidewalk. A real dog lover will sit outside wrapped in Winter coats if that means dogs can join the outing. There are quite a few of these coffee and beverage establishments. If the strongest willed dieting human goes into the coffee shop and swears to buy only coffee, the other humans can sit outside with the dogs. This way, only one human will must be tested by the peach tarts, chocolate almond biscotti, oatmeal cookies and cinnamon raisin bagels. A bag of specially treated tooth cleaning raw hide chews can be taken for the dogs. Dogs believe

they are enjoying a treat and the mothers and fathers know they are promoting dental health. Warning: Share dog chews only if all dogs present can enjoy rawhide and not feel compelled to wrest the other chews from the jaws of their doggy friends. This is an excellent time to work on and enforce the dog's down-stay command.

Area coffee houses are located beside sidewalks crying out to have dogs go for a leisurely, weight reducing promenade. Dogs can practice their walking on loose leash skills while burning calories and trudging toward the weight loss goal.

Surprise! Healthy Habits Feel Good
As we grow lighter of bulk, our enjoyment of walks and exercise increases. Will we ever prefer the walk to snuggling on our big bed? Will we ever sit and fantasize for a carrot? Probably not, but we just may increase our days upon the Earth to enjoy one another. As we pass by the potatoes calling our names, I know I would give up anything to keep Quinnton healthy and active for one day longer.

Taking the best possible care of our dogs may be a dieting secret we all need for weight loss success. Happy dieting. Keep passing the open drive through windows.

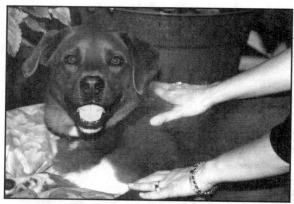

Rub Me Mama:
The Art of Dog Massage

*"The quieter you become,
the more you hear."*
Baba Ram Daas

When I was little, growing up in eastern North Carolina, we used to pass a fascinating hot pink, sprawling, low to the ground cinder block building labeled, "Gentleman's All Girl Massage" on the way to church every Sunday.

Without fail, each week, I would plead from the back seat, "Daddy, can't we stop and see those girls?" There was a painting on the building of a woman in a skimpy, curvaceous outfit that looked so much more interesting to me that what Mamma and I ever got to wear. Or, I'd suggest, "Daddy, could *we* have a massage?" I had no idea what a massage was, but I learned for sure that my church-going, iron-willed

 388

Mamma in her white gloves and Sunday finery was going to make sure no one got one. So we didn't. But just the word, "massage", awakens a mysterious longing in me to know more about this art of laying on of the hands.

De-Cluttering Yields Rewards (Who Knew?)

A few days ago, while pretending I was going to undertake the boring job of cleaning out the rat's nest I call the home office, I was rewarded with unearthing a surprise. A good reason to love dogs is that they will gladly lie at your feet and admire you while thriving in any amount of mess and disorder the humans make. After much unstacking and reorganizing of several book cases, you know the ones, where you stack all the books and newspapers that you just know you will get to read when the weather is too wet, too hot, or you are sick and afraid of being bored while resting. While doing more re-stacking than dusting or discarding, I was rewarded with a lost treasure.

Dog Massage Video Teaches Hands-On Skills

I found a two volume set of videos titled, "Effective Pet Massage for Dogs" and "Effective Pet Massage for Older Dogs" by Jonathan Rudinger. My dogs, Izobel Margot, Quinnton Benjamin Pig and Abroham, were now panting to knock each other out of the way to climb onto my lap for the first massage.

Most of us can think of no better feeling than to have our hands on the fur of the dogs we love. In many homes right now, I hope you are stroking or rubbing dog fur and can think of nothing more enjoyable or relaxing.

Massage All You Like!

Dog behavior experts warn that too much petting can spoil the dog; making her demanding, neurotic or unsure of her place as a lower member of the pack. Many dog behavior books give strict advice describing "the ten second petting rule". Trainers warn that the dog needs to do something for its petting and not be over fondled.

Perform For Petting

Renowned dog behavior counselor and writer, Job Michael Evans, is famous for his "perform for petting" rule: you may pet the dog if the dog sits, but after a few seconds of petting, you need to give another command. When the dog responds, you are free to pet a little more.

Another wise dog writer and behavior analyst, William Campbell, is well known for his "no free lunch petting program." Same idea: you want to pet the dog, the dog wants to be petted. But the dog needs to "learn to earn his petting". If you read many dog behavior books, this idea of not over-fondling the dog lest you spoil or confuse the dog are stated over and over.

Massaging Teaches Calmness

What is a pet owner who is dying to lay on the floor and rub the dog to his or her heart's content to do? The dog wants to be rubbed; you want to rub her. After a rough day at work, many dog owners arrive at home as eager to be with their canine companion as the dog is to see them. Many a care of the frenzied world has been left outside the house because the love of a good dog waited inside. Any dog lover will tell you the dog gives back as much love as she was ever given.

There is an easy solution to the how long to pet the dog dilemma: learn the art of dog massage. Massage is not spoiling. Massage is good for the dog's body and mind, and a rewarding skill to be mastered by the owner.

Massage With Simple Gentle Techniques

Mr. Rudinger's excellent massage videos demonstrate how to hold your hands and how to rub the dog. Dog massage was not brain surgery to grasp and I was delighted to see how much the dogs liked being massaged.

Head To Tail Good Feeling

The basic principles were you hold your hands gently on the dog, stroke from head toward the tail; make sure you are breathing gently, deeply and calmly yourself, and work from head end to tail end and all the bits between. Emphasis is on "gently" .Do not be heavy handed in the least. You are not trying to tenderize tough meat!. I f the dog shies away at all, you are probably going at the massage with too much

391

force. Maybe you have found a spot that hurts and needs looking over by a veterinarian.

Head, Ears, Feet: Oh, Wow!

The head, ears and feet are very important  and relaxing massage parts to the dog , so while you are learning, you can focus on doing a thorough massage of those parts as you learn to explore the rest of the dog's body. You're not trying to move anything. Gently stroke and perhaps add a little kneading action as you progress. Do not massage dogs who have had recent surgery, or have areas warm to the touch unless your veterinarian has given you the go ahead.

Structure and Plan
Equal Excellent Massage

As I followed the instructions in the video it struck me that massage was not so different from petting, but had more structure and a plan. Mr. Rudinger teaches you to begin massaging for 15 minutes or less. Let the dog get accustomed to this new activity. I found the first few times I did this with three willing spaniels, all trying to get near me at the same time, that five minutes each was a good start.

YOUR DOG'S BODY

Benefits of massage are many, including bringing increased blood supply to arthritic or sore areas, increasing flexibility and range of motion, getting a good overview of any possible lumps and bumps, and generally calming the dog. Your dog will be much calmer for the veterinarian who must examine her if you have your own hands all over her all the time. You will enhance the dog's feelings of health and well being as you happen to massage all her acupressure points. You will also have a great excuse to spend more time with your hands on the dogs who love you.

A massage may be a reward you and your dog both enjoy.

I'm so glad I found the tapes in my bookcase. I think I'll go back and see what else I have hidden!

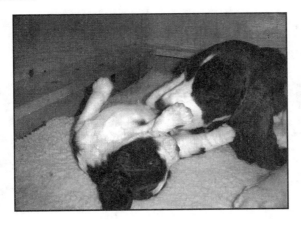

From Here
To Maternity

*"She was such a beautiful
creature, and so full of tricks."*
Queen Victoria

Hallelujah!! The breeding 'took'! Your cherished companion will soon be a mother. The due date is circled on the calendar. You have nine weeks to relax before the duties of puppy-raising fill your days, nights and dreams.

Whoa there, breeder! Dash those delusions of relaxing until all whelping preparations are checked off your pre-maternity to-do list.

Reading Is Fundamental

The one time you are encouraged to stretch out on the sofa and relax is while you read these fundamental breeder's bibles: "The Complete Handbook of Canine Midwifery" (by Chris Walkowicz and Bonnie Wilcox); "Joy of Breeding Your Own Show Dog" (by Ann Seranne); "Genetics: Introduction for Dog Breeders" (by Jackie Isabelle); "Breeding a Litter" (by Beth J. Finder Harris); and "The ABC's of Breeding CD," available from ESSFTA.org. On-line resources include: *www.animaldefenceleague.org*; *www.amcny.org*; and *www.talktothevet.com.*

Experienced Breeder's Advise

Chris Walkowicz, author, AKC conformation judge and distinguished breeder, begins her volume on 'canine midwifery' with the wise counsel, "The decision concerning living creatures should never be taken lightly. All factors must be carefully considered." Once a breeder breeds a dog, that breeder must spend countless hours preparing to nurture a healthy mother dog who will produce strong, cared-for, wanted puppies."

Breeding: A Huge and Heartfelt Responsibility

The reading and preparation required for responsibly and humanely adding puppy lives to the world is a grave undertaking. No breeder wants the pups that are defenselessly brought into the world to end up taxing the resources of rescue leagues and humane shelters. No wonder breeders often report sleepless nights, as they

395

do all they can to safeguard the tiny lives they have brought into the world.

Experienced breeders will tell you that the worry and commitment to every tiny life they have caused to be born is with them for all the days of every pup's life. The true sign of a great breeder is that the breeder tells every puppy owner that the puppy always has a home with the original breeder. The best puppies come from breeders who always want their puppies back if a pup needs a home.

Stock Your Supply Closet

A whelping box is a must-have. Lightweight, corrugated plastic boxes are easy to assemble, clean and move. A child-size plastic swimming pool is another option. Ask a breeder who has built a whelping box for suggestions. An Internet search for 'whelping box' will provide many choices.

Other maternity-room supplies include:
- another person to help, heat source in the whelping box to keep puppies warm;
- supply of old towels;
- scissors (to cut the umbilical cord);
- dental floss (to tie the cord);
- blankets/sheets for bedding;
- cell phone/speaker phone;
- rubbing alcohol;
- cotton balls/pads;
- thermometer;
- clock;
- a scale for twice-daily weighing of the pups; and
- a puppy-feeding pan.

Visit *www.whelpwise.com* for supply
suggestions.

Prenatal Maternity Care
Walk her daily to improve muscle tone. Increase
her food intake during the last three weeks;
consider feeding her puppy food during this
time. Bathe and trim her tummy in preparation
for nursing hygiene.

Get Veterinary Advice
Once your dog is in labor, call your veterinarian
for help if you see any of these signs, listed by
Dr. Carol Getty:
- "Strong contractions without production
  of a puppy within 15 minutes;
- Female dog seems weak, wobbly or ill.
- Contractions become weak or stop for
  more than an hour when you know or
  suspect more puppies are there."

397

Be Ready To Hand-feed Pups
In the event that the mother dog is unable or unwilling to feed her pups, be ready to feed them by hand. Accepted schedule for hand-feeding is every two hours the first three weeks. Check this schedule with your veterinarian and get advice regarding the best bottle formula and feeding supplies. Learn to stimulate pups to urinate and defecate in the event the mother dog does not perform these very necessary duties.

The Maternity Ward
A daybed, or at least a sleeping mattress in the room with the whelping box, is the sleeping area of choice for most breeders the first weeks after the pups are born. A television or radio will keep you entertained during your puppy vigil and will also provide sound stimulation for the pups.

Your Puppies' Futures
Contact prospective puppy owners. Interview puppy buyers. Satisfy yourself that they are the very best homes for your pups.

Make A Postnatal Plan and Budget
The pups need the care, socialization and training that only the mother dog can give them during the first eight weeks of life.

Responsible, caring breeders have lots to do looking after their pups from the time they are born until they go to their forever homes. The pups will need high-quality puppy food. If they are large pups, the amount of puppy food required may require special budgeting. The

 398

pups will require initial veterinary examinations and vaccinations. Some breeds will undergo removal of dew claws and other surgeries.

In order to register the puppies with the American Kennel Club or other registration organization, a breeder must be aware of registration procedures and have necessary registration papers on hand to give to the puppies' new owners.

Once your prenatal and maternity-ward prep tasks are complete, Dr. Getty recommends, "Plan something very important for the day you want the litter to be born in order to assure the pups will be born on that day." In other words, only the pups and their drive to wriggle into the world will dictate your whelping schedule.

Many thanks to veterinarian and springer breeder Carol Getty, and to breeders Amber Carpenter, Carol Callahan, Charlotte Mills, Mary Susah Billingsley, Nancy Johnson and Yvonne Stickleman for sharing puppy-preparation wisdom.

To Breed Or
Not To Breed

*"Motherhood: All love
begins and ends there."*
Robert Browning

A long time ago I bred a litter of puppies. Muffin was a Scottish Terrier with a personality as endearing has her black bearded, fuzzy face. I thought there could never be another dog as smart lovable, nor who loved me as steadfastly.

Only Her Puppy Will Do: A Myth
Let's let Muffin have a litter of puppies. Only a Muffin puppy could be as fine as Muffin. If Muffin could not live forever, at least her pup would carry on the Muffin-perfect genes.

Who Knows This Stud?
A young, illustriously bred Scottie boy was found. He came away on a honeymoon with Muffin.

 400

MacDuff, a well made Scottie boy, demonstrated his amorous intentions to Muffin.

Unwilling Bitch
Muffin told him that she would gladly bite his face off if he investigated any of her parts again. Off we went to the veterinarian. Our veterinarian artificially inseminated the reluctant mother-to-be.

Endless, Horrible Delivery
Weeks later, on a Christmas eve, Muffin presented the signs of going into labor. Many hours later, Muffin produced one dead puppy. Then another dead puppy. Then two more dead puppies.

Holding a dead puppy in your hand grips your heart with a chill that you do not forget. So much hope become despair.

Heartbreak and Inexperience
Not only did we not produce a litter of perfect Scottish terriers; Muffin almost died before the "let's let her have one litter" ordeal ended. Labor is a gentle term for the near death experience I inflicted on my dog.

My ignorant attempt to duplicate my dog because I loved her so much almost cost her life. As the vet worked to save her life, I promised to leave breeding dogs to professionals for the rest of my life.

Homework, Experience and Ability: Leaving Dog Breeding To Professionals

Do I think that no one should breed their dog? No. Breeding dogs is an art and an honorable commitment to dogs by dog lovers.

There are too many pleading faces looking out from cages in shelters all over the world. These bewildered faces have no idea why they spend their days bored, pacing a concrete run, perking their ears to every noise that breaks the monotony of their lives in a shelter. These abandoned, unwanted dogs had no owner waiting for the birth of a mixed breed puppy.

Commitment and Responsibility To Every Pup Bred

Before breeding one more litter of defenseless lives that will enter the world needing love, training, physical care and emotional development, a would-be breeder must commit to a great responsibility.

Every puppy that is produced on purpose will probably keep one shelter or rescue pup that was a mistake, or was discarded, or was just not wanted from finding a home.

Lessons Learned

Having bred one litter and having had no one stand in the way of my free will to do that, I would offer these lessons that Muffin and I learned.

We decided to leave the great responsibility of bringing defenseless puppy lives into the world to experienced breeders.

Know Your Dog
Visit your veterinarian for a pre-breeding physical exam. Tell your vet you want to breed your dog. Many breeds are plagued by hip problems, knee problems, eye deformities, seizures, immune deficiencies, blindness, or birthing difficulties. Recruit your veterinarian for advice and health guidance every step of the way to making healthy puppies.

Know Your Budget Limitations
Spend the money for diagnostic tests that may predict the health of your puppies. Put away a thousand dollars now, just in case your dog requires hours of emergency care to save her or the puppies. Set aside funds for the vaccines and food the pups will need from birth until they go to their new homes. Be aware that breeding healthy dogs is expensive. Few breeders ever clear a nickel from puppy sales. The dream that a litter of puppies will be a money maker is a myth.

Know Your Breed
Contact or become a member of a local dog club for your breed. Club members of your breed club will have experience breeding, birthing and raising litters of puppies. The American Kennel Club at *www.akc.org* will have a list of local and national breed clubs.

Commit Yourself To The Welfare Of The Puppies
A reputable breeder will tell every puppy owner that any puppy that leaves her kennel always has a home to come back to should the puppy ever

403

need a home. A true breeder and defender of the gene pool of the breed they love, will consider every life they create to be their responsibility. Dog breeding should be an 'until death we do part' commitment.

Who Will Have Your Puppies?

If your breed normally has six to eight puppies, you must be prepared to add six to eight puppies to your own home if no responsible homes are found for them. If you have eight dog loving friends whom you know will care for the puppies for all their lives, that is great.

Just as puppies from a shelter are not usually free, it is not a good idea to advertise your "free" puppies to strangers. A dog is a substantial financial responsibility. Puppies require a series of vaccines, the expense of spaying or neutering, premium food, crates, leashes, bowls and brushes. If the greatest appeal to own your puppy is that he is free, that is no insurance that the pup will be responsibly cared for.

Interview Prospective Puppy Owners Carefully

Do they have a fenced yard? Do they own a dog crate? Have they owned a dog before? What breeds and how old are their other dogs? Have the dogs they owned before lived to healthy, old ages and not been given away? What is their work schedule?

If you ask all these questions and a puppy seeker is offended or lacking answers, clutch your little puppy to your heart and hide him. You asked his little life to come into the world. You are the only insurance he has to protect him from being one more dog left by the side of the road or abandoned in a card board box on the door mat of a shelter that is already bursting with dogs with little hope, and no prospects for a magical puppyhood.

Think Hard Before You Breed Your Dog

Hold her on your lap and ask yourself if you really want her to be a mother. Your dog's breeder, if she is a professional breeder with years of experience protecting and hoping to make her breed better, will have more litters with another perfect puppy waiting to be yours in years to come.

405

Blind Optimism:
Loss Of Sight Doesn't Keep A Good Dog Down

"Blessed is the person who has earned the love of an old dog."
Sidney Jeanne Seward

American cocker spaniels are among breeds that may suffer from progressive retinal atrophy.

Progressive Retinal Atrophy (PRA) is an eye disease that can occur at almost any age, and progresses at various rates of speed. Dogs who suffer from PRA often become blind.

Many Dog Breeds Are Affected
Schnauzers, Corgis, Collies, Great Danes, Gordon and Irish Setters, Elkhounds, Akitas, Australian Cattle Dogs, Australian Shepherds, American and English Cocker Spaniels, Beagles, Dachshunds, English Springer Spaniels, German Shepherds, Golden Retrievers, Labrador Retrievers, Poodles

(miniature and toy), Rottweilers, Shetland Sheep Dogs and several terrier breeds all have high incidence rates of PRA.

Careful, dedicated dog breeders are vigilant in identifying dogs who may pass on this blinding disorder, and to remove affected dogs from their breeding programs.

Blindness Not A Death Sentence

The diagnosis of PRA is in no way a death sentence for the affected dog who will learn to cope with losing his or her sight.

Ask anyone who has shared home and heart with a blind dog and you will find endless tales of coping and bravery, of mastering new skills and finding joy in all the senses. A dog may lose his sight, but his sense of touch, smell, taste and hearing remain to guide him to enjoy his life and love his people as well as he ever did before blindness darkened his sight.

Our Dogs Teach Us That Life Goes On

The best we can do for our dogs is to educate ourselves to make their lives full and safe no matter what befalls them.

Morgan: A Rescued Treasure

Kim Bolster rescued Morgan when he was 3 years old. She was Morgan's third owner. Before Morgan came to Bolster, he had spent his young life in a crate 20 hours a day, with no one to play with him or appreciate what a beautiful, playful dog he was.

407

DEVOTED TO DOGS

At age 5, and by then living with Bolster as his family, Morgan was diagnosed with PRA  that was signaled to his family vet by a glassy cataract in one eye. Morgan demonstrated no behavior traits of visual difficulty, but was referred to Animal Eye Care's Dr. Michael Blair in Richmond. Blair monitored Morgan's development of PRA, which worsened over several months, first in one eye and then another.

Research Blindness In Dogs
Since Morgan's PRA developed slowly, Bolster had time to research the disorder and to assemble an arsenal of books, including "Living With Blind Dogs," by Carolyn Levine and the video "New Skills for Blind Dogs: A Companion Film to Living With Blind Dogs." Bolster joined the Internet Yahoo group for blind-dog owners, and spent hours reading advice and experience at Web sites such as *www.acvo.com* (American College of Veterinary Ophthalmologists), *www.blinddogs.com* and *www.eyevet.ca* (Veterinary Ophthalmology Information Centre).

Train Early: Be Prepared
Bolster undertook a proactive training program to teach Morgan words that would help him

navigate and understand his daily world better when he eventually became sightless. Bolster taught Morgan words for specific actions.

She explains, "Every time we went down stairs, I would say, 'step,' 'step,' so Morgan would associate stairs with the command 'step.' On leash, during daily walks, Morgan learned 'curb,' and to understand 'wait' and 'watch.'

"'Watch' was my caution word for him to stop and wait for more instruction."

Bolster continues, "Morgan had a diminished-sight period for close to a year and a half. He did not go totally blind until age 7. His gradual loss of sight gave me some time to prepare him to cope with his blindness."

Consider Emotional Needs

Morgan lived to be 10 years old. Bolster remembers, "He mourned Annabelle, his companion and family pack mate, who had died five months before Morgan, too, passed away. Annabelle had been his partner in old age and had helped guide him. He loved to go on walks to the end, head held high, with a graceful gait, always taking in all the smells."

Bolster uses the joy of Morgan's life and her education for coping with a blind dog to help others who are devastated when their dogs are diagnosed with impending blindness. She is a resource person with Mid-Atlantic English Springer Rescue (*www.maessr.org*).

Bartholomew: Living The Good Life To The End

Bart was diagnosed at 7 years old with PRA. His owner had not noticed any signs or symptoms that he had a vision problem. Bart went to an ophthalmologist to be tested for PRA to make sure he was clear of the disease before being used as a stud dog. His owner felt a strong commitment that she did not want to breed him if he was affected by PRA, thus carrying the PRA gene and adding more PRA-affected dogs to the gene pool. Bart had been tested at age 5 for PRA and had been found to be clear of any indications of the condition.

Get A Diagnosis From An Opthamologist

After Bart's diagnosis, his mom says, "It was very hard to tell that the dog was visually impaired for a few years. His examination by the ophthalmologist showed that he didn't have very good vision at the time of diagnosis, but you sure couldn't tell. He began having vision problems at 10 and was completely blind at 11 years old."

To keep Bart safe in his backyard, his owner "put a short exercise-pen around the hot tub" to

protect him from potential danger. Even dogs who were good swimmers before becoming blind can drown in familiar pools and ponds if they lose their sense of direction and cannot find a way out of the water.

Owners: Upbeat, Not Tragic, Please!

Bart's mom emphasizes that adapting to gradual blindness can often be more difficult to owners than it is to the dog. She admits, "Blindness was unfortunate, but not painful. Dogs learn to trust you. You can still take them on walks. Bart continued to enjoy our company and was right at the refrigerator door every time he heard it open up!"

Bart, like many blind dogs, was easily startled by younger, rambunctious pack mates who would bump him or block his well-learned paths in the house and yard. Bart's mom learned to carefully supervise other dogs' interaction with him.

Beatrice: Guided By A Pack-Mate Companion

Beatrice was just over 6 years when she began to have trouble seeing in twilight. Today, Beatrice is 10 years old and very nearly blind. She can discern movement against a strong light.

Don't Move The Furniture!

Beatrice's mom describes adaptations to living with severely limited eyesight, saying, "She navigates just fine around the house, so long as things aren't moved. She sometimes 'gets lost' in the backyard. She gets turned around and isn't sure which direction to take. I've discovered that

411

when that happens, she's more able to follow the sound of hands clapping than my voice."

Beware of Tripping Over The Blind Dog

Beatrice's owner advises, "Remember that not only can she not see, she can't tell if you're in her way. Last summer we were playing in the yard and Beatrice walked right in front of me as I was running. I fell and broke a finger. I'm fine, but I'm a lot more wary."

Accepting that a beloved dog has to cope with new limitations can be sad and difficult for the dog parent, explains Beatrice's owner. "I was devastated when I discovered that she had PRA because she loves agility and would have loved rally obedience. However, losing her sight really hasn't discommoded Beatrice much at all. But it has changed her life and mine."

Best Help: A Canine Seeing-Eye Companion

"One thing that may make things easier for Beatrice is that I have another dog. They get along well and Beatrice follows the noise of his collar tags when they're outside."

Finally, Beatrice's mom stresses that human pack members must work to be more responsive to communication efforts by the blind dog, saying, "She barks more now when strangers come to the house. I think it is difficult for the blind dog when they're not sure anyone is responding to their bark, or the dog feels no one knows they are there."

Rescue Organizations Protect Blind Dogs

Judy Manley works with a national breed club's rescue organization and laments the fact that frequently dogs who are diagnosed with impending blindness are abandoned or given away to rescue organizations. Manley notes, "First many of the owners of visually impaired dogs are angry and cry because their dog is going blind. Very often they get rid of the dog because they cannot deal with owning a blind dog."

Big Hearts Equal Big Payoffs In Love

Manley has great admiration for rescue families who adopt and love blind dogs who have been abandoned by one or several homes. She praises the kind people who rescue blind dogs, saying, "Our rescue organization has had several adopters that will only adopt blind dogs. They have a special place in their hearts for them and we thank God for these caring people."

Better lives for blind dogs

Any dog may become blind as his or her life progresses.

Being ready to help your dog in times of emotional or physical stress is a very good reason to obedience-train your companion dog now. Mastery of life-saving safety and behavior management commands makes your dog's life easier as he ages, regardless of health impairments that may befall him.

Obedience Training Always Helps

A dog who promptly performs "sit," "down," "off," "stand," "come," "easy" and "quiet" will have a vocabulary and repertoire of useful behaviors to keep him safe. Teaching words that are vital to wellbeing include: "step," "water," "careful," "place" and "whoa!"

Check Your Dog's Eyes Regularly

Ask your family veterinarian to refer you to a canine ophthalmologist for a full eye exam. Have his eyes checked on a regular basis. Remember that visual changes can happen throughout his life. Know whether your dog suffers from any signs of developing blindness or medical/visual difficulties.

Neuter Affected Breeding Stock

If your dog is diagnosed with any genetic eye abnormality, consider the welfare of future generations of dogs by neutering your dog. Notify your breeder of any congenital eye disorder. Help your breeder to strengthen the genetic future of all dogs by neutering affected

breeding stock. Send copies of your diagnosis to your dog's breeders, both sire and dam.

Adapt With Kindness and Imagination

Use your imagination to think of ways to respond to and explore his world in ways that do not require his eyesight. Perhaps a textured carpet on certain surfaces would signal to the dog where he is walking. Baby gates at stairs or leading to rooms where he should not go are a must. Maybe he needs you to walk with a hard step to let him feel you coming. Tiny bells on your shoes or on collars of other dogs or cats in the home could alert him to the whereabouts of his family. A water bowl that is made from a fountain or other running water source could be just the ticket to let him hear exactly where his water bowl is located.

Be Strong For Your Dog: He Feels What You Feel

Your dog reacts strongly to your emotions and the way you cope with stress. One gift of caring you can give your dog is to keep worry, fear and sadness regarding his health challenges to yourself. When your dog is in trouble, he needs a human caretaker with a stiff upper lip, a happy voice and the acting skills necessary to assure his doggy senses that all is safe in his world.

415

10

Safe Dog: Protecting The Dog You Love From Dangers At Home And Away

"A danger foreseen is half avoided."
American Indian Proverb

Safety In The Big Back Yard:

A Watchful Eye On Outdoor Fun

"Dogs need to sniff the ground; it's how they keep abreast of current events. The ground is a giant dog newspaper, containing all kinds of late-breaking dog news items., which, if they are especially urgent, are often continued into the next yard."
Dave Barry

What transforms a boring day into a perfect dog day? Leaping after butterflies and chasing toys that bounce. Canine paws and noses delight paddling in the pool or river, and sniffing mysterious aromas on leaves and rocks. Some dogs find joyous abandon tasting anything they can wedge into their mouths.

419

DEVOTED TO DOGS

Canine companions, are connoisseurs of fun, but may lack understanding of danger.

Dogs scampering in the river may cut their paws on rocks and debris. Dogs leaping into a backyard swimming pool may find themselves in paddling distress in the splash of a whisker.

Swimming Safely Under Mom's Eagle Eye

Molly Judge, dog mom to several avid canine swimmers advises, "Swimming pool owners must use the same level of concern for dogs as for small children. Like children, dogs can be unpredictable. Elvis, our Miniature Dachshund, launches himself into the pool without warning. Although he can swim, he cannot find the stairs in the pool, so he could tire out in his search and slip under to an untimely passing if not carefully watched. A dog-sized life jacket gives Elvis plenty of floatation support, but is not a substitute for close observation."

Judge added this precaution for year round pool safety: "The only time I am confident that my dogs are safe around the pool is when it is closed for the Winter. We spent the extra money to install a fitted pool cover that can hold an elephant's weight."

Strolling For Fun: Hot Paws, Beware

When temperatures soar, hot pavements and scorching sidewalks transform a dog's walk into a march of torture. Before you start a hot day dog stroll, put your own hands on the asphalt or sidewalk. Even though dog's paws may be toughened up to rough surfaces and heat, to feel

the temperature for yourself is a hands-on reminder that even though most dogs dance with delight when the leash appears, his paws may suffer.

Pam Jewett-Bullock says, "Walking dogs on hot pavement and concrete is a bad thing. "Lovely Miss Lucy the Labrador" is loathe, on hot Summer days, to walk the same long distances she willingly covers during cooler seasons. In this regard, she seems to have innate good sense. We often watch, in horror, as folks drag their dogs along for walks and runs during the hottest part of summer days, or, when the humans stop along the way, for a 'chat' with a friend or neighbor, while poor doggie stands there on the hot blacktop; tongue hanging out and feet shifting uncomfortably."

Carry Water For Your Dog

Make sure your dog is in good physical condition. Begin his walking program with short jaunts. If at any time he pants, wheezes or stops, he may be telling you he has had enough. Stop and rest.

Snuffling in the Grass:
Is There Anything Better?

I had a friend, Miss Cassie, a Golden Retriever. She would follow her mother to the ends of the Earth. She would scamper after butterflies, moths, or bees in her effort to play with every living creature that flew past her nose.

Cassie's mom, Sue Lough, remembers, "Cassie, was very allergic to bees. Cassie tried, and succeeded on more than one occasion, to catch a bee in mid flight. These mid-air catches always ended in an emergency veterinary visit. I kept prednisone on hand and my vet's phone number memorized for these emergencies. Had I not noticed the sudden swelling the first time Cassie was stung by a bee, I wouldn't ever have known she was allergic... had she survived the 'sting'."

Not all dogs are dangerously allergic to bee stings. Many dogs react to stings with a stings with swelling and signs of discomfort. Your dog's veterinarian is the best judge of how to treat all stings, bites and mishaps.

Lough learned during years of devoted supervision of her active Golden Retriever that, "Pet owners need to check their animals every time they come in from an outside trip. You never know when something might have happened while playing in the yard. It is part of a dog mother's job to be vigilant to secure the safety and well being of their 'charge'."

SAFE DOG

If It Fits In The Mouth, It Must Be a Toy

Most puppies chew while teething. Some dogs chew and look for things to munch and retrieve as long as they live.

Janelle Schopfel, is a cautious mother of both a tiny human and a small pack of canines. Schopfel has educated herself about plants that could be dangerous if tasted by her active, inquisitive little ones.

Explaining, "I am trying to create an English garden here in hot/humid Virginia, and I have been surprised to learn just how many plants and flowers are toxic to dogs and children. I have decided to live without some of my favorite plants, such as foxglove, rather than risk poisoning our Basset hounds or toddler, Ava. Ava and the dogs may eat anything."

Schopfel shared her research sources, saying, "'The American Medical Association Handbook of Poisonous and Injurious Plants', by Dr. Kenneth Lampe and Mary McCann, gives a short list of poisonous plants.

DEVOTED TO DOGS

"The list includes:
- autumn crocus;
- bleeding hearts;
- boxwood, daffodils;
- English ivy;
- flowering tobacco;
- hydrangeas;
- mountain laurel;
- rhododendrons;
- azaleas; and
- Virginia creeper."

Schopfel recommends, "Gardeners should talk to their vets about toxic plants. Research plants before you plant them. Be especially careful with puppies. If your heart is set on a particular plant, place it outside a fence in an area that's inaccessible to your dog."

The American Society For Prevention of Cruelty to Animals (ASPCA) offers an informative and life saving telephone hotline (888-426-4435) and poison education website. Two thought provoking articles on their website (*www. apcc.aspca.org*) are "The Wrath of Grapes" by Charlotte Means, DVM and "ASPCA Poison Center Warns Pet Owners: Summer Is Deadliest Time Of Year For Companion Animals".

Veterinarians, Dr. Liz Ubehlor and Dr. Pam Fandrich, described many frequent dangers to pets enjoying themselves outdoors.

Ubehlor explained, "Excluding accidents involving cars and dog fights, I often see fishhook emergencies. Also, dogs that eat trash, garbage, carcasses, etc. can get endotoxin poisoning and that is very dangerous. Blue-green algae has a toxin that can cause neurological problems and even death. Concentrated amounts of insecticides and fertilizers are challenging cases when ingested by the farm dog. Thankfully, dilution is the solution to pollution. If insecticides and poisons are diluted for application, the dangers are lessened."

Dr. Fandrich owns Italian Greyhounds and Whippets who compete in lure coursing, agility, and obedience trials. She watches closely for outdoor dangers.

Fandrich warned, "Certain species of mushroom are a danger. I have seen two Beagles who were running in the woods with their owner who saw one of the dogs eat a mushroom. About two days later, both dogs were violently ill, and had liver damage."

DEVOTED TO DOGS

To keep dogs healthy, a dog owner must pick up poop or risk health and sanitation dangers. Dr. Fandrich, suggests owners also need to pick up all mushrooms in the yard as soon as they see them.

Fandrich explained, "There are several species of mushrooms that can be toxic, along with many ornamental plants, so people should be aware of what is growing in their yards and what they plant for decoration. I pick up mushrooms in the back yard when I pick up the poop piles."

Fandrich shares very wise dog management advice, recommending, "If owners are aware of their dog's habits, they can still have a great time running and playing in the woods. If you know your dog is a scrounge hound, perhaps you should keep him on a long line so you know what he is putting in his mouth."

Do you have a dog health and safety question? Always, the best source of guidance and peace of mind is to ask your veterinarian. When in doubt ask the veterinarian.

Take your dog outside and have fun.

Danger Detectives:
You Can Safeguard Your Pet

"It's a dangerous business going out your front door."
J. R. R. Tolkien

Every dog needs a fence. Many breeders will not sell a pup into a home without the safety of a fence. In one unsupervised second with one door left ajar, one canine life can be snuffed out.

Keep fence gates closed, even if you have to resort to using spring–hinge auto–closers, bungee cords on each side, and a sign that says, "Please close the gate."

When you hire a service person to work at your house (cleaners, painters, plumbers, cable installers, etc.) give them the house rule, "No matter what you do while you work at my house, close the doors and close the fence gate." If they do not close doors and gates, don't use their services. Check with your dog-savvy friends for a dog-wise service provider referral. Anyone who visits your home and who does not close doors and gates is a safety hazard to your dogs and cats.

Hanging Cords Kill Dogs

Examine every blind cord, shade pull and extension cord for hanging, choking and electrocution dangers. Drape all window treatment cords over the top of the blind or shade. Cover or elevate electrical cords.

Read All Labels

Buy products that are pet-safe. Many pet-safe products have the added benefit of being more environmentally friendly.

Clean all pet house-breaking accidents with a cleaning product designed to erase all traces of urine or feces. Carpet cleaners must say they neutralize pet stains. Perfumed carpet cleaners may disguise odors to your nose, but may leave urine smell-markers that say, "Go here again!" to the dog. My favorite brands are Nature's Miracle ™ and Spot Shot Instant Carpet Stain Remover. Cleaning all accidents properly will assist your dog to master house-breaking skills, and will preserve your carpets and floors until you have taught the dog exactly where to "go."

Trash Can Be Poison

An open trash can offers a smorgasbord of  smells, found chew toys and edible dangers. A covered trash can is a safe trash can. Even small, decorative trash cans need a dog-proof cover. Place a serving tray over small trash cans' openings and voilà, a makeshift dog-proof lid. Hard fiberboard place mats are perfect for covering small trash cans. Outthink the trash hunter; put a lid on him.

Store Food Securely and Safely

Store pet food in a container that does not offer your dog a self-serve option. High temperatures may cause deterioration of some nutrients. Protect nutritional goodness of your food by storing at room temperature. Avoid letting your dog's food bake in a broiling car or sweltering garage. Many manufacturers sell airtight containers that will be easy for you to open, while protecting your dog from his own attempts to serve himself.

De-Clutter and Discard All Danger Items

Discard anything that could harm your dog. Throw away items that could be hazardous if your dog eats or chews them. I love to buy shoes. My Bearded Collie, Vivien, is convinced that the silica gel packets that often come in shoe boxes (and other mail order parcels) are candy. Packing materials of all sorts may be dangerous to the unsuspecting or unsupervised dog who chews or eats them.

Are Your Hobby Items Dangerous?

Gabriel, who relates to the world with his miraculous Springer Spaniel nose, recently joined me in the craft of beading. He found a large, carved brown bead made from some African animal's horn. I am sure the bead's smell called out the call of the wild to hunting dog Gabriel. While I was making a beaded necklace, I heard him tossing the bead into the air, catching it and crunching. I jumped up and traded him his prize bead for a ham-scented Nylabone™.

Get Up And Investigate

Investigate all crunching the moment you hear it. A few seconds of chomping could produce several hours of emergency room worry. Adopt the "if it sounds worrisome, it probably is" philosophy of dog noise and mysterious activity intervention. Beads, needlework supplies, paints, polymer clays and many craft supplies are very tantalizing and dangerous to a curious dog.

Beware Of Kitty Litter Smorgasbord

Have you ever met a dog that could pass by an open kitty litter box with kitty litter aromas whispering his name? I have not. My two Maine Coon cats, Lucy and Sam, can barely leap from the toilet box without a big springer's hungry head peering into the box. Snack–hungry humans may haunt the icebox, but canines like nothing better than a treat from the cat box.

Buy a covered litter box. Find a private, elevated location for the litter box. Beware the dangers  of dogs eating litter. If you use a hard clumping kitty litter, be very sure the dog cannot help himself to a bite of cat–box fare. If you are offered a doggy kiss from canine lips encrusted with a concrete–like whiffy substance, it is time to take immediate action. If your dog demonstrates a penchant for a litter box safari, ask your vet for post–litter eating advice before you really need medical help.

Your Fence: Find Gaps, Holes and Dangers

At least once a month, walk your fence perimeter. Check for gaps or tears in or under your fence. Have any tree limbs fallen on the fence? Some dogs love a challenge: A tiny hole may be an invitation to leave home and visit the neighborhood. Vouchsafe the dog you love from his own curious nose and attempts to roam. Make sure his fence is a perfect barrier of protection. Even if you have the safest fence, don't leave him outside unsupervised for long periods of time.

Do You Have Junk-Filled Yard?

Become intimately acquainted with every object in your yard. If the dog can reach it, smell it, chew it, run into it or run around it, he probably will do just that. Dogs are busy. Dogs investigate objects that could harm them. Discarded wood, nails, wire, anything that protrudes or dangles can bring injury to your dog.

Upend wheel barrows, unused flower pots, any container that makes a gestation pool for mosquito larvae and stagnant water.

See Your Veterinarian Regularly

Make sure your dog has at least one annual visit to his veterinarian for a complete physical. Many veterinarians like to see each patient at least every six months for a general wellness visit. Don't let your dog be a patient who only sees his doctor when he is sick and feeling bad. Trips to visit the vet for a wellness once-over safeguard your treasured friend's health. Giving your dog's doctor a chance to see your pet in peak condition helps your veterinarian to keep him that way.

Your Dog Depends On Your Watchful Eye

Your faithful companion depends on you to protect him from all the creatures who would like to feast on him. Don't let him be dinner to parasites. See your veterinarian often to refill prescriptions for flea, tick, heartworm and other parasite prevention. Drop a fecal specimen by your veterinarian's office to make sure the inside of your fuzzy pal is as safe and cared for inside as you have made him safe on the outside.

SAFE DOG

If you wake in the night and worry over dog activity noises, dog bodily function sounds, anything that crackles in his jaws, or lurks dangerously in a trash can, better to wake the household and investigate your fears than have a dog you love harmed by danger lurking in his home. Patrol your yard. Know where your dog is at all times. Know what he has eaten, drunk and sniffed. Make a dog safety to-do list today.

You have the good judgment and danger-recognition abilities in the relationship with your dog. Your sweet, curious dog is easily led into trouble by his nose and doggy drives. He has placed his trusting heart, and body's well-being, in your hands. Guard him well from every danger.

Riding In Cars
With Dogs

"If the traveler can find a virtuous
and wise companion, let him
go with him joyfully and
overcome the dangers of the way."
Buddha

"**G**RITS, ma'am?" inquired a tall, bouncing, big- headed cow.

Vivien cocked her topknot- and bow-adorned head to the side, wagged her body from tip of black nose to wisp of white tail end, and answered, "Woof!" Southern dog-speak for, "Yes, sir, please!"

Had Vivien and I fallen down the rabbit hole where cows ladle out grits like ambrosia? Not exactly. Vivien and I had been driving our way across Virginia and North Carolina, and had just crossed the South Carolina line. We were

 434

headed to an obedience event hosted by the Palmetto Obedience Training Club, bound for Columbia, SC.

For 10 hours, we had availed ourselves of every rest area. Vivien took walks and sashayed in pine needles while inhaling the smells and news left behind by traveling dogs who came before her.

Leg stretching prolongs the road trip a wee bit, but riders, both dog and human, arrive feeling less stiff and weary. The South Carolina rest stop was the first of 10 stops to offer anything other than bathrooms and vending machines.

Genteel Southern Cow Keeps An Eye Out

The kindly cow, who was serving up bowls of grits and tiny plates of delectable chicken nuggets, told me to park right by the front door and go in for a spell. Under that bovine costume, beat the heart of a dog daddy. He understood that I could not leave Vivien unattended in the van, even for the lure of grits and free fried food. The day was rainy, the temperature cool, and since Vivien was safe and comfortable in her dog crate, I opened all the windows and left the trusty cow to keep an eye cast toward Vivien.

Five minutes later, I returned to Vivien with useful and edible loot. Travel mugs, mouse pads, tollhouse cookies, apples and banana walnut muffins were nice rest-stop mementos, but the three bags of premium-quality dog

435

cookies were the best part of South Carolina hospitality.

First Pack The Packing List

Before Vivien and I set out on our mother-daughter road trip, lists were made. Dog travel supplies were hauled out of closets, garage and attic. Since we were traveling during hot weather, careful attention was paid to how hot the van might get and what I must do to keep Vivien safe and cool.

Dr. Jordan Kocen, veterinary specialist of holistic medicine and acupuncture at Southpaws Veterinary Referral Center (*www.southpaws.com*) in Fairfax, VA., recently shared recommendations for keeping traveling dogs healthy and comfortable. My dog Quinnton visits Dr. Kocen every four weeks for acupuncture. While Quinnton relaxes on his comfy exam room rug, I asked Dr. Kocen what were his main concerns and tips for traveling dogs.

Heat Is A Dog's Travel Enemy

Dr. Kocen stressed, "Owners need to be very conscious of summer's high temperatures. Pet owners must carefully monitor and protect traveling dogs and cats from heat and from direct sunlight."

He warned that, "Even in an air-conditioned car, while human passengers riding in the front of the car might be cool, the pets riding in the back of a car, van or station wagon could become overheated from direct sunlight shining into the vehicle."

Shade, Lots Of Shade

Sun shades, to reflect heat from the vehicle, are a must for the traveling dog. Many types of shades are available from pet, auto and variety stores. Shiny, reflective blankets, often called 'space blankets', are easy to store and can be used in many locations in the vehicle to reflect direct sunlight away from the dog's crate or area. Collapsible reflective screens for the front and back windshields are easy to store in the vehicle and take moments to unfurl and protect the dog from direct sun.

As I loaded my van for our long drive to South Carolina, I packed all bags, suitcases and valuables in areas deep within the van. Since my van has four large dog crates, it was easy to secure all luggage inside the crates. An advantage of an extra crate, if you have room in your vehicle, is that when there are no dogs

437

in the crate, your possessions can be secured inside with a small lock. You can leave windows down if you must leave a dog in the car while you make a rest stop.

A Cool Dog Is The Most Valuable Item In Your Car

Don't have room for an extra crate? Cover luggage with an old sheet, lock the car and leave the windows down for dog ventilation. Your dog must never be left for any amount of time in a closed car. A closed car quickly heats up to temperatures that can harm your pet.

Small, battery-operated fans, available at auto, variety and online merchants, will stir the air and cool the dog who is resting in his crate. In my van I have four dog crates, and each one has its own battery-operated fan.

Reduce Travel Stress On Your Dog

Dr. Kocen expressed concern that many dogs find traveling stressful. He noted, "Some dogs become anxious when they see suitcases being packed, or the car being prepared for a trip." Rescue Remedy, a flower essence available at many health food stores and dog supply boutiques, can be added to your dog's water, administered directly to the dog, or sprayed (by diluting with water) in the room or crate where the dog rests, to alleviate the dog's anxiety and stressful reaction before and during travel.

"Using tranquilizers during pet travel, especially during hot weather," says Kocen, "can be dangerous." Tranquilizers can lower blood pressure, causing the dog or cat to be more susceptible to heat-related medical emergencies.

No Crate: At Least Use A Seat Belt

A traveling dog must be either safely resting in his crate, or, if no crate can fit into the vehicle, a dog seat belt must be used. There are several seat belt types. My dogs have been most comfortable in a seat belt that resembles a fleece-lined durable canvas breastplate, that is secured by a sturdy strap that attaches to the vehicle's safety belt.

Dogs who ride loose in the car are in danger and can be dangerous to the driver and other motorists. What happens to the dog when you have to slam on the brakes and the dog is hurled into the floor or a really cute dog on the side of the road causes your normally calm dog to suddenly land in your lap trying for a better view of the dog by the roadside? What do you imagine will happen to your dog if the passenger-side air bag blows up and smashes him in the face?

As a dog mom who longs to sit and converse with a dog at my side, I have taken the cure for my own selfish desires and make my dogs ride in a crate. If you have a van and want the dogs closer to you, take out the middle seats and put the crates behind you. Make your human passengers ride in the very back if being closer to your dog makes for happier rides.

Pack Your Dogs Health Documents

Scottee Meade, author of "The Boston Terrier: An Owner's Guide to a Happy, Healthy Pet," advised that dog travelers leave home armed with the dog's rabies tag and certificate, medical history and the dog's veterinarian's phone number. She wisely suggested that the dog's own veterinarian may be able to recommend a veterinarian in the destination city. Meade added that an Internet search to find the name, address and phone number of the nearest veterinary emergency hospital in the destination city could be found at *www.superpages.com*. Print out the exact driving directions from your travel destination hotel to the emergency hospital to save minutes and even your dog's life if an emergency occurs

Meade, a veteran dog traveler, includes a familiar blanket, toys, cleanup supplies, paper towels, baby wipes and spray cleaners in her travel kit. "Cleaning up pet accidents in the car or the hotel will be much more pleasant if you are forearmed with necessary supplies," Meade assured me.

"If you feed your dog fresh food, you must take a cooler; preferably the type that can plug into the vehicle's cigarette lighter and hotel power supply," Meade recommends. Pack drinking water from home to avoid canine tummy upsets.

Identification Tags On The Dogs A Must Have

"I always have two identification tags on my dogs while traveling," Meade explained. "One tag has my home address. The second tag has the destination address, just in case the dog becomes lost while we are away."

One final dog training tip from Meade: "Train your dog to get into and out of your vehicle from the right side of the vehicle. Right-side entrance is much safer than allowing the dog to jump in and out on the traffic side of the car. Consider the safety of right-side entry when you place your crate or seat belt in the vehicle."

In Case Of Emergency Instructions

Dog trainer and dog behavior seminar leader Diane Smart travels with a brilliant "In Case Of Emergency" form that she believes is a must-have item for traveling dogs. Smart's emergency form asks anyone who finds her car after an accident or emergency to please look after the welfare of her dogs. The form includes these points:

DEVOTED TO DOGS

"In the event that I am incapacitated and unable to make my wishes known regarding my dogs, please honor the following requests. The welfare of my dogs is my primary consideration. If my dogs are not injured, they are to be cared for by the nearest reputable boarding kennel, and be kept in the best possible manner until arrangements can be made to get them home.

"If my dogs are injured, they are to be cared for by the nearest reputable veterinarian. I prefer that my veterinarian be contacted regarding decisions on my dogs care and treatment. They have all my dogs' medical records available."

Smart lists each dog's name, breed, physical description, tattoo, microchip location and any medical conditions, along with her veterinarian's contact information. Smart's emergency form includes an emergency contact and a backup contact, and states: "These contact people will guarantee all expenses for the dogs."

Vacation days are here. Make your travel to-do list and save it to use for future dog travels. If you travel often with your dog, find a nook in your garage or storage room and keep all the travel gear in one location.

Travel with dogs may be more labor intensive, but according to Joe Mathias, Manager of Ritz Camera vacation photographs often feature the family dog "playing in the water and catching Frisbees on the beach."

Let's hit the road with Rover.

 442

Toys, Tinsel, Turkey:
Supervise Your Dog's Holiday Joy

"To call him a dog hardly seems to do him justice, though inasmuch as he had four legs, a tail and barked, I admit he was, to all outward appearances. But to those who knew him well, he was a perfect gentleman."
Hermione Gingold

Sleigh bells ring. Are you listening? Dog mother dashes up the stairs as bells jangle. The small canine gift-sniffer flees the room.

One smart cookie, this dog mother. She has hung large red and green bells, poised to ring and clank at the slightest dog-nose touch, on every bottom branch of her Christmas tree. One jingle announces canine tree investigation and package snuffling.

443

What is the first training commandment for a perfectly behaved dog? Canine behavior management by the human in charge comes before, during and after all dog training.

Blame Yourself For Mishaps
Your dog is never really at fault. He will follow where his miraculous, curious nose, his boundless fascination with the world around him, and his delight and need to play lead him. Our job, as dog moms and dog dads, is to prevent dog misbehavior or danger.

Master The Gentle Art Of Redirection
Teach your dog 'approved' ways to play. Show him what he can do and what he must not do. The old adage, "Don't blame the dog: Train the dog" will be more complete if you ask yourself, "Where was I while he was getting into trouble?"

Which Toys Are Safe Toys?
Think your dog ate a shiny decoration from the Christmas tree? Did Aunt Sadie let Muffin eat the turkey skin off her plate? Where did that box of tinsel for the tree go when you left it on the hearth for just a minute?

Ask A Veterinarian
Never hesitate to call your veterinarian and ask your question. Kind and well-trained staff will answer queries that cause you apprehension. Many veterinary hospitals have a licensed veterinary technician ready to listen to your

concerns and offer you the benefit of the technician's years of education and experience.

Investigate Dog Sounds In The Night

During the wee hours of our family's post-Thanksgiving celebration, I was awakened by the unmistakable canine retching noises that every dog-lover is loath to hear. Usually, when you hear these distinctive sounds, the weather is cold and it is raining outside. Next, you realize one of your bedroom shoes has been purloined by a dog that loves you so much that even your shoes smell like "Mom," making one slipper the perfect treasure to carry from room to room in mother homage. With no time to find the lost shoe, you have no choice but to remain barefoot on the freezing porch steps as you rush the soon-to-vomit dog into the front yard.

If you have more than one dog, you leap from the bed with speed that is exponentially increased by the number of dogs. It is absolutely critical to be able to tell the veterinarian which dog is sick. No one wants to line up the whole canine crew and stare into their eyes asking, "Now which one of you threw up?" Let me not repulse you here with the specter of worry that if one dog throws up and you do not leap up to take charge of the situation a dog fight just might break out when the other dogs rush to the scene to help clean it up.

Sparing you the details of our tumultuous body-function evening, suffice it to say that my sick dog was Gabriel, the baby of the pack. Gabriel and I retired upstairs to the guest room, leaving the rest of the pack in the family bedroom with dog daddy. Gabriel slept peacefully pressed against my chest, sometimes waking to show me his big black eyes and to wag his short tail. Riding to town early, Gabriel and I were among the after-Thanksgiving tummy-upset throng that filled our veterinarian's waiting room the next morning.

Post-Holiday Upset Tummy Brigade Await Veterinarian

While waiting our turn for a checkup and check-over, Gabriel and I listened to many holiday dog danger and mishap questions that dog mothers and dog fathers asked the hospital staff. Fredericksburg Animal Hospital's two licensed veterinary technicians, Dawn Magnone and Tracy Ramsey, rubbed lots of little heads, fuzzy noses and wagging bottoms while dispensing

danger-prevention tips for enjoying a safe holiday season.

Antifreeze Kills

Dawn Magnone warned, "Licking or drinking antifreeze is one of the biggest dangers for pets. The antifreeze manufacturing industry has been asked to add a non-palatable deterrent to all antifreeze, but this has not been done." Magnone stressed that pet owners need to know where their pets are at all times and supervise them, lest they find the sweet, deadly liquid in garages or on driveways. The danger of leaking antifreeze ingested by an unsuspecting pet is one more reason to never allow pets to roam the neighborhood. How will you know why your pet is sick if he has eaten a dangerous substance while away from home?

447

Dog Must Not Clean Up All The Leftovers

Holiday food leftovers can be dangerous to pets. Never scrape human feast-leavings into the dog's or cat's bowl. Better to waste food than to make your pet sick. Magnone advised, "Bones from holiday meals can cause serious problems. High-fat foods, or people food in general, cause gastrointestinal upset."

Secure Trash Cans From Noses and Paws

Take the trash can to a place where your pet cannot steal food or get into the trash bin. Holiday food-preparation and waste items can be deadly. Magnone cautioned, "Turkey harnesses [the strings that are used to lift turkeys out of the roaster] are very dangerous to cats, as well as dogs. Linear [long, string-like] foreign bodies can do a lot more damage than other foreign bodies. Surgery is required to remove them." Tree tinsel, strung berries or popcorn, wrapping ribbons and many holiday decorations can cause distress and internal trauma to the dog or cat that likes to eat or play with found objects. Magnone concludes: "Chocolate and trash send lots of dogs to the emergency room during the holidays. Poinsettias aren't as dangerous as once thought, but can cause oral irritation, vomiting and nausea. Ornaments and needles from real trees can cause problems. Salt used to melt ice causes irritation of pets' paws, so paws should be wiped well after each walk."

Balls: One Size Does Not Fit All

Veterinary technician Tracey Ramsey warned young Gabriel to be wary of balls, explaining:

SAFE DOG

"Balls can choke dogs, get swallowed, and are sometimes difficult for the dog to spit out. Many dogs enjoy a game of tug, but owners must be very careful how they play tug games. Supervise all dog play. I have seen dogs with missing teeth because the owner has played tug of war too roughly. Toys, even tug toys, should be for tossing to the dog, not used for tug of war. Favorite toy choices are soft, multidimensional toys that squeak. Most dogs respond to things that squeak or make noise."

Supervise Christmas Tree Viewing

The Christmas tree and holiday visitors require supervision for pet safety. Reactions and interactions with ornaments, gifts and little human children who may not have good dog manners can lead to holiday mishaps and medical concerns. Ramsey explained: "Avoid placing breakable ornaments at a tree level where they can be knocked off, broken or stepped on. Be careful that some gifts or decorations may contain chocolate and be eaten by the pet. If there are guests visiting that your dog does not know, keep close tabs on the pet. Work to socialize your pet to the visitors."

During the Christmas season, while we take stock of the year's best blessings, Gabriel and I are grateful for all the animal hospitals and all the animal-hospital staffs who dedicate themselves to keeping pets safe and well every day of the year. Take a plate of cookies to your animal-hospital staff. Ask them your holiday questions.

Scared Dog Walking:
Coping With A Dog Attack

"Integrity without knowledge is weak and useless, and knowledge without integrity is dangerous and dreadful."
Samuel Johnson

"I saw blood on my dog. I saw blood on me. I was terrified. I believed my dog was going to be killed."

Shirley has been confidently walking her tiny Rat Terrier, Ben, in a local park for years. Ben wags his little tail in delirious anticipation when Shirley clips on his leash. They both look forward to their daily stroll.

Not any more. Shirley and Ben will continue to walk, but never again with peace of mind or the same joyous companionship.

Ben, who weighs under twenty pounds, was attacked by a massive dog who weighed 80–

 450

SAFE DOG

100 lbs. The huge, snarling dog dragged his owner and a second large dog walking with him, across the park path to attack Shirley and Ben.

Dog Attack

Picture a huge dog, totally out of control, lunging forward with teeth bared; snarling , straining on his leash to clutch the little terrier between his teeth. Picture Shirley , a petite woman who barely outweighs the aggressive dog, attempting to haul her little dog out of the jaws of torment. Add the horror of the attacking dog suddenly slipping free of his too loose collar. The terror escalates as the snarling dog loose without leash, voice or physical control of the owner, who is using all her strength to restrain her second dog, who is still on leash.

How Much Worse Can It Get?

Jump forward from the images of the little dog being attacked and Shirley struggling to save her dog. This nightmare gets worse.

Rabies Vaccines For The Humans

Later, Shirley sits nauseous and dismayed in her doctor's exam room after she reacted badly from taking rabies prevention injections. She has been forced to undergo this painful, unpleasant treatment because the owner of the dog who attacked her ran away. Ran away. Not just the dog, but the owner of the dog, too. Incredible? Unbelievable? True.

Coward or Criminal?

Once the attacking dog was restrained and its owner saw blood running down Ben's leg and

DEVOTED TO DOGS

Shirely's hand, the big dog's owner told Shirley to take Ben to his veterinarian for immediate treatment . She promised to follow Shirley in her car and be present to give necessary information on her dog's rabies, and registration.

The big dog's owner never arrived. She never called Shirley or her veterinarian. A concerned radio announcer kindly begged any listener with information about this horrifying park dog attack to call with information. No responsibility was taken and Shirley and her dog were required to be treated for rabies prevention.

What Would You Do?
Shirley and Ben's ordeal raises many difficult and necessary questions about dog behavior, dog ownership and dog owner responsibility.

Be Cautious Approaching Unknown Dogs
Not all strange dogs like other dogs. Not all dogs out for walks are under control. There is nothing to do to prevent Shirley from having to take the full series of rabies vaccines. Sadly, Ben

may now think he has good reason to be fearful or defensive toward unknown dogs he meets.

Be Prepared: Take Precautions

One benefit from enduring traumatic events in life is that if you live to tell the story you can sit and ponder the lessons learned. A difficult experience can be an opportunity for self examination and growth. We may never know why the woman who owned the dog who bit Shirley and Ben never came forward to help them. We can ask ourselves the questions that surely have kept that woman awake at night.

*Is your dog under control sufficiently to be no danger to other dogs, children and strangers? If he is not; obedience training, or a private trainer is the place to begin teaching control.

*Does he wear a close fitting, sturdy, well-made collar and equally strong leash at all times? Even at home alone, he should wear his well fitted, flat buckle collar. Who has not had a beloved dog slip out the door and need to be hauled back in? A dog without a substantial collar is an accident waiting to happen.

*Is he fully vaccinated for rabies and all communicable diseases? Is he licensed with the city or county where you live? Can you locate proof of these vaccinations and license if you need them?

*Is he aggressive? If he growls at dogs or people, yes, he's aggressive. Consider the growl to be a warning he is thinking of biting. Have his

453

behavior assessed by your veterinarian and ask your vet for a referral to a dog behavior professional. Don't wait for the dog to actually use the teeth he is showing to believe he is a danger to himself or others.

If he is out of control or you know he is aggressive, have you considered that you will be liable for any harm he causes? Consider the type of liability your insurance coverage will give you if he bites someone and you have court or medical damages to pay.

Don't Wait: Socialize and Train Him Now

All dogs deserve the opportunity to be good dogs. Certainly it is easier to train a tiny puppy who has his following instinct and his bite inhibition intact, but that does not mean an owner can ever decide it's too late to train an unruly dog. The training job may become more time consuming, but after all, we own dogs because we enjoy their companionship. Training every dog until he is a joy to be with is the responsibility that comes with dog ownership. Just as some people take longer to learn a skill, some dogs require extra time and repeated positive demonstrations.

Prove Your Love For Your Dog Train and Control Him

Unless we intend to stop owning dogs, we can never stop taking responsibility for their control, love and training.

454

Snake In The Grass:
Curious Noses Beware

"For my companions, the Hills,
Sir, and the sundown, and a
dog as large as myself that my
father bought me. They are
better than beings, because
they know but do not tell."
Emily Dickinson

Copperheads! I am trying to learn to live peacefully with the snakes who lived here in rural Virginia before my Irish ancestors hopped off the boat.

The local snakes did not vote to have their lovely woods invaded by flower bed planting, tree removing humans, so I am doing my best to be a good neighbor to the snakes. In fact, I would be thrilled to death to find several benign black snakes curled up anywhere in my yard.

DEVOTED TO DOGS

I know there are readers thinking, "Snakes!!!! One bit your dog! How can you be on the side of snakes?"

The Copperhead that laid a nasty bite on Vivien's sweet muzzle surely sent us off to the veterinarian in a hurry. Her muzzle swelled up to look like a giant football by the time we reached the doctor. She did cry and look pitiful. I admit to being frightened beyond description.

Dr. Frank Wagner examined her, gave her an  injection of antibiotics and prepared me to watch for where and how the swelling in her head would progress through her lymphatic system. Dr. Wagner assured me that there was more worry about dangers from germs in the Copperhead venom than about possible death from poison itself for a dog the size of my 45 pound Bearded Collie.

Vivien was fit enough to share a bit of an ice cream cone on the way home. She had to be restrained from making a bee line right back into the flower bed where she poked the unsuspecting snake with her Beardie nose.

So began my investigation into how to live peacefully in the woods with the snakes.

SAFE DOG

Go to an expert when you need advice.

John E. Howe, Virginia Cooperative Extension agent in Spotsylvania County says, "As a general rule, snakes live in areas where they can find food and shelter. If food and shelter are scarce, snakes will not find it an attractive area to live in.

Howe offered this advice to limit snakes in and around your home:

- Mow your yard regularly. Most grass varieties should be mowed to a height of 2 to 3 inches;
- Copperheads feed on mice, rats, birds, amphibians and lizards. Eliminating areas where these prey animals may live and have shelter will limit food resources for snakes and discourage snakes from living in that area;
- Keep the yard and grounds clear of brush piles, firewood stacks, lumber, junk, and thickets and other areas that provide hiding spots for snakes;
- Birdseed and pet foods attract animals that Copperheads and other snakes feed on. By eliminating pet food and birdseed, fewer prey species will be attracted to the grounds. Snakes will find fewer reasons to visit your property.

Howe made a good case for cleaning up the yard. Summer is a perfect time to clean up and make your property less attractive to poisonous snakes.

457

My Now Neat Yard: A Blessing In Disguise

Where there used to be three overgrown, rock-garden flower beds, there are now a few ornamental trees. Over 20 wheelbarrows of large gray river stones have been hauled off our property. My hope is to encourage snake habitat in the woods outside the fenced back yard.

Bird feeders have been given away. The deck is shining clean and bare.

Whack Your Weeds

One friend brought her "grass hog" string trimmer and gave me a lesson in grass trimming. Another neighbor kindly taught me to ride the riding lawn mower. Evenings, after sundown, I circle the flower beds and house foundation, rumbling and rattling, being a better yard keeper.

Recognize the Safe Snakes

If you live in the woods, near creeks and streams, you may make the acquaintance of a poisonous snake. Learn to recognize the poisonous snakes that you hope to relocate, and learn to welcome the non-poisonous snakes who really pose no harm and are a benefit to your outdoor environment.

Tony Wrenn's Advice

Award winning writer, Tony Wrenn, who writes "In A Virginia Garden" in the "Town and County" section of The Free Lance-Star newspaper, told me, "I grew up on a tobacco farm in

SAFE DOG

North Carolina where Copperheads and the occasional Rattler were a real problem. We always encouraged both black snakes and especially king snakes around all farm buildings. Both will feed on small snakes, and Kings are evidently especially fond of Copperheads, so the two do not normally cohabit.

"My father would have fired any farm worker who killed either a Black or King snake. The Black snakes were amazingly effective at handling rodents in the grain barn and corn crib. Once, a family of Flying Squirrels homesteaded in our house, it was built in 1868 and had no insulation, so, come dark, the walls were interstates for the Flying Squirrels. It was a Black snake that moved from the corn crib and through a scuttle in the roof of my bedroom closet into the attic that convinced the Flying Squirrels to leave.

"I doubt that the Black snake was ever hungry enough to eat a squirrel, but the two species were not happy cohabiting. The snake did finally cause a bit of excitement when one day, while my mother was going upstairs, she met it coming down. She swept it the rest of the way down the stairs and out the front door and that was that."

459

Since many kinds of snakes are common in most rural settings, I was not surprised to hear of many dogs and snake encounters.

Snake In The Swimming Pool

A story from Deborah Collins, "One morning I went to check the pool equipment before a swim. Our Dachshund, Skippy, ventured into the pool house and came out barking. He had two puncture wounds in his nose. A Copperhead was in the pool house. Off we went to our veterinarian.

"The very next day, Skippy was barking in the flower bed. Another Copperhead. The third day, Skippy was going wild at the pool, running around the perimeter. Two more Copperheads. Skippy was always aware of his turf."

Stick Your Nose In A Bush: Find An Unsuspecting Snake

From Peggy Carlson, this story. "My husband and I were walking our two Beagles, on leash, down our gravel road. We live in Spotsylvania County in the woods. Daisy put her muzzle into a clump of shrubs at the edge of the road. She immediately jumped a foot into the air. We assumed that something had spooked her. Less than two minutes later, she lay down in the road and wilted. She had blood on her muzzle.

"By the time we got to the vet, Daisy was going into shock. The veterinarian administered fluids, steroids and antibiotics. She was grotesquely swollen on her muzzle and neck. Our veterinarian confirmed a Copperhead bite. We are just so thankful that we saw the bite happen and were able to rush her to the vet."

Invite A Blacksnake To Your Yard

One last story from Marge Brandel. "We have not had any personal experiences with Copperheads in the 20 years we have lived here in the woods. We have a lot of Black snakes; the good kind of snake to have. Black snakes eat Copperhead young, so maybe that is why we have not had a copperhead problem. Remember, never kill a Black snake!

"My Rottweiler, Kora, did get tweaked on the nose by a black snake that was determined to hunt baby birds nesting in the eaves of our garage. Kora the Rottie went up to the fence to sniff the snake. The snake came through the fence after Kora's inquiring nose, just as if it were saying, "Bug off, this is my territory'!"

Snake bite initiated Vivien remains on the hunt for snakes, skinks and anything that goes swish in the grass. I am the one in charge of protecting her from her own curiosity. You can bet she will not be out of my sight as she prances and piddles in her fenced yard. We are hoping that a nice mature Black snake family will take up residence in our yard. We promise leave him or her alone and share our turf.

Lost Without A Microchip

"Nothing but love has made the dog lose his wild freedom, to become the servant of man."
D. H. Lawrence

Button is 14 years old and she is my good friend. She is blind and deaf. Some days she doesn't move an inch unless her mom wakes her. Arthritis has slowed her doggy activities nearly to a standstill, but her steadfast desire to be with her mom is stronger than her need to rest at home. Every morning she reports to work with her mom. Her most important job these days is to sleep on a very comfortable bed nestled under a sunny window.

Button is a beauty, even as an old girl. She has white, bronze and black wiry fur, is gray-grizzled around eyes and muzzle and has big black devoted eyes that tell you she has known

 462

only very kind people and that she believes humans deserve her trust.

I have known Button for more than a decade and it is hard for me to believe old age has her in its relentless grip and that all of us who love her must face her inevitable departure someday.

Button Goes Missing!
Recently she frightened all who love her right out of their socks. We thought she had vanished into thin air. If there is any terror worse than losing your dog, it is losing your blind, deaf, ancient companion.

When Button's mom has to travel for her job, there are dog lovers lined up willing, pleading, begging to be allowed to look after Button. That is how sweet and cute she is. And trouble? No trouble! How much inconvenience can a blind, deaf, nearly immobile, sleep-all-day and all-night, terrier-beagle with a heart of purest delight be?

Lots of Get Up And Go
Left In An Elderly Girl
Ha! Never take anything about any dog for granted. Three weeks ago, geriatric Button taught many of her friends and loved ones several lessons. She showed us to never count the aged out as too old to give you a surprise. Her story has a happy ending, but for three days many Button lovers were in panic and distress. Button was lost.

DEVOTED TO DOGS

Vanished. Gone. Not one trace.

Button's human mother had gone out of town and a lucky aunt who lives in the depth of a very rural county (Partlow, Virginia) won the honor of having Button spend the night. Let's call the Aunt "June", just to protect her privacy.

Land, Lot's Of Land

June has several fenced acres. She also has a dog door. At ten o'clock, just before bed time, Aunt June took her two big, gentle Rottweilers and carried Button to the back yard for the 'last call' peepee. Button was so sleepy and so arthritic (and remember: blind and deaf) that she made a tiny little grass sniffing circle, completed her mandatory bedtime bathroom duties, and was carried back into the house. The other dogs came in and everyone went to sleep. Everyone had whatever kind of dreams dogs and humans have. All was well.

Button, Button, Who's Got The Button?

Dog women often get up with the sun, mainly because at first light the older, housebroken dogs are stomping on your head in the bed, or puppies paw at their cages if they are still in the housebreaking stages. Aunt June's household is no different. Since she is Button-sitting, she figures Button has a very old bladder and will appreciate being sneaked out to wee before Aunt June's two big dogs wake wild and willing to stomp poor geriatric Button in their joy of young dogs greeting the new day.

June casts her sleepy eyes over to the Button bed. No Button. Can her eyes deceive her? Button is gone. Let me shorten this frenzied search report by saying that June, getting more frantic by the second, searched every inch of her house, her garage, and her totally secure fenced yard. No Button and no evidence of escape.

Frantic Searching

June took the day off from work to frantically search woods around her home and all the back roads of Partlow. No Button. By this time June alternated between driving and crying and going in to sit by the phone wondering how she would give such horrible news to Button's mother.

Button's mother arrived that night and after assuring guilt-trodden June that no one could have expected a Button escape, the two of them, in separate cars, continue the Button search. They visit every animal control office and animal shelter. They assure everyone helping them look that Button has on a sturdy collar and a well engraved name tag with her name and address. Several of the animal control officers ask, "Does Button have an ID microchip?"

DEVOTED TO DOGS

Button's mother admits that she has had ID microchips implanted in her younger dogs but never dreamed Button could ever get lost.

After two days of constant, frantic searching, Button's mom caught sight of a little white furry creature at the edge of the woods down a very rural country road, miles from Aunt June's house. Slamming on the brakes, pulling over to the shoulder of the road, Button's mom began yelling, "Button!", waving her arms and trying to call Button to her. Button, exhausted, hungry and disoriented, did not look in her mother's direction. Since Button moves very slowly , her mother had her scooped up into her arms and safely traveling toward home within minutes.

Button Comes Home

Button's story has a very happy ending. Unfortunately, millions of dogs and cats stray from home every year. Many of them travel miles, disoriented and frantic to find home and never do. They end up in animal shelters and unfortunately most of them end their lives being put to sleep.

Get Your Dog A Microchip

Animal control workers and shelter volunteers stress that there can never be too many forms of identification on your pet. Collars can come off or be removed. Plastic identification tags can fall apart and be lost. Some metal identification tags tarnish and rust and become unreadable. Most dogs who are tattooed have the tattoo done when they are young and often as the dog grows, the tattoo fades and changes shape. Many veterinarians have told me they feel their handwriting is so bad when he attempt to tattoo squirming dogs that the tattoos are not very readable even in the beginning.

An identification microchip is the newest and perhaps the best method to permanently identify your pet and give both of you insurance that if lost she will be returned to you.

Tiny: A Grain Of Rice

The chip is the size of a grain of rice and is made of surgical glass material that is completely safe for the dog. The chip has its own unique 10 digit number that will track the dog back to you and only you.

The chip is inserted just under the skin, between the shoulder blades, by an injection that takes seconds. Many dogs do not even notice they have been implanted. Dogs who dislike other veterinary procedures will probably run true to form and may not cooperate for this injection either. But most calm, easy going dogs will stand still and get the chip inserted in the same amount of time it takes to receive a vaccine.

DEVOTED TO DOGS

Several area veterinarians reported that they prefer to implant the chip while the dog is under anesthesia. Any time a dog comes to its veterinarian for any procedure requiring anesthesia, from surgery to routine tooth cleaning, the owner is asked to sign a permission form for the veterinarian to anesthetize the dog. Many veterinary offices ask at the time the owner signs this form if the owner would also like to have the identification micro chip inserted while the dog is asleep. A few hospitals have added this question about identification chipping to their anesthesia form so the owner can check "yes "and the doctor will implant the chip.

Area veterinarians assured me that they have implanted many chips with the dog awake and the dog did not even turn its head back to notice. Your dog's temperament and past behavior for vaccines and other procedures performed while awake should be the guide for making your awake versus asleep decision. My dogs Vivien and Gabriel had their chips inserted while standing on the doctor's exam table, wide awake, tails wagging. Neither dog even turned it's head to look at what was going on behind it's collar.

One veterinarian admitted that when clients want the chip implanted with the dog awake, she offers the dog really dog yummy food that an assistant holds under the dog's nose while the veterinarian implants the chip. This veterinarian said she tries to keep a few delicious hot dogs frozen and ready to be microwaved and chopped into a diversion reward for the dogs who are having the implant. She laughed and said, "a good indicator of a stressed or worried dog is whether or not it will eat."

Implant Cost Is Low

Cost of the implant is $25-$50. Some offices charge for an office visit at the time of implanting and some do not. The identification number must be registered with a central data bank. The registration fee is a one time-fee. Owners receive a distinctive plastic identification tag for their pet's collar which says the dog has an ID chip and shows a toll free number for contacting a pet retrieval data base.

Two primary companies make the chip: AVID (*www.avidmicrochip.com*) and HomeAgain (*www.homeagain.com*). Both companies' chips can be registered with the American Kennel Club, whether the dog is a purebred dog or not. AVID also keeps a secondary data base of its own.

Most animal shelters and veterinarians own a handheld scanner device that when passed over the chip will read its ten digit number. The chips will last for at least 75 years, so unless your pet is a parrot or an elephant, you can have no worry that the chip will fail during a pet's lifetime.

Scan All Found Dogs

Shelter operators stress that found dogs should be scanned all over their entire body just in case an identification chip has moved. It is very rare that a properly implanted chip will move, but chips have been reported to move to new areas. One veterinarian I spoke with described finding a rice sized object on an x-ray of a dog who was about to have knee surgery. The veterinarian guessed it was an identification implant and sure enough, the scanner proved the chip was working properly even though it had migrated. The chip is placed just under the skin and not implanted deep into the animal. Therefore no harm could come from a chip having migrated to a new area.

Use of identification microchips has been going on for at least two decades. Biologists have tracked migrations and breeding patterns of birds, fish, and many wild animals. Chip use is widespread in theft prevention. Many cameras, computers, saddles and bicycles conceal a hidden chip to prove who really owns the expensive item. The time has come for pet owners to take advantage of this very safe and useful technology.

Get Chipped. Get Peace Of Mind.

There is nothing more heartbreaking than sitting by a stop sign looking onto the pleading face of a lost dog on a "Lost" poster. Thinking of the frantic and heartbroken family makes all of us think of our own dear furry family member wandering desolate and hungry. The ID microchip could be the miracle that brings your beloved pet home again.

Think of Button and her disappearance. No one thought she had the energy to get off her bed. But she did. She must have been determined to breathe the night air and smell the delights of squirrels of her youth. I am assured Button got an ID microchip. All of us would be advised to get one for our own little ones who have only us to protect them.

Lost!
There's No Place
Like Home

*"I sleep. I wake. How wide
the bed with none beside.'*
Kaga no Chiyo

Have you ever looked into the face of a friend whose dog is lost? Then you have witnessed a heart racked by pain and peace of mind destroyed with incessant worry.

To endure losing, looking for and endlessly hoping to find a dog that loves you, is nothing less than torment.

If you have ridden the roads and byways calling out the name of a lost dog, never again will you see a "lost dog" poster tacked to a signpost that you do not relive the ache of worry brought by a lost dog.

 472

SAFE DOG

Dogs can be lost from their own homes, from the homes of friends or relatives who look after them while their owner is away, or even from pet boarding facilities.

Lost Dog Action Plan:
Before Your Dog Is Lost
Before you leave your dog in the care of anyone, sit down and make two lost-dog action plans.

Plan one will give instructions for the person, or kennel, caring for your beloved dog while you are away.

Plan two will describe steps to be taken in the terrible event that your dog is lost.

If you have a computer, type your action plans into your computer and save them to print every time you leave your dog with anyone. Update your dog-care instructions each time you leave your dog.

Leave Your Dog Sitter With A Plan
Your printed plan explaining what the dog keeper should do in the terrible event that your dog is lost will save precious hours that will be needed to prepare a search for your dog. Time is the most critical predictor for finding a lost dog. If you are away, you need to leave town with your dog caretaker prepared to start a search before you have time to return to town to lead the hunt. Never leave your dog without leaving a photo and descriptive details.

473

Be Specific

Don't be afraid to say exactly how you want your dog to be supervised. I have a friend whose dog often stays with me when she is away. We have known each other for years and this friend still gives me instructions just as though I had never seen a dog or kept one safe.

I am not insulted. I am relieved to have so much information from the person who best knows the dog. Every dog has different activity levels, curiosity drives and possible escape habits. Anyone who thinks your instructions or wishes are too detailed should not be entrusted with your best friend: your dog.

'Away From Home' Action Plan

My dog has a sturdy collar with a durable metal tag with my phone number, street address and my veterinarian's phone number. Do not take off this collar for any reason.

- A disposable write-on tag has been added to his collar that has your (the dog keeper's day and evening phone number and address. He has a microchip. He has a tattoo. Here are the ID numbers.

- Keep my dog in his crate. My most important concern while he is in your care is that he is confined either in his crate, or on a leash if outside with you for bathroom duties.

  Please do not let him run unsupervised at any time in your yard or your house. Here are toys and 'chewies'. I will make up to him this short period of inactivity when I return. We will play in his fenced yard when he is back at home in his familiar surroundings.

  If you take him for a walk, make sure he wears his collar, all the tags, and that he is never, at any time, off his leash.

  Do not under any circumstances let a child walk him. He could dart away, even on a leash.

  Here is the phone number for his veterinarian. If you have any question about his health, do not hesitate to take him to see his veterinarian immediately.

- Here is a bag of his food, and a written schedule for how much and how often he eats. Have him eat in his crate. Let him rest quietly in the crate an hour before he eats and an hour after he eats. When you take him out to go to the bathroom, he should go on a leash.

He usually eats breakfast around 7 in the morning and dinner around 6 in the evening. He can wait to use the bathroom for around seven hours. He will sleep in his crate all night without having to go outside, unless he is sick.

- Contact me with any questions. Here is my hotel and cell phone number. Please call me at any time, day or night, to ask me anything at all about his health, his habits or any question that comes up.

  If he rides in the car, please have him ride in his crate, with his collar on, and be sure he is on a leash at all times, especially in the doctor's office.

Lost Dog Action Plan
The town where the dog lives and all surrounding counties are the first search and notification area.

- A door-to-door visit should be made to every home near the address where the dog was lost.

  Continue to search the yard, bushes, outbuildings; any place a dog could hide. If he is old, consider that he may not hear your calls.

- Make a list of all the reasons the dog may have escaped or wanted to run free in the area. If he is not neutered, he is probably roaming to look for company of the opposite sex. Promise all the dog angels in heaven that you will neuter him (or her) immediately when he returns.

- What breed is he? Even if he is a mixed breed, you must have a clue to the types of dogs he hails from. If he is a terrier, he may have found a trove of vermin to pursue and burrowed out of the area in digging pursuits. If he is a herding breed, the siren call of moving bicycles, children or cars may have lured him away. Think like your dog. What would lure him away?

- Is he a shy dog? Would he run or hide if a stranger approached him? Is he a friendly dog? Would he hop right into an open car door for a kind word or a cookie? Is he athletic? May he have run away in pure dog-running joy? Is he a small, young or old dog? How far do you think he might run? All these questions beg for your analysis of your understanding of your dog.

- Call every dog lover you know and put together a dog hunt posse to knock on doors and show the picture of the dog. Leave the picture flier and thank everyone in the area for looking for the lost dog. As searchers walk and drive through the neighborhood, make lots of noise calling the lost dog's name. Return several times a day and call the dog's name.

The 'Find My Dog' Poster

- <u>Prepare a brightly colored flier with a current picture and his detailed physical description.</u> State that a reward is offered, and that you will pay any medical or kennel bills.

Scan a picture of your dog. Before you leave town, send the scanned picture and the dog's detailed description, by e-mail, to the person who will be keeping your dog. In the terrible event that your dog is lost, the person keeping him will be ready at a moment's notice to use this description and this picture.

Send an e-mail with the dog's picture and description to everyone in your address book.

Make 500+ copies of his picture/description flier. Post them on every stop sign and street marker in the neighborhood where the dog was lost.

- <u>Recruit volunteers to post these signs everywhere around town, especially in places where dog owners will see them.</u> Excellent posting places are: all pet and animal feed stores, all shelters, rescue agencies, all local law enforcement, public safety, government offices, public libraries, veterinarians, groomers, pet kennels, pet-training facilities, convenience stores, playgrounds, anywhere people gather.

Visit post offices and leave fliers for the mail carriers who may see a loose dog on their routes.

- Place an ad in every local newspaper, and shopping flier. Many radio stations offer "lost pet" announcements as a community service. Buy a radio ad if necessary. The more people who hear the dog's description, the sooner after he goes missing, the better the chances someone will see the dog and call you.

- Follow up on all leads immediately. If you hear that someone has seen your dog, get in your car and go to that place. Walk the neighborhood and call the dog's name.

The Internet offers a vast network of dog-friendly Web sites. Use several search engines to search out "lost dog networks," "lost dog rescue" or any site that offers assistance to find lost dogs.

- Don't give up the search. With every day that your dog is not found, widen the area of your search. Visit *www.superpages.com* for telephone numbers for surrounding towns. Call all your area animal rescue and animal shelters to ask for advice from their staff. Many pet help agencies are staffed by a large cadre of volunteers. Different dog lovers will have different ideas and may offer new and useful suggestions for your search.

479

DEVOTED TO DOGS

Don't give up hope. Many lost dogs do come home to the families that love them.

May every lost dog come home. Safeguard your dog today with an identification tag, microchip and/or tattoo, neutering, and a photo and description prepared just in case it is needed.

Know where your dog is every minute. Never leave him alone to investigate escape routes, even in a fenced yard. If you don't have a fence, make a plan to give him a fence. If you have a fence, make sure you and your dog walk his fence line at least weekly looking for tiny opening chinks, nooks open beneath the fence and other escape hatches that could call to your curious dog. Whither he goes, you need to go, too.

11

Everyday and Holidays: Joyful Treatment And Dog Fun For The Dog Who Loves You

"Thorns may hurt you, men desert you, sunlight turn to fog, but you're never friendless ever, if you have a dog."
Douglas Mallock

Dog Lovin' From Your Oven

"If you wish the dog to follow you, feed him."
American Proverb

"The Ultimate Dog Treat Cookbook", by Liz Palika, is packed with ideas to please your canine.

Preheat the oven. Tie on your apron. Do more than talk the talk of dog love. Walk your dog-love to the pantry and stir together some high-smelling dog-attractive ingredients.

You say you're a real dog lover? How long has it been since you baked your dog a biscuit? Don't delay. Pledge to bake your furry pal a home-baked treat this weekend.

Don't know what to cook? Have less than zero culinary skills? Is your cooking limited to microwave heating? Stop your yapping of excuses. Liz Palika, award-winning dog writer, has written a book for all of us whose dog loving hearts are willing but whose kitchen expertise and time to cook are in short supply.

Ultimate Treats From
The Ultimate Cookbook

"The Ultimate Dog Treat Cookbook," by Liz Palika, is the most informative, entertaining and dog-friendly dog book to cross my desk in a long time. Palika offers dog-treat recipes for everyone who has ever loved a dog. No kitchen skills needed. If you can read, you can thrill the dog that loves you with Palika's easy-to-cook treats.

Liz Palika *(www.lizpalika.com)* has written over 50 dog books, from dog training to dog breed reference books.

EVERYDAY AND HOLIDAYS

Why Homemade?

Why did she write a volume on homemade goodies for man's best friend? Palika explains, "By making homemade dog treats, I can control the ingredients I use. I can make sure that the ingredients are of good quality, and I can avoid things that I prefer my dogs not eat. It's important to me that my dogs eat well; after all, I want them to be with me, hale and hearty, for as long as they can be."

"The Ultimate Dog Treat Cookbook" is fun to look at, and to read. Brimming with adorable, brightly colored dog drawings, each page is a visual treat. In addition to 50 canine-tested, veterinarian-approved yummy recipes, the book is enhanced by "Nutritional Notes" that explain valuable canine nutrition do's, don'ts, why's and why not's.

Palika generously gave her permission to share three favorite recipes. My choices were based on three criteria that suit my dogs' tastes and my cooking style.

Smell That Aroma: Heaven In Your Nose

First, I chose recipes with ingredients that would excite my dogs. Translation: Is it high-smelling? I chose Palika's "Yogurt Salmon Yummies" because my dogs adore fish. My husband despises fish, and refers to all dishes prepared from creatures who live in the sea as "stink meals." Since very little fish is cooked here, my dogs always clamor for any treat that reeks of fish.

485

Easy Is Good

I am severely challenged when it comes to kneading, rolling and cutting. Mixing and dropping dollops of dough, or pouring the entire mix of dough onto a greased pan, best suits my baking abilities. I felt brave enough to follow recipes that required as little working and handling of dough as possible.

Microwave dog treat recipes were new to me. If you have short supply of time to cook, "The Ultimate Dog Treat Cookbook" is the book for you. With Palika's instructions, you will soon be listening for the microwave "ding!" while your dogs circle worshipfully at your ankles, applauding your culinary skills.

Surprise your deserving dogs with recipes from "The Ultimate Dog Treat Cookbook."

Give A Gift Of Canine Cookies

When you buy your copy of this amazing doggy cookbook, bring home several copies. Solve your question of "What to take as hostess gift?" when invitations arrive. Forget wine, chocolate or flowers for the hostess. Win a dog lover's heart by giving "The Ultimate Dog Treat Cookbook." Word will go out among your dog friends, both human and canine, that a hostess gift from you is something to bark about.

YOGURT SALMON YUMMIES

Makes 2 to 3 sandwich bags of tiny training treats. These very nutritious treats will smell up your house while you're baking them, but your dog will appreciate your effort.

1 cup high-quality dry dog food kibble
2 7-ounce cans salmon
1 cup yogurt
1 cup instant mashed potatoes
1 cup flour
1 teaspoon baking powder

1. Preheat oven 350 degrees.
2. Put dog food kibble in food processor or blender and grind to course flour. Measure cup after grinding. Put the ground dog food kibble in a large bowl.
3. Empty both cans of salmon (with liquid) into a blender or good processor. Add the yogurt. Puree until mixture is smooth paste. Pour into the large bowl with the ground dog food. Add remaining ingredients and mix well.
4. Spread mixture onto greased cookie sheet. Using your fingers, flatten the mixture, spreading it evenly over the bottom of the cookie sheet.
5. Bake for 20 minutes.
6. Take the cookie sheet out of the oven. Using a pizza cutter or knife, score the dough into bite-sized pieces.

7. Put the treats back into the oven and bake for another 20 minutes or until golden brown.
8. Remove from oven. Break all pieces apart.
9. Cool thoroughly. Store in airtight container.

Note: For crispier treats, when all cookies have been baked, turn off oven. Put cookies back on cookie sheet and return to oven. Leave them in the cooling oven for several hours or overnight to harden.

CHEESY CHICKEN DELIGHTS
Makes 20-30 bite-size treats
1 7.75-ounce package of Bisquick Complete Three Cheese Biscuits
1 cup precooked chicken, chopped into -inch pieces
1 cup grated cheddar cheese
1 cup water

1. Preheat oven to 350 degrees.
2. Mix together all the ingredients into a sticky dough.
3. Drop by teaspoon onto greased cookie sheets.
4. Bake for 10 to 15 minutes or until golden brown.
5. Remove from the oven, let cool thoroughly, and store in and airtight container in the refrigerator.

MICROWAVE OATMEAL BALLS
Makes 60 round bite-size treats
1 cup nonfat dry milk

 488

EVERYDAY AND HOLIDAYS

1 cup all-purpose flour (white, whole wheat, barley or potato)
1 cup quick oats
1 cup flaxseeds
1 cup cornmeal
2 tablespoons low-sodium beef bullion powder
1 cup melted butter
1 large egg
1 cup warm water
1 cup quick oats, for coating the treats

1. Mix the first six ingredients well.
2. Add the butter, egg, and water and mix until the mixture forms a ball of dough.
3. Spread the second cup of quick oats on the breadboard.
4. Form marble-size pieces of dough into balls, rolling each in the oats.
5. Place 12 oat-covered balls on a heavy-duty paper plate (not Styrofoam).
6. Microwave the plate of treats at 50 percent power for 4 to 5 minutes.
7. Remove from the microwave. Let cool thoroughly. Store in airtight container.

489

Love Is A
Liver Biscuit

*"If you think dogs can't count, try
putting three dog biscuits in your pocket
and then give Fido only two of them."*
Phil Pastoret

Lightening struck our oven and I did not notice
for seven months. I attempted to bake a batch
of dog cookies and realized the oven refused
to pre-heat. Liver, garlic, flour had been mixed,
kneaded, rolled. No oven. Disappointed dogs.

My excellent dog pal, Rose, heard of our oven's
demise and my dogs' disappointment. Rose
prevailed upon her mother, Yvonne Stickleman,
to bake and deliver crisp and crunchy garlic
cookies.

Dogs and I agree: any pal who arrives bearing
baskets of divinely stinky baked goods is a
friend indeed.

 490

Rose has given permission for her simple, yet delicious, dog cookie recipe to be shared.

Bake A Better Biscuit by Birchwood Rosebud
2 1/2 cups whole wheat flour
1/2 cup powdered non-fat dry milk
1 teaspoon each: honey and salt
1 tablespoon minced garlic (fresh or from the refrigerated jar)
6 tablespoons margarine
1 egg

Mix ingredients with about 1/2 cup cold water. Knead 3 minutes. Dough should form a ball. Roll to 1/2" thick . Cut into dog bones. Bake on a lightly greased cookie sheet for 30 minutes at 350 degrees. Turn off oven. Leave bones in oven overnight to make them real hard. Rose's Flavor Note: Add extras to create different flavors: mint (for fresh breath), dry soup mix, peanut butter, or garlic.

Dogs Hunt For Cookie Recipes
Word went out to my dog mother friends that Quinnton, Gabriel and Vivien needed cookies. They whispered " our mother needs help with her oven" to every soft hearted dog lady they met. "Cookies and cookie recipes welcome", they explained. If you want something badly and you never ask for it, probably you will remain empty handed, or empty pawed, as the canine case may be.

The week before Christmas, tucked inside a big picture greeting card of our dog friends Miss Belle and Boeing Broderick, we found the dog cookie recipe booklet of our dreams. You will want a copy of this recipe extravaganza. I loved the easy recipes. The dog wisdom and anecdotes about each recipe made even a reluctant baker begin a shopping list and jump on the biscuit production line.

Easy Bake Cookies Are The Best Cookies

The recipes that I liked best required minimal mixing and limited ingredients. Many were pressed into the pan like brownies, requiring no rolling, squishing, cookie cutter–cutting nor shaping.

Dog mother and writer, Diane Goodspeed, has written the doggy cookbook, "Canine Cuisine:

Delectable Desserts and Dishes for the Deserving Dog". Funds raised from cookbook sales will assist the non–profit dog training group, The All Star Dog Association, to sponsor their annual 'All Star Agility & Obedience Championships' in York, Pennsylvania.

Canine obedience and agility athletes arrive from all over the United States to heel, jump, tunnel and compete for prizes. Booth spaces are filled with dog vendors selling everything from luxurious leather leashes and collars, to doggy collectibles that glorify every breed. Ride up to

EVERYDAY AND HOLIDAYS

York, Pennsylvania to witness these inspiring canine athletes. For information and to order a cookbook, visit the All Star Dog Association's website at *www.allstardogs.org.*

Goodspeed's recipes are too yummy to miss. She has kindly given her permission to share these favorites. Tantalizing recipe names and dog savvy reasons your dog will like them are direct quotes from Goodspeed. You owe it to your dog to order this cookbook and bake the biscuits that will delight your dog. There are over thirty unique and yummy recipes in the small book, including "Snickerpoodles", "Muttloaf", and "Dogumbo".

Gummy Blobs
"From gooey to chewy... sure to please young pups with new teeth to old pooches with no teeth."

1   jar beef or chicken baby food (2.5 ounce)

1/4 cup dry milk powder
1/4 cup wheat germ

Alternates:
Use banana, sweet potato or apple baby food.

Preheat oven to 350 F. Combine all ingredients and mix well. Drop by teaspoon onto well-greased cookie sheet. Bake 10-15 minutes until brown. Refrigerate for freshness. Okay to freeze. Makes about a dozen small cookies.

Liver Bow-Wow-Knees
(Liver Brownies)
2   pounds chicken livers
2   cups corn meal
2   cups wheat germ
2   eggs
1/2 cup dried parsley

Preheat oven to 350 F. Liquefy livers in food processor. Mix in other ingredients until smooth like brownie batter. Spread on greased cookie sheet. Spread evenly to about 1/3 inch thick. Bake 35 minutes. Cool. Cut into squares or strips. Store in airtight container in refrigerator.

Barkin Tuna Bake
2   cans tuna- (6 ounce- Do not drain)
1 1/2 cups whole wheat flour
2   eggs
3/4 cup grated parmesan cheese

Preheat Oven to 375 F. Mix tuna, cheese and eggs. Ad flour in small amounts. Mix to brownie consistency. Spread into greased 8 x 10 inch

pan. Bake 20 minutes. When done, brownies will have a putty–like texture and edges will pull away from pan. Cut into squares. Refrigerate or freeze.

Green Grazers
2 cups wheat germ
1/2 cup bread crumbs
1 bunch fresh spinach (chopped small)
3 eggs, beaten
6 table spoons
2/3 cup parmesan cheese

Preheat oven to 350 F. Mix all ingredients. Shape into 2 inch balls or logs.(Yes, with your hands.) Bake for 20 minutes on lightly greased baking sheet.

Thank you to Yvonnne Stickleman and Diane Goodspeed and the All Star Dog Association for sharing their cookie secrets. Doll yourself up in your best apron. Pre–heat the oven. The key to a dog's heart is made with liver. Let your dog watch the magic unfold.

Love The
Dog You're With

"Dogs... do not ruin their sleep worrying about how to keep the objects they have, and to obtain the objects they do not. There is nothing of value they have to bequeath except their love and their faith."
Eugene O'Neill

My mother wanted me to be Miss America. She bought many plastic tiaras to try and mold my desires and aptitudes to match the ladylike plans she nurtured in her heart for me.

I wanted to sit in the high weeds behind the garage and read thick books about animals and vampires while a big, warm dog laid his head on my lap.

Mother finally realized that her dignified dreams would never be my dreams. My hopes

 496

involved words like puppy tummies and dogged devotion.

Dogs, children, true friends: everyone we really love; ask the same thing of us as proof of our esteem. They ask that we love them for themselves. When we nag them for change, niggle them with suggestions, and yammer at them to do things they do not enjoy, we insure that they will become less than they are.

Esteem The Uniqueness of Your Dog
Loving a dog for himself is a life altering experience. Trying to force a dog to become a dog that he was not born to be can bring tragic obsession to us and may worry the long suffering dog to neurosis.

Gabriel Goes To Dog Camp
I recently attended a paradise for dogs near Asheville, North Carolina. Aptly called, "The Dog's Camp", my fur boy Gabriel and I spent one full week frolicking from dog class to dog sport finding out "What Does Gabriel Want To Do?" and "What Does His Mamma Do Well With Gabriel?"

From canine acting class, to dog massage, we tried a paw at new dog interests. We lingered beside a duck pond listening to dog communicator and author, Patty Summers. Afternoons, I strapped on my hotdog treat bag and off we raced to tracking class. Every night, Gabriel and I went to bed exhausted, but knowing more about each other.

497

DEVOTED TO DOGS

The lingering lesson that Gabriel taught me in our week of seminars, heeling practice, agility jumping and dog curriculum was that there were activities he was willing to do because I asked him to do them. But better than that lesson, I saw that there were dog sport activities that Gabriel truly wanted to do. Together we explored dog skills that made his little cropped tail nearly wag off the end of his body when we approached that particular training area of the camp.

What Does Your Dog Like To Do?
Tracking was the dog sport that Gabriel liked best. His nose went down into the tall grass, his tail began to twitch rhythmically, and his happy nose made otherworldly "snuffle-whuffle" sounds of sheer delight. Even a heard of nosy and noisy goats, hanging their ear waggling heads over the tracking field fence, did not deter my track sniffing boy from his bliss.

Lead With Your Aptitudes
We took just one class of freestyle dog dancing. It turned out that Gabriel is as graceful as a dog can be. He made agile figure eights around my

less than gracefully positioned legs. He danced right and left as the teacher called doggy dance steps and while I stomped all over his sweet feet. Our teacher was gracious, but I saw the stark truth in her slightly amused eyes. She knew the dog was a dancer but the mamma has feet not just of clay; perhaps cement. Gabriel gave up future dancing stardom. We agreed to prance gaily in the tracking field.

The lesson I learned at dog camp was this: love your dog for his very own and very personal talents. Explore his actual aptitudes more and fixate on your own aspirations for him less.

Your Dog Is Perfectly Unique
Every dog has a talent. Your dog will help you develop an ability to read his aptitudes and develop his skills.

Your dog's breed may not dictate how he prefers to play. I have met Cocker Spaniels who wanted to go to join the chase at lure coursing clubs. I know greyhounds who are most happy to lay very still for endless hours on the sofa. Many pups who were molded for a beauty contest dog show career, eventually found true joy working in the obedience ring.

The most stately, gorgeous dog I have ever met is a huge hound-collie mixed breed named Michael Susan. He resembles no breed I have ever seen in a breed book, but has more dignity, grace and lovely movement than all the dogs I have seen prance around dog show rings. His devoted mom never let a lack of pedigree papers thwart Michael's fun and dog sport activity. She led Michael out into the world to try his paw at all sorts of dog fun. Michael worked hard to pass his Canine Good Citizen test and his Therapy Dog test. He developed his full potential to be a well behaved ambassador of dog perfection.

Engaged Dogs Are Happier Dogs

Inside your dog lurks a talent and a desire to find work that will turn him on. Every dog is a happier, better behaved dog if he has a job to do.

A dog owner must find the activity their dog most likes to do. Maybe he would like to play hide and seek and find toys you hide around the house and yard. Perhaps he would like to learn not to pull on the leash and to go for a weekly walk downtown. He may long to hear onlookers "ooh'" and "ahh" over his fine manners and gentle civility as he strolls around town with the person he loves.

Take him to obedience school and believe from the start that he will be a brilliant student. Perfect his sit, down and come. Set a goal to pass the AKC Canine Good Citizen test. Take him out. Show him off.

There's No Dog Better Than The Dog Who Loves You

More than anything else, make sure that every time your eyes look into his, let him read in your face that he is the dog of your dreams. Love him like he is the best dog on the planet and sure enough, he will be.

 500

Relax, It's Pajama Day

"Perhaps the final test of anybody's love of dogs is willingness to permit them to make a champing ground of the bed. There is no other place in the world that suits the dog quite so well."
Henry Merwin

Are dogs protective and kind to us because they feel we are born so defenselessly and starkly naked?

The first time a tiny puppy sees his dog mom or dog dad step naked into a bathtub, he must stare in horror thinking, "What? No Fur? And they willingly take baths? These misguided mutants really need me."

Dogs, on the other hand, are born gloriously covered in fur. Is there anything like the velvet nuzzle of a puppy muzzle? Have you ever kissed anything softer than a pink puppy tummy? If you cannot admit to kissing a puppy from head to toe, you have missed one of the joys of life on Earth.

No Finer Fashion Than Pajamas
My dogs tell me that they like humans best when humans are dressed in pajamas. When human parents lounge around the house in pajamas, dogs feel sure fun is going to break loose.

My dog Abroham once told me that he referred to his fur suit as 'furjammies.' Life in furjammies represents paradise. To linger in pajamas tells a dog, "we are soft, warm, ready to snuggle up and read or roll on the floor and be rubbed."

Why not spend today in pajamas? If not today, get out your appointment book. Write in, "All day in pajamas with dogs."

Celebrate Leisurely Pursuits With Your Dog
Why does a dog like to see his human wearing sleepwear all day?

Chances are, if you are wearing pajamas, you will not leave the house. You will be home all day to play with and admire the dog. Perhaps you will don bathrobe and slippers and sneak up the driveway, in the car of course, to get the newspaper.

It goes without saying that your dog gets to ride in the car. Even the shortest driveway is a delightful jaunt to a dog.

Newspaper reading to the dogs is encouraged. Dogs have entertainment and civic interests, too. The sound of your voice is a joy to your dog. Perhaps there are humans in your house who hope you will eventually hush and let them think a private thought, but not your doting dog.

Make A Joyful Noise For Your Dog
Your dog loves your voice. Always speak to dogs in a pleasant tone, unless you are laying down some law that they must follow. Only for laying down the law, when the law has been broken, does the wise dog owner use less than dulcet tones.

Another use of your fine human voice during pajama day should be singing a few songs for the dogs. These songs can be to the tune of

any song you like to sing. Insert the name of the listening dog every chance that you possibly can.

Not currently singing to your dogs? You may have to audition a few songs until you hit upon a melody that lends itself to the insertion of your dog's name. Many, many dog parents have confessed to me that they have created special songs for their dogs. I could name names here, but dog serenading is a private act between dogs and those who love them.

For example, I sang a lilting rendition of the theme song from the Captain Kangaroo television show to my dog Bonnie every time I served her a meal. It went like this: "Good morning, Bonnie. Won't you come on out and play. 'Cause we're happy to see you, and start a Bonnie day." If you are too young to know the tune to this melodious theme song, ask someone born between 1950 and 1960. Probably, they can sing the Captain's theme to you.

Each dog in the house must have his own song. Usually, these songs are best sung upon waking and during feeding time.

Let Your Dog Lead Your Exercise Routine

If you wake stiff with age or fatigue, and your dog sleeps with you, you can perform various stretching exercises in the bed, while singing the song. Most dogs will cavort upon your body while you sing and stretch. You will learn quickly which soft parts to cover from delighted wiggly feet. Try this. You will not start the day as a grump if you have had a dog dancing foot massage as you hit the floor singing.

Relax With Entertainment From A Dog's Eye View

Pajama day calls for either videos of favorite movies or very good books. If you are trying to make the dog feel fully included in the video fare, consider movies that feature animals, especially dogs. The first "Babe" movie is beloved at my house. The second Babe ("Babe in the City") is too violent and not dog friendly, in our opinion. Cat and bird videos get high marks on pajama day. Wolves, and movies that have dog violence and dog fighting are not wise choices for entertaining calm, convivial family dogs. "Stuart Little One" and "Two" are also good choices.

Make Your Own Movie

If you are fortunate enough to have a video of your own dog, that will be the video of choice. My Gabriel will lay rapt across my robe clad lap and watch himself grow from six weeks to two years on the "Gabriel Video."

If you have a video camera and do not have a video in progress of your dog, pajama day is a perfect day for video taping and photographing your canine companion.

Portraits, Prissy Hygiene, and Purloined Toy Hunts

Pajama day would be a perfect day to drag out props and brush the dog for a holiday or birthday portrait.

505

DEVOTED TO DOGS

Brushing and bathing activities lend themselves well to pajama day. You will not care about dog hair or suds on your bedtime ensemble.

Toy scavenging, and if necessary toy refurbishing, by a run through the washing machine is another good pajama day activity. My dogs believe that any item that is whisked from a plastic grocery bag with hoopla and rejoicing is a new toy. On pajama day, we scrounge under beds, sofas and coffee tables to rescue hidden toys. A delicate wash and a whirl in the dryer makes most toys new to the dogs. Sometimes washing deadens the squeakers, but old toys usually have had their squeaker debilitated already.

Most dogs believe that all good days include a little retrieving. Fetch is a positive way to teach dogs who would keep or guard a toy, to "give". Show the dog, who is hanging on to a toy  like a terrapin, a piece of something yummy to eat. Say, "give." If all goes as hoped, the dog will open his mouth to eat the food morsel. Catch the toy as it falls from his teeth. As you catch it, say in a pleased voice, "good to give!" Teach the give game early in your dog's life. Practice often. You will train your dog that he does not need to guard things because he knows that the human hand always offers something better than he already has in his mouth.

Snacking: Always A Popular Pursuit

Intermittent snacking is good on pajama day. My dogs will eat carrot pieces, frozen tortellini pieces, popcorn, rice cakes. Quinnton will even eat pieces of orange. Snacks do not have to be fattening fare.

Let Your Dog Assist

You may feel compelled to do something productive on pajama day. My dogs and I hope you can get over that compulsion as you progress in your pajama day fondling and dawdling. If you must work, try to perform chores that can be done on the floor. Dogs like to have humans down on the floor so they can assist.

Floor chores include cleaning out any floor level cupboard, shelf, vanity, closet bottom, or bookcase.

Do you even know what hides along the wall under the kitchen sink? Make sure there is nothing within dog nose sniff reach when floor level cabinets are open. Even if you do not have small children, dogs are very nosey sniffing and exploring cabinets left open. Pajama day is a good day for safeguarding and rearranging cabinets.

Pajama day is for you and the dog to relax and reconnect. Turn off phones. If the doorbell rings, do not even look to see who it is. Good manners dictate that anyone dropping in is too rude to acknowledge. After all, visitors should surmise you are not at home to visitors on pajama day.

507

Love Him Like You Want To

"A dog lives in the moment and always hopes for the best."
Jack Brown

Have you seen the refrigerator magnet that exhorts, "Dance like no one's watching. Sing like no one's listening"? I would like to suggest, "Love your dog like you want to. Enjoy him every way you can."

Our dogs have lives so much shorter than our own. Why is that heart-wrenching fact an unchangeable truth? None of us knows.

Dogs live their lives like there is no tomorrow. Your dog can show you the way to "live in the moment." A good dog that loves you can be the spiritual guru who brings you inner peace.

 508

EVERYDAY AND HOLIDAYS

The happiest people I know love their dogs with true abandon. Caught up in dog love, these people do not care if they look silly rolling on the rug with Rover, or being lavishly licked all over the face by the dog who adores them. Non-dog lovers occasionally look at those of us who are dog-obsessed with incredulity or cynicism that implies, "How might one be so simple-minded to find inner peace and a return to innocent play through activities with a mere canine?" Those scoffers have not yet bonded with a canine heart.

Dog Wisdom: Play Now
Dogs show us the way to relax and play. Learning to play demands that we step back from human frenetic activities and chores that really will wait to be accomplished tomorrow. Wonder if dogs watch humans scurrying and worrying and think to themselves, "Why does my human resemble a hamster on a treadmill?"

I fantasize that dogs make mental lists of all the things they would choose to do if they had opposable thumbs and could drive. They would: Clean out the refrigerator daily, and learn to drive the car with their ears waggling in the breeze of a rolled-down window. They would never be wheedled by their doctor to take more walks, learn to enjoy exercise or relax into the sheer joy of doing nothing. They would sleep when they wanted. They would never have to swat the snooze button on the alarm clock and wonder if they can live until the coffee-maker's first cup of enlivening brew is slurped down.

509

Relax With A Dog On Your Lap

The best part of any day for me is to luxuriate in a deep leather recliner, with my 60+ pound, solid and warm Springer Spaniel, Gabriel, stretched languorously from my neck to my knees. He throws his heavy, square velvet muzzle up over my shoulder and sleeps. His slow, secure, rhythmic breathing is more soothing than the latest mood-elevating drug or relaxation device.

I prop a book that I have been looking forward to reading all day on his flat black flank. He sleeps. I read. We are both as close to heaven as we will get while breathing air on Earth. He cures aches and pains, both physical and spiritual, of overdoing out in the daytime world. Like a miraculous heating pad, warmth and time spent still and silent with a sleeping Gabriel and a well-written book can ease frantic thoughts or life's discontents.

I am not alone in my appreciation of finding joy in the comfort of ritual activities of comfort with my dog. Many dog owners describe the personal ways their dogs bring them solace. Several people have told me about their rituals. (The names of dogs and humans have been changed; the bond between a person and his or her dog is an intimate joy.)

Ode To Joy: Taking Your Dog To Work

Eddie Shelton is a lucky man, fortunate to have a job that allows his dog, Sable, to go to work with him. They are inseparable. Getting paid to work while being able to rub Sable's head any

510

time the urge strikes almost seems like stealing to those of us who wish our dogs could go to work, too.

But going to work is not the best part of the day for this dog-man pair. After both have had a nice dinner and the house is quiet, Sable, without fail, arrives in front of Eddie's easy chair and bows to her dad. Eddie succumbs to her invitation to play.

Lured onto the rug before the fireplace, the pair wrestle, cuddle and eventually lie side by  side to watch the news on television. Sable is a big dog, with perfect manners and an inquisitive mind. She is more than Eddie's co-worker, she is his playmate and gentle companion. (For the record, Eddie also has an adoring wife. Is Miz Becky jealous of Sable? No. Like any secure, well-loved human partner, nothing brings her more joy than to see her man happy with his very good dog.)

Tiny Dog On The Tub Rim

Miss Legume, a wee Beagle girl, and her mother, Beth, celebrate the end of each day with a long soak in the bubble bath for Beth and a prolonged scamper around the tub rim for Miss Legume. When you read that a tiny dog can get lots of exercise without ever leaving the house, believe it. While Beth soaks, suds and scrubs,

511

Miss Legume runs laps around the edges of the bathtub. If her mother is still and does not thwart her efforts, Miss Legume will steal a wet lick of suds off Beth's soapy shoulders.

To share one's bath time ablutions is a very personal experience. True dog lovers can look back on the lives of all the dogs that have loved them and recall memories that each dog left printed on their hearts.

Dip Your Tongue In Paradise

Doodle is a Jack Russel Terrier. She has sisters named Delilah, Donna and Destiny. They are all delightful girls with a yen for dairy products. Their treat of choice is whipped cream. Not any whipped cream, but brands that are dispensed from aerosol cans. Their mother, Susan Ann, squeezes the cream nozzle and the terrier girls scamper from far and wide.Susan Ann so loves to watch the terriers hurl their diminutive white bodies down the hardwood-floor hallway to the kitchen, that she indulges their dairy delight at least twice a day. Instead of cream in her coffee, she swirls on a whipped-cream pyramid. The milk-hunt girls burst wide-eyed in the kitchen. Susan Ann admits bending over and making four whipped-cream mounds on the kitchen tile floor. Sometimes, Susan Ann confesses, the tiniest of the crew will leap onto her lap at breakfast and attempt to dart a little whipped-cream-probing tongue into her coffee. "This terrier is on a cream hunt," she laughs.

Is this whipped-cream fixation bad dog training? Heck, no. Susan Ann, who has trained many

 512

competitive, high-scoring obedience dogs, says she shouts out, "Come!" as the whipped-cream can makes its distinctive squirting noise. Very quickly, all her terriers learn to love the word "come" and are unstoppable to comply with their mother's calling wishes.

What Is Your Dog's Joyful Ritual?

What do you and your dog do to unwind and let your spirits mingle? Consider your rituals. Make being with your dog a priority. The dog will learn to look to you for guidance. Your dog will feel your positive regard and repay you with attention and willingness to follow where ever you go. Good dog training that is built on a true heart-to-heart connection between a human and the dog. Start a ritual. Find your own relaxed place of peace. Let your dog show you the way.

Found Toys

"The real voyage of discovery consists not in seeking new landscapes, but in having new eyes."
Marcel Proust

The sight of an empty shoebox never fails to cheer me. I can close my eyes and loose myself in the memory of my favorite dog who could tear up a shoe box with unbounded bliss. Anyone blessed to watch him was transported into his shoebox destruction joy.

Watching dogs at play is one of the delights of dog ownership. Dog owners are constantly looking and listening for news of the newest, best, most entertaining dog toys. Often, our dogs surprise us and find entertainment with toys of their own choosing. They teach us that real treasures wait to be found all around us.

Lately, I have asked all my dog friends, "What is your dog's favorite toy?"

 514

Looks Like A Toy? Is a Toy.

Many dogs prefer found objects from yard, kitchen and bathroom over expensive toys procured by adoring owners. Recycling is a dog art form.

Plastic Bottles for Miss Lucy Labrador

Curious dogs hunt for souvenirs on walks. Miss Lucy Jewett–Bullock, the Labrador's mother agrees, "Lucy has effectively demonstrated that all the material written on Labrador Retrievers is certainly true. Basically, life is a party and virtually anything one can pick up in one's mouth can and does become a remarkably entertaining toy. Lucy's particular favorites are the prizes she picks up on her walks, especially plastic drink bottles. Not crushed, for heaven's sake! It is the crunching noise one can make with one's jaws that is so satisfying, not to mention the really cool way the uncrunched bottle bounces noisily on bare floors and even carpeted ones! We remove both the caps and the cap rings, as she seems immediately intent
upon chewing those off".

Zack: Cocker Gardner

Toys left behind by a gardening mother appeal most to Zack the Cocker pup. His mom, Diana Chappell, reports, "Zack loves big black flower pots that azaleas come in. He got hold of one last summer when he was a puppy and pushed it everywhere. The pot was all dented up and chewed on. This Spring he was outside playing and ran up with a new one that he found behind the house. So I threw the old one away and brought the new one inside. Zack rolls around

515

with his pot in his mouth having the best time, making lots of racket."

Butterflies And Bubbles

A totally original enjoyment was shared by a mom who works with Springer Spaniel rescue. She says, "My dogs' favorite things are butterflies. If there are no butterflies, they love soap bubbles that I blow for them." Bubbles provided an entirely new way to play for my dogs. The wild chasing and wagging those shining, floating spheres brought to Quinnton, Vivien and Gabriel has given us a new play ritual.

Love That Black Plastic Gutter Pipe

Plastic pipes and tubes of all types rank high as found toy favorites. Dog moms and dads have to keep a sharp eye on dogs who might actually try to eat these found items. Some dogs are safe to toss and chase nearly anything they find. Some dogs can and will chew and swallow objects just

because they can. The 'we eat anything we can chew' crew need careful supervision.

I Can Fit This Into My Mouth!
I have known and owned dogs who enjoyed the challenge of "how big a thing can I get in my mouth?" Puppies bravely and proudly carrying objects far too big for their mouths are also occupied, entertained and quiet. Mothers and puppy owners alike need a little rest from noise and interaction.

Bulldog owner, Cathi Allison, says ,"Beatrice the Bulldog liked to drag fireplace logs all over the living room then chew the bark off everywhere. Her sister, a lab mix, preferred carrying black lace underwear."

Nothing Beats Underwear Between Your Teeth
Underwear manufacturers must soak bras and panties in invisible, mystical chicken aroma to insure that dogs will first practice their retrieving shills with lace and elastic in their jaws. Show me a new puppy mom and I am ready to wager a new undie wardrobe is in her future.

Love To Rip That Paper
Paper products produce hours of frolic to many dogs. If the dog parent has a back strong enough the bending, crawling and searching that paper destruction clean up requires, the paper loving dog will reward you with a fine show. Wrapping paper tubes, paper towel rolls, and new or used tissues are huge favorites at our house.

DEVOTED TO DOGS

Chinese Crested Dog breeder, Lynn Coppage reveals that "Raven, loves the cardboard toilet

paper rolls when they are finished. I let her have them for a while and make sure she does not eat them. I have one Crestie who loves to hide keys, and several who will hide our eye glasses. They also think vegetables are great. Broccoli stalks: all my dogs come running. "

Dex Fischer, a Golden Retriever pup, shared that his favorite is "a plastic milk bottle that he found in the yard under a large bush. He likes to shop for toys on his walks. One day Dexter was very intent on sniffing a bush until he came out with someone else's tennis ball in his mouth. (His mom) didn't even know he liked tennis balls."

Kitchens: Treasure Trove For Found Toys
Really creative hunters find lots of toys in the kitchen. TJ and Willie's mom told me, "I've had a problem since TJ came that Willie won't let her play with any toys. I was very relieved a while back to hear TJ playing with something and Willie did not seem to care. I finally went to see what it was and it was a plastic measuring cup. She likes to hit the handle and watch it bounce around. Willie ignores her since it isn't officially a toy."

Kid's Toys Will Do, Too

My own Gabriel recently found a plastic bat left behind a shed in our yard. It was not his toy and we are not sure who abandoned the bat, but now it is Gabriel's prize as he strides across the yard. If you bend over to pull a few weeds from the flower bed, Gabriel just might whack your bottom with the bat. The fun never ends.

Balls and Socks

Where would dogs be without balls and socks? Many dogs report a love for balls hidden inside socks. One dog's mom said, "Our dog's favorite found toy is an old sport sock stuffed with other old socks to make into a big stuffed sausage. A knot is tied at the end, making a dangling tail.

Meadow Muffins?

Border Collies are always inventive. A Border Collie that I know was the only dog who admitted to "playing wildly with meadow muffins (horse poop). The best part of these found barnyard toys was that once you finish tossing and retrieving them, you can lie down and snack on them."

Supervise Always. Supervise Everything.

Every dog must be supervised carefully with any kind of toy. The dog who plays for hours with a plastic bottle is having harmless fun. But, the dog who chews and swallows any toy is not a candidate for bottle play.

Dog love and dog owner responsibility require that we know what kinds of toys are safe for our own dog. Dogs need supervision with all

519

their playthings and playtimes. They are like little children in needing constant attention and guidance.

Humans Learn To Play

Dogs at play teach us curiosity, persistence and confidence to make unusual choices simply because these choices make us happy. As they carry their gallon milk jugs proudly and with great concentration from room to room, ignoring expensive purchased toys, dogs show us that leisure enjoyments are very personal choices.

Get out your video camera, or borrow one from a friend. Put it on your calendar that this week you will make a video of the dog you love lost in the joy of playtime. Tape him destroying a shoebox. See if he will carry a hula hoop. Tape him finding twenty dog biscuits you have hidden in the grass. Let him perform any trick you have taught him.

Time Is Fleeting: Play Now

When he is old and he needs you to lift him onto the bed because all he wants in life now is to lie next to the warmth of you, you will have your younger day play video. The two of you can watch him in action and know that his body may be old, but his heart is as young as ever. You can both close your eyes and dream of a time when he nudged your leg with the ratty tennis ball and nothing on Earth could tire him.

Play hard with him now.

Spring Down The Road With Rover

"Dogs feel very strongly that they should always go with you in the car, in case the need should arise for them to bark violently at nothing right in your ear."
Dave Barry

Hitting the road with Fido in tow is an adventure. Gathering his bare necessities requires lists, stacks, piles and planning. Ensuring your dog's comfort demands packing familiar dog goods brought from home. Safeguarding his health requires protection from overheated cars, riding loose and falling off seats, and checking with his veterinarian for travel health advice.

Dog lovers pack their cars with experience and long lists. One of the best dog moms I know, Amy Thorpe of Fredericksburg, VA, looks out for every contingency of dog comfort when she travels with her dogs, Ranger and Phoebe.

Gotta Have Leashes
Asked how she packs for a dog trip, Thorpe admitted, "What a task. If I'm taking the dogs to the beach or on vacation, this is what I bring: regular 6' leashes and long ones. 20' leads are great for the beach. With these, the dogs swim; you don't have to."

The Dog Crate: Home Away From Home
Thorpe gave thoughtful advice on what to take and what not to take since space should include room for packing for the humans going on the trip, too, advising, "If I'm going away for a week or two, I buy dog food where I'm going. I buy a smaller bag so I don't have to pack it or bring it back. In the car, I have some old sheets and I cover the back seat. When I buy new bath towels, the old ones are saved for the dogs for baths and travel. I bring bottled water with me for longer rides. On the road, I bring dog cookies. This gives the dogs a snack every now and then."

Thorpe reminded me that many dogs need their crate even when they travel. She explained, "My hound, Phoebe, needs to be crated when I'm not home. It's a drag to lug a dog crate back and forth between here and my mom's house [in another state] or the beach. My mom found a second crate at a yard sale and it stays at her house. She takes it up to her beach house for me if I'm coming up, too.

"If you don't travel to places where you can leave a crate, I suggest the plastic-coated wire crates that collapse. They're easy to put together. Save

522

the box because it's easier to pack the crate in the box. Many crates are big enough to put them flat in the back of the truck/SUV/ wagon. You don't want your dog getting his feet tangled in the crate mesh. Cover the box with an old sheet and let the dog lie on the box." Doggy seat belts help uncrated dogs ride safely in one spot.

No Dogs In Hot Cars

Heat was a worry to Thorpe since dogs cannot tolerate heat and do not perspire like humans. But summer temperatures did not stop Phoebe and Ranger from going on the road with their mom.

Thorpe added, "I travel with my dogs all the time. Some trips have lasted eight hours due to weather and traffic. I travel at night as much as possible to avoid traffic and hot sun in the summertime. I always have two car keys so I can leave the motor running and the air conditioning on for them in case I have to run in for just a few minutes to a restroom for myself. I lock the car, leaving the motor running, and the air conditioning on and I can run in. I don't like to leave them in the car anywhere for longer than it takes to run in and out of a restroom. Dogs left alone in a car is just too dangerous."

Sometimes you just can't take a crate. What's a dog parent to do? Cathi Allison, owner of Fredericksburg doggy boutique Dog Dayz, has a solution: "One dog travel accessory that has been a lifesaver is a 20-foot metal, plastic-coated cable with screw-in-the-ground stakes. This tie-out cable allows the dogs to hang out in the yard, on a beach, or campground with the traveling owners. I will never forget a 22-hour drive to Arkansas in a rental car with two bulldogs and a Labrador retriever in the heat of July!"

Cool Coats, Chill Pads
Mary Susan Billingsley travels to agility trials year round and recommends, "'Cool pads' and 'cool coats' for dogs. Soaked in water, they retain cool moisture for up to 12 hours. Many dog goods catalogs have lots of models of these ingenious cooling devices. Portable fans that run on D-cell batteries are favorites for traveling dogs."

Sun Reflector Tarps
Lynn Coppage of Whisperin' Wind Chinese Crested Dogs and Afghans reminded me that "reflector tarps (aluminum sheets, often called 'space blankets') used to cover and keep cars cool "are a must when traveling and stopping in hot weather." She reminded travelers to take clips to attach the reflectors.

Emergency Identification
Dog artist Ruth Dehmel told me of her fear of having an accident with her dogs in the car. She offered this precaution: "In case of a car accident, with the driver becoming hurt, or

unconscious, we should have information in  our wallets and on each dog crate and collar, asking the police to take care of our animals. This wallet card and crate identification sheet should ask police or rescue workers to take the dogs to a veterinarian if needed. Ask that uninjured dogs be taken to a good boarding facility. Give a contact person's information. State that you will be responsible for all veterinary bills and boarding.

All this can be put on an index card, folded and put in a plastic baseball card sleeve. Punch a hole through and twist-tie it on or use a cable tie zip strip. On the front, in red, it should read "In Case Of Accident Please Read."

First Aid Kit For Canines
A doggy first-aid kit is a must, according to Carol Callahan, dog breeder and dog show judge. Callahan advised, "The first-aid kit for dogs contains such things as a can of I.D. [Intestinal Diet] dog food for a dog with intestinal upset, a tube of antibiotic ointment, gauze pads, vet wrap, doggy diarrhea medication, a digital thermometer, paper towels and extra dog towels."

Before you leave town, a trip to your veterinarian to ask what should be stocked in a doggy first-aid kit is a smart precaution. Many human over-the-counter medications are poisonous and deadly to dogs (and cats). Never give a medication that you have not had approved by your vet.

Take Vaccination Records
"Always travel with your dog's vaccination record and a supply of any medications your dog requires. Your vet may be able to suggest a veterinarian in the town you are going to visit. Travel prepared to find a veterinarian in a hurry. Teresa Patton, of Felicity Dog Training School, reminds dog packers, "A fully charged cellphone is welcome if an emergency arises."

Whew! When I asked all my dog-loving friends what they take on their trips, I had no idea the list would be so endless, thought-provoking and heavy! An elastic back support from your favorite orthopedist may be needed before you haul all these necessities to the car.

The traveling dog packing list is longer than this, but I am exhausted at the thought of a trip. My dogs and I are going outside to lie on the grass and contemplate staying right here at home.

The Royal Treatment Your Dog Deserves It

"Any man with money to spend to make the purchase can become a dog's owner. But no man, spend he ever so much coin and food and tact in the effort, may become a dog's Master without the consent of the dog. Do you get the difference? And he whom a dog once unreservedly accepts as a Master is forever that dog's God."
Albert Payson Terhune

Is your dog a queen? Are you aglow in the daily presence of a canine king? Is your dog a queen? Are you aglow in the daily presence of a canine king?

Sure, all dogs need to master basic manners: sit, down, walk on a loose leash. They must come when you call them. Dog lovers own and care for dogs not because we constantly want to command them. We love each of them based on time spent learning and appreciating their unique personalities. We attach ourselves to dogs who share our lives, and add to our happiness as we appreciate the the affection we share with four footed family members. My mother always said, "Love reflects love."

Dogs are fun. Dogs brighten the cares of adulthood. They open a window in the rules of maturity and invite us to play with a regained innocence of childhood.

Dogs will let you dress them up. Dogs will relish any wild concoction of foods you mix together in their bowls and present as a feast. Dogs will rise to the fantasy you create that you are part of a royal family.

Recently, I asked dog owners the question, "Do you treat your dog like royalty?" Owner responses were alive with dog love and recognition that every dog is a unique individual. Here are their stories.

Princess Delia and King Louis,
as told by Charlotte Mills.

We have had several coronations of Kings and Princesses, complete with jewel and fur embellished crowns and capes. The Princess Delia, a dainty Jack Russell Terrier, adorned in her pink peau de soie cape with pink seed pearls, sashayed about her kingdom ruling wisely for many years. King Louis, our dashing brown Miniature Poodle, has been royal since his arrival on the planet. In early puppyhood, when he graced his first puppy class, the teacher admitted that she imagined that we carted him around the house on a gold lame pillow. He loves to wear a gold braided leopard skin cape and filigree crown with sparkling jewels. He cavorts gleefully in all types of doggie clothing. His kingly professional portrait hangs in a place of honor in our living room.

Queen Bailey Rules From Her Chosen Throne,
by Amber Carpenter.

Bailey is known simply as "The Queen." We tried "Queen B" for a while, since she was a Bailey, but the title seemed to trivialize her queenitude. The Queen has a throne and has always had a throne in our house. We call it a "sofa", but Bailey sees it as her private throne. We are not permitted to sit on the throne and heaven help the guest who thinks they might have a shot at the coveted couch. Forget about it. Bailey is a Beardie, so she doesn't have an aggressive

bone in her body. She has other more Beardie-like ways of dealing with would-be throne interlopers. She sits directly in front of them and stares. A quite intimidating stare. One that says, "Move your bloomin' bottom."

Bailey has made known her wishes that her throne remain uncluttered and ready for her royal resting. Once when a large box was left  on her throne while the family left home, Bailey not only removed the box, but proceeded to rearrange much of the room's furnishings to her liking. She harmed nothing, but did redecorate the room with much relocation of things she believed belonged to her. I scolded the Queen and commenced to picking up the redecorated room. Where was Bailey? Lying on her throne, now clear of the offending box. Just lying there staring at me. It was that same sort of look she gives to interlopers. I still get the creeps thinking about it. I've never underestimated Bailey since then. And I've never, ever, cluttered her throne with so much as a sofa cushion.

Two Bassets and a Border Collie Rule,
by Janelle Schopfel

Basset owners refer to themselves as food slaves. To the uninitiated that means, we only live to feed them and do their bidding. Our senior Basset, Dudley, will decide that he wants to sit in a chair that is occupied by a human, even when other seats are available. He will sit next to the chair and level a hard stare at the occupant. If eye contact is made he will whine loudly. He continues vocalizing until the occupant is unnerved and gives up the seat. It is not unusual for us to find ourselves sitting on the floor because Dudley, Penelope and Nigel are in the chairs and on the sofas. So much for maintaining the role of alpha.

King Casey Requires Help Mounting the Throne; Queen Jenny is Served in Fine Human Restaurants,
by Ann Reamy.

Since my canine children are treated like royalty every day, it is hard to point to one specific event. King Casey is a springer-lessql, so we had to find a bench for our bed so that he could be comfortably ensconced on his throne all the time.

For Jenny who deserved to be treated like the Queen she was, we found a very nice restaurant in Savannah, Georgia that allowed us to bring her to dinner with us one night. She sat up at the table and dined on a hot dog while my husband, Chip, and I had a relaxing meal. What a remarkable dog queen she was.

DEVOTED TO DOGS

Queen Saffy Rules From The Mattress Throne,
by Sandra Fischer.

Our Westie, Saffy, is such a queen bitch that she rules the bed. If she wants under the covers, so be it. If she wants to lie in between us with her head in the crook of my husband's arm, so be it. No wonder we didn't have children!

Royal Dogs Require Yummy Foods,
by Jane Shelhorse

My dog "babies" think they can only eat dog food that has human food added to it. This special treatment started when my brother in law was feeding them for us while we were on vacation. When he fed the dogs, he felt that they seemed unhappy with the meal, so he quickly added some chicken broth to their dinners and then hand –fed the smallest dog. They haven't been the same since! Now if you give them plain food they just look at you like, " you must be joking!"

Luxury Car With Heated Seats Required by Queen Maggie Moo, a Shih Tzu,
by Sandra Lay

Queen Maggie prefers a car with heated seats. So far, during puppyhood she enjoyed the comforts of a 560 SEL Mercedes Benz. She has also made her moving throne in one Saab and a Lexus LX450. The Lexus has heated seats but they are leather and her little feet slip when I stop. I bought cheetah print velour covers for both seats so she won't slide. She is not a young Queen now and needs a pillow with an egg crate foam insert that she sits on. Quite regal, you know? She wears a red polar fleece hunting jacket with a hood with matching red boots. The Queen is not too happy about that ensemble. But it works for the snow.

Her Royal Highness, Princess Sibelle: Born To Rule and Doing It,
by her faithful subject Mrs. G. Frank Wagner

As a puppy, Sibelle showed herself at dog shows. Later, she attended obedience classes, had private lessons from award winning coach, Diane Smart, and proceeded to finish her CD, CDX,and UD titles. Sibelle never failed to please but she made it clear that she performed her public appearances because she felt the responsibility of those born royal to go forth and share their special selves with their public. Sibelle's mother realized that Sibelle need do nothing to prove her queenliness. Sibelle has now retired to the country in Spotsylvania where she rules her territory with gentle, yet regal, grace.

Have You Rewarded Your Royal Dog?
Your dog is deserving of all good things. Get her a coat. Make sure she has a lovely, comfortable bed. Stir in a little hot water soup on her daily ration. Long live the Queen. If only the King could live forever. Life with dogs is exactly what we make it. Never be afraid to play.

My Secret Garden:
Memories Become Art for Dog Lovers

"Nothing can come between true friends."
Euripides

Get thee behind me selfishness. I am going to divulge my very best gift giving secret.

Have you ever found a gift that will make people leap up and kiss you? I have discovered a gift that brings remarkable, delighted emotions to anyone who deserves the perfect present.

Mind you, this gift is heavy. You must be careful where you store it until presentation time. You cannot gently plop it into a friend's lap or onto a birthday gift laden table. Have a bad back or arthritic hands? Enlist carrying help from a friend or family member when you deliver this best gift on Earth.

Every Wish On Your List Fulfilled
Dog lovers, cat lovers, horse lovers, flower lovers. Everyone on your gift list can be taken

 534

care of with artwork from local artist and crafts person, Karen Joos.

By day, Joos educates area children at R. E. Lee Elementary in Spotsylvania County. Evenings, weekends, holidays, snow days, after her homework grading and lesson planning are complete, Joos makes art.

Dog Faces Shine In Stained Glass

Stained glass art. Once you behold a dog or cat captured forever in a stained glass stepping stone carved and cast with devotion by Karen Joos you will want one for yourself. Next, you will begin making your birthday and Christmas gift list for everyone you know who adores a pet.

Casey Ramey is a big black eyed, gentle Springer Spaniel. I have known him almost since he was born. Since his arrival in Fredericksburg, he has demonstrated impeccable taste in dog clothes, sunglasses, restaurants that welcome canine diners, and has discerning taste searching out life's treasures. It came as no surprise when I received a picture of the dapper, handsome Casey immortalized perfectly in a stained glass stepping stone.

My mother taught me not to covet the treasures of others, but laying eyes on Casey's glorious image in stone left me breathless with envy. "Who made this amazing work or art?" I asked Casey's mother, Ann Reamy.

Ann Reamy, has a reputation for generosity and therefore did not selfishly try and keep Casey's portraitist to herself. "Karen Joos," Reamy shared and sent me Joos' e-mail address.

Sharing My Favorite Artist

I cannot in good conscience keep this gift source to myself any longer. My advice is to seek out Joos and get yourself and all your favorite dogs and cats onto her list to be preserved and celebrated in stained glass and concrete.

My first stone was of my own puppy Gabriel. This stone caused me a crisis of conscience. I  had also ordered several stones as Christmas gifts for dog mom friends. When my Gabriel stone arrived in November, so gorgeous that I wanted to drive it around town showing it to everyone I knew, I did not want other gift recipients on my list to realize just how dazzling a gift I had in mind for them. It was agony to guard my surprise , but I kept my Gabriel stone wrapped in a table cloth, hidden under my dining room table, for six weeks. Daily, more than once, I would unwrap and admire Gabriel's perfectly captured face.

Friends Flip For Stained Glass Faces

Finally the time came to present the Christmas gift stones. First, my usually low key, dignified poodle mother friend was clearly moved to ecstasy to view her wee brown pup captured with every hair in place.

Next, I presented another dog lover mom with a stained glass stone of her adorable Jack Russell Terrier, Doris Day Doodle. The Doodle is known to wear fancy hats. Lo, in the Doodle stone, Jones reproduced a flowered hat. Doodle's surprised mother was moved to tears. (See terrier and hat in concrete for yourself at Joos' website: *www. jonesstones.com.*

Thank You Kisses Will Come
A few weeks later, I gave a very sedate friend a stepping stone of her majestic black and white Corgi, Danny Cadillac. This friend leapt off the sofa and ran across the room and kissed me.

To own a Karen Joos stepping stone is better than a Van Gogh hanging in your dining room. Move over Rodin, a Joos lawn decoration will give everyone visiting your home real art to think about.

Art In The Rain?
How could I convince myself that my lovely Gabriel stone really could go outdoors for rain and sun to fall upon his perfect face? Joos assured me that she has stones made years ago out in the yard, holding up with no wear and tear from the elements. Recently, I moved my Gabriel stone to the front porch. I am a careless, disinterested housekeeper. I need art near the front door to divert the eye as guests enter dog haven.

According to Joos, she has been, "working in glass for over 15 years. I started with small window panels, then graduated to large tiffany glass windows. About five years ago, I began to see garden stones at the glass shops, arts and crafts fairs, and even in stained glass catalogues where I order my supplies."

Joos continued, "I started with flowers and birds and then moved onto our furry friends. There was a good market for them with my colleagues at R.E. Lee Elementary School. Then, through word of mouth and the Fredericksburg Arts and Crafts Festival, I began to get orders from the surrounding areas. I've designed and created over one hundred and fifty different stones with quite a variety of animals, dog and cat breeds."

Juke and Barney Model For Mom
Jooes is a pet lover and has two dogs of her own who model for stepping stones. She told me, "I am the proud owner of a very grateful Beagle, Barney. I adopted him from the Spotsylvania County Animal Shelter nine years ago. I also have Juke, my very spoiled and lovable four year old fawn Boxer."

Every Stone Has A Story
Creating lasting memories in stained glass art allows Joos to talk with many pet owners. She shared with me that, "The saddest part of my craft is when I am making a stepping stone for a family whose pet has passed on. It's so hard for me to look at those pictures, those eyes, and

think about all the years that wonderful dog gave it's owners."

Once you have a stone that Joos has created, you begin to make lists of all the dogs and pets you know who need to be captured forever. This seems to happen often to the artist.

Joos laughed and agreed, telling me, "I was working on two black cats for a lady from Stafford. I've made nine stones for her to date! She was sending digital photos to me via email, and I didn't realize that 'Grey' and 'Frank' were two different cats until I got seriously into the details of their extremely similar markings. After 'Grey' was completely finished, I realized that I put the wrong colored eyes on him. They were an emerald green and should have been tan. As a result, I had to chisel them out and make new ones. Funny thing is, the owners didn't

even notice when I sent them the pictures. I'm a stickler for details."

In order to make a pet live forever in stone, Joos gets to know the pet's individual story. She told me about a beagle friend named Clyde, "I made a stone of a one-eyed Beagle. Our neighbor down the street had a seventeen year old beagle named Clyde. Clyde had developed cancer and his dear parents took him for weekly chemotherapy treatments. Clyde took it in stride and never complained. He had lost his eye because of cancer. I decided to surprise Clyde's owner with a stone of Clyde, with his eye sewn shut. I left it on her porch one summer morning. That evening, she let me know how thrilled she was with this quite unique gift. Where else could you find anything with a one-eyed Beagle? The following Christmas, Clyde passed away, but his stone is now a small monument to a very large and sweet dog."

Splendid art makes our hearts beat faster and takes our spirit on flights of memory and imagination. Karen Joos captures the magic shining in the faces dogs who have loved us. Her stepping stones transform a flower bed, walkway, or porch into a treasure gallery.

New Year's Resolutions For My Dog

"'Hi' I said. She came over, licked my hand discretely, allowed herself to be scratched for a time, chased her tail in a dignified circle, lay down again. I remember thinking, 'There are times when God puts a choice in front of you.' I often had such thoughts back then. We took the dog."
Stanley Bing

Why make New Year's resolutions? Such resolves can depress you. You may sit and obsess over shortfalls and personality pitfalls. You may ponder your habits with guilt and dissatisfaction.

This year, examine the things you could do to make life better for your dog. My dogs,

541

Quinnton, Vivien and Gabriel, and I offer you our New Year's resolutions. Exercise lifts the spirits, enhances health and takes the edge off most worrisome behaviors.

Dogs Deserve To Play Hard

Unless my dog has had 30 minutes of hard exercise that day, I will never complain about any of his behaviors. After all, he is a dog. Dogs were born to run, and to dig and chew and chase and bring home prey and frolic with wild abandon.

I promise not to expect him to behave calmly like a small, quiet human. If I cannot take a long walk, I will get the tennis racket and wham the tennis ball across the fenced yard over and over until my own arm is tired and he has retrieved until he is ready to lie down and rest.

A Dog Mom Looks After Her Dog's Health

I will call my veterinarian this week and make sure that my dog's immunizations are current. He will either get a titer to check his immunity levels or he will get a vaccine. I will take no chances that the next germ he meets will make him sick.

I will make an appointment for the doctor to look in his ears, eyes, mouth, and at every lump, bump and furry part to make sure he is healthy.

Stimulate Your Dog's Mind

Dogs are curious, good at problem-solving and looking for fun. Most of the behaviors that get them into trouble with humans (digging, barking, chewing) develop when the dog is bored to death and inventing ways to entertain himself. To stimulate and entertain my dog, I will be a more involved companion.

At least once a week, I will put him in the car and we will have an outing that is fun for the dog. Maybe we will find a park and look for wild animals. Squirrels, birds and rabbits will offer a chance to see if my dog is under good control on leash. If not, we will have a short obedience session on "sit" and "walk on a loose leash."

Until I take the time and make the commitment to enroll him in obedience school, and teach him how to behave in a mannerly way, I will take every bit of blame for all his rowdy habits and lack of control.

543

My Dog Will Be Safe In His Crate

Every dog needs a dog crate (cage, kennel). A crate-trained dog is a miraculous beast.

A crate is a haven of rest when unruly children visit and yank his ears and tail. A crate offers relief from company who think they are dog lovers but may worry the dog unmercifully.

A crate is the place to put a dog who has been to the veterinarian and had surgery or any treatment that the doctor's orders were "take him home and have him rest." Your veterinarian knows that a crate-trained dog will be more likely to follow doctor's orders and get well faster. A crate-trained dog also will be much more comfortable in the cage at the veterinarian's office, if he ever has to go for surgery or spend a day for treatment.

A crate is every puppy or un-housebroken dog's haven of protection from the big overstimulating world of being left loose in the house unsupervised.

A crate can be a beautiful thing. Every dog deserves a crate.

If your dog has not been crate-trained, begin training him to like his crate gradually. Tie the door open for a few days. Feed him with the door open, with his food toward the back of the crate so he must at least stand in there and have the pleasant experience of eating. After a few days, close the door after you have thrown in delicious treats and let him run in. Sit near him for a few minutes while you praise gently. Increase time in the crate every day.

Place the crate in the room you will be in. Never use the crate as a punishment. The dog who is crate-trained learns discipline, feelings of safety and the comfort of a place of his own. Oodles of types of crates and indoor exercise pens can be seen at *www.petedgecom, www. rcsteele.com, www.cherrybrook.com* and many other dog wholesale distributors.

I will be an owner my dog can depend on. My dogs come and stare into my face every afternoon at 4:30. I could throw away my watch with complete confidence that they would come and get me at 4:30 p.m. to rattle food bowls and make the hot water for the dog food "soup."

A Dog Depends On A Schedule
He Is What He Eats
To be fed on time and to be taken outside to relieve himself I will learn to read a dog food label. Since dog food is the primary nutrition my dog is going to get, the food he eats now builds the dog that I hope will live for many years as my best companion.

I will not feed my dog any foods that are not made from human-grade ingredients. If a preservative has been shown to contribute to cancer in humans; even if not proved to be a carcinogen for dogs, I will know the names of all questionable preservatives and additives and I will avoid feeding them to my dog. I will feed my dogs foods and treats plainly labeled as preserved with tocopherols, Vitamin E, sodium ascorbate or Vitamin C.

I will ask dog breeders, trainers and veterinarians whose dogs I know have lived long, had shining coats, are not overweight, and are beloved, "What do you feed your dog?" I will ask them, "Why did you pick that food?" A long list of "premium" dog foods can be found on the veterinary Website: *www.altvetmed.com/premfood.html.*

After I find the premium food that is full of sound nutrients and healthful ingredients, I will not add anything to it. I will not give the dog extra vitamins and supplements. I will not guess about what might be a healthy product to add since I am not a veterinarian and I do not have a degree in canine nutrition.

A Fat Dog Wobbles
I do know that every elderly dog I have had to part with from this life has left me due to hips and knees wearing out. I will do my part of keeping my dog trim and never fat to help him live as long as he possibly can, mobile and pain-free, for as long as possible.

EVERYDAY AND HOLIDAYS

Fattening the dog because he loves to eat and we cannot resist his desires is not an act of love. I would delight in a diet of French fries and chocolate pecan pie. I realize my lifespan would be cut short if I fed all my desires without an eye toward good nutrition. The dog needs me to look after his waistline even if I ruin my own.

Finally, if my veterinarian puts my dog on any veterinary prescription diet, I will feed it exactly as the vet instructs. Anything added to a prescription diet changes the nutrients and may make my dog sick. I will not find comfort for myself by feeding my dog human foods when he has been placed on a prescription diet. I will give my dog a New Year's party. I'll decorate and take pictures and send up hallelujahs and thanksgiving for the dog who pads behind my every step.

I Will Celebrate My Dog All Year Long

Try what I do and invite all his human friends, but not any strange dogs who are not his buddies. Sit around for a few hours admiring your dog. Take a picture with each friend for making a New Year's scrapbook. Rub him and throw the fleece chew man. Invite him into laps. Just love him.

It's a new year. Here's one more chance to deserve the dog who adores you.

Dogs Eggscited About Easter

"A little madness in the Spring is wholesome, even for the king."
Emily Dickinson

My friend Zack asked for a ham in his Easter basket.

His wise, canine nutrition–savvy mother told him, "No, Zack, ham is bad for a little Cocker boy."

Zack is going to find "a stuffed squeaky toy, treats and colored milk bones" in the basket that the Easter bunny leaves this year.

Last year, Zack celebrated Easter with "a big family gathering." Zack volunteered to assist his dad, David, with hiding the plastic eggs for an egg hunt. Zack's mom, Diana Chappell, confessed, "Zack grabbed the eggs out of their hiding places as fast as David could hide them. This year we are going to the beach for Easter and are planning an egg hunt in the sand. I will fill all the plastic eggs with milk bones."

Zack is going to have a great time dashing and digging in the sand as he celebrates spring.

What's In Your Dog's Basket?

Dog moms and dads treasure memories of Easter baskets assembled for a special dog. My first springer spaniel, Bonnie, was a tiny pup when she tore open her first made-by-mom Easter basket.

One red-white-and-blue dumbbell-shaped toy brought Bonnie years of delight. I am sure it cost less than a dollar. It remained her favorite all her life. For over 10 years, until she was too arthritic to toss and chase the toy, she would find it and play and play and play. That toy came to be known as the "Easter Bunny Bonnie Bone."

When she died, at nearly 16 years old, we placed her dear ashes in a brass inlaid teak chest along with the treasured toy. A day does not pass that I do not stop for a few seconds and place my hand on the chest with her ashes. When I think of Easter I see a tiny, wild-with-joy spaniel pup dashing over grass, carpet, beds, and flower pots, her little puppy jaws locked on the Bonnie bone.

Toys, Biscuits, Fancy Collars

If you have not prepared your dog's Easter basket, it is never too late. Even if you wait until all the

549

DEVOTED TO DOGS

Easter supplies go on sale at half-price, your dog will not yawn and turn away, complaining, "Don't you know Easter has passed?" Dogs are like that. Always grateful.

There are usual dog Easter basket treats: dog biscuits, squeaky fur toys, easily digestible chews, a ball or two, homemade egg-shaped dog biscuits.

Perhaps you will add a few luxury items to the basket. My dogs have opinions on which dog items are coveted.

A Luxury Brush?

My Bearded Collie, Vivien Scarlett O'Hara, saved her pennies. She is paid for assisting in my obedience classes. Vivien bought herself

a Mason Pearson brand, real natural bristle hairbrush. These brushes are actually human quality brushes, made in England. Probably, your own grandmother brushed her hair with a Mason Pearson. Dog lovers all over the world covet these luxurious brushes. I found mine by performing a Mason Pearson™ hairbrush search on the Internet. Fifteen human and dog supply catalogs appeared for my brush shopping pleasure.

Be Picky 'Bout Your Rawhide

My youngest, Gabriel Izodore Keanu, when he is is not curled up with me watching videos of our favorite action idol Keanu Reeves, is often found staring at the cabinet where the dog chews rest. Because some rawhide chews are manufactured in countries that do not have the same rules governing chemicals used to cure dog snacks, Gabriel chews only small, easily digestible hide treats made in the U.S.A. We buy thin, safely chewable and digestible rawhides that have been treated with a tooth-cleaning enzyme. We buy these at our veterinarian's hospital.

Different Dogs Need Different Treats

Gabriel can stare at the treat cabinet for as long as he wants, but he only gets one chew every few days. His sister, Vivien, cannot have any rawhide at all or she suffers a badly upset digestive tract. Every dog has a different reaction to foods and treats. Report all gastric upsets to your own veterinarian for professional advice.

The Older The Dog
The More Special The Easter Gifts

The senior dog who rules here, Quinnton Benjamin Pig, did not get an Easter basket this year. 'The Pig' asked for and received a big, ultra-suede dog bed. Shaped like a cushy doughnut, with a bouncy pillow center, Quinnton staked his claim immediately on his new bed. After all, when a dog boy is 9 years old, his comfort-driven opinions should be respected.

An unforeseen benefit to the new bed is that we place it on our own bed at night and the

551

restless Pig is corralled into one spot. No longer do we wake with a dog foot up our noses or hot, breathy canine kisses in the ear before sunrise. We call the bed the "Pig Boat" and the last human to leave the family room at night transports the Pig Boat onto the bed. When the lights go out,

the Pig becomes our watchful captain at the foot of our bed as his younger brother and sister sleep quietly in their crates, also in the bedroom. Another family rule here: only the senior dog sleeps in the big bed in the little boat. If your dog does not own a comfy dog crate with a luxuriously deep soft cushion, surely you must get one. A dog who rests nicely and happily in his crate is a better traveler, rests and recovers nicely if they ever have to spend the night at the veterinarian, and will adjust more calmly when they must be boarded and confined to a small space. Every nice dog deserves a cozy dog crate that smells like home.

If a dog has a few behavior quirks, here are some quick-fix behavior items that a dog mom or dad could add to the Easter basket.

Maybe A No-Pull Halter?
If a dog has not learned to stop yanking his mom's shoulder out of the joint as they hurl themselves down the street, a no-pull harness could change

the human's life and alter her opinion on pain-free dog walking. No-pull harnesses are designed to loop under the pulling dog's armpits (forgive me for anthropomorphizing dog anatomy) making yanking the mother uncomfortable for the dog. Dog teaches himself to ease back and stop pulling like an untrained mule. (That is not to cast aspersions on mules. I know a few perfectly behaved mules.) Many brand names can be found. Sporn™ is a manufacturer that comes to mind.

Don't Forget Balls

For avid chasing and retrieving dogs (Labradors, Goldens, Chessies, Ridgebacks, Rotties, terriers, shepherds, spaniels and pointers, to name just a few) there is a device that will hurl a ball, at forceful speeds, far across the yard. Some of these devices look like giant slingshots. Ask your favorite dog shop salesperson where to find one of these magic throwing tools.

My favorite lazy-mother retrieving technique is to stand on the deck with a tennis racket and lob balls into the woods for my dogs. With practice, you can drink your morning coffee, lounge in your dressing gown and read "The Free Lance-Star" while stopping intermittently to whack the tennis ball.

Dogs love this. Suddenly, you will be an action hero mom. But a fenced yard is a must.

Don't do another thing until you make your dog an Easter basket. Now.

Dog Mothers Share Wisdom And Love

"The essence of love is kindness."
Robert Louis Stevenson

Miss Bean, whom Meg Raymond of Stafford, Virginia calls her 'beaglet', is 13 years old but still sings for her supper, and thinks frozen green beans are yummy.

Peer into the hearts of many a woman and you will find the love and friendship of a good dog. Caring for her dog is not work; it is pleasure. Sharing her life with her dog is not a responsibility; it is a privilege.

Do you jolt awake to the faint tippy–tap of dog toenails by the bedroom door? Do you open your eyes, delighted to find an expectant dog staring at you, willing you to wake? Does a tight, fluttering, panicked sensation grip your stomach when you are trapped in traffic and know your dog is waiting patiently behind the front door, wondering why you are late? If the needs, health

 554

and happiness of your dog are always high on your priority list, you must be a dog mother.

Don't bother to tell a dog mom that she is "not that dog's mother." You waste your breath. The dog mom may be too polite to set you straight about her steadfast attachment to her dog, but anyone who does not acknowledge the depth of a dog mother's feelings for her dog is traveling down a short road toward losing a relationship with the dog mother.

Never ask or demand that a woman choose between her dog and a new human in her life. A wise woman will kiss the demanding suitor goodbye faster than she can zip open a can of dog food.

Recently, I had the privilege to hear two women describe the joy that being a dog mother brings to their lives. Their eloquence made me very proud to be a dog mother.

Miss Bean
Tiny Beagle Queen
As told by Meg Raymond

Miss Bean is my tiny Beagle girl. So tiny, that I call her my "beaglet." Miss Bean weighs 15 pounds, is 13 years old and is getting very creaky. She's had back surgery and has always been somewhat stiff.

Her favorite activities are eating and sleeping. She is still incredibly enthusiastic about mealtime and will bark imperiously for me to "hurry up!"

555

DEVOTED TO DOGS

Her little mouth makes a perfect "O" and her front feet come up off the ground when she barks. I love to hear her sing for her supper.

I feed her a big handful of green beans (either frozen or no-salt-added canned) with her evening meal so she doesn't notice that she's getting less actual food. With her advanced age, bad back and level of (in)activity, it's important to keep her weight down. Green beans fill her up. She thinks frozen green beans are dog biscuits and eats them as "treats."

Miss Bean's remaining teeth are worn to nubbins. She gets things stuck between her teeth: grass roots, bits of dog biscuit. At least twice a day, I look in her mouth and run my fingers around her teeth to see if anything is stuck. She does not like this at all!

Her favorite playthings are postcard inserts from magazines and catalogs. Sometimes, I "accidentally" drop them on the floor for her to find. She holds them between her front paws and rips them. I think she likes the tearing sound.

EVERYDAY AND HOLIDAYS

She gets regular "massages" so I can check for lumps and bumps. She had a cancerous growth removed from her lip a month ago and has recovered well. Her smile is a little crooked and she drools a tiny bit.

Miss Bean doesn't always like to "go potty" outside when the weather is too cold or too rainy or if she is just too tired. At those times, she prefers to use the "indoor facilities," even though I've tried to explain to her that we really don't have indoor facilities. Sometimes, she just can't (or won't) hold it all night or all day while I'm at work. She will use a wee-wee pad (sold at pet stores as housebreaking pads, or puppy training pads). I usually have a wee-wee pad in each bathroom for her to use.

It's hard to see Miss Bean getting older, creakier and slower. Her dramatic "Cleopatra eyeliner" is fading. Her face is getting whiter. Sometimes, her back legs just give out and she will either fall over or abruptly sit down. She is grumpy more often and dislikes having her routines disrupted. If I stay up late, she very pointedly tells me that it is "time to go to bed!"

She doesn't like to get up in the morning, and will blink and stretch until she is sure that breakfast is in the offing. Sometimes, she is still sound asleep when I get home from work.

She is my heart.

DEVOTED TO DOGS

When Her Dog Worries
The Dog Mom Worries, Too
As told by Cynthia Setliff

My Labrador Retriever, Luke, is nearly 13 years old. As a young and a middle-aged dog, he was fearless and carefree. Nothing bothered Luke.

 During the past year, Luke has become worried about sounds that the young Luke never noticed. Thunderstorms, wind blowing, the beeping noises that fire detectors and carbon monoxide detectors make when their batteries run low. Any sound or activity that Luke perceives as being out of the ordinary causes him to pace the house behind every step I take, obviously worried, and frantic to keep me in his sights.

Luke will follow me all day from one room to another. I have tripped, fallen and stumbled trying to avoid knocking into him or falling on top of him. Luke is obviously worried about being left alone.

For our family, we want to be with Luke just as much as he wants to be with us. We recently purchased a very big utility vehicle so that we would have enough room for Luke to join the whole family on trips. The car salesman must have thought we were crazy when the first thing

558

we told him was "We are looking for a vehicle large enough to make a large, elderly Labrador comfortable on long trips."

I love Luke more than words could ever express. I do not consider him a dog, really. In my heart, Luke is my child. I want him to be as comfortable as possible for as many years as he can be with our family. I know there will never, ever be another dog like Luke.

Buy a Mother's Day card, and give a bag of biscuits As you choose Mother's Day cards and remembrance gifts for the mothers on your list, don't forget to include dog mothers.

Demonstrate to dog moms that you understand the feelings that dog mothers hold so gently, yet steadfastly. in their hearts. Invite a special dog to rest his precious head on your lap this Mother's Day. Love the mother by loving her dog.

Don't Spook Your Dog This Halloween

Who knows what dangers lurk on Halloween night for unsuspecting owners and their canine companions?

Holidays can be festive or frightening for the family dog. A very well socialized dog may enjoy dressing up in costume and being a part of the fun. A shy dog may be terrified by the noise and commotion of doorbells and hobgoblins invading their territory to take away candy.

Precautions are necessary to safeguard your dog and to prepare for a happy Halloween.

Beware The Open Door.

Expecting all children to close your front door is just about as likely as a visit from the Great Pumpkin. Don't count on it. Your dog could slip out and be in danger in the time it takes to put your hand in the candy bowl and admire the little visitor's costume. If you have any doubt that you can keep one eye on the dog and one eye on the costumed kids, better keep Bitsy on a leash or place her safely in another part of the house.

Watch Out For The Door Charger.

If your dog is a door charger or escape artist, you know it. Take action to protect this little devil from herself before the door flies open. One of the most dreaded notations on a veterinarian's chart is "HBC", or, "Hit By Car". Halloween is the one holiday that truly increases the number of times your dog could escape. If you have a dog that loves to dart out the door and is happy to show you she is deaf to all pleas to "come", don't wait for her to try make her get-a-way. Put her on a leash and keep the leash in your hand, or confine her safely in her crate or another room.

Who Left The Gate Open?

Many of us have learned, to our great horror, that a fabulous fence is no protection at all if everyone who comes in the gate does not close the gate. My own fence gate has a big sign on each side begging, "Please Close The Gate." I am glad to say that my UPS man, Lorin Lee is a dog loving angel who always reads the sign and closes the gate. He is one of the few who realize that gates are very important to help dogs live to ripe old age.

I decide whether to call any service provider (plumbers, electricians, carpet cleaners, etc.) back again by whether or not they close my gate. I don't care how great their work is if I have to worry, "Will my dog be dead in the street after they leave?"

Spooky Goblins In Halloween Regalia Can Cause Dog Panic And Fear.

Adults and children squealing with delight as each

costumed child arrives often scares the weewee out of unsuspecting dogs. If your dog is cowering, barking in a frenzy, jumping off the furniture, lunging onto the visiting children, or weewee'ing on the rug, he is not telling you this is a good time. He is begging to be saved from the unusual and frightening invasion of his territory that Halloween brings. Pay attention to his body language.

A frightened dog will only become more frightened with each dose of doorbell ringing and hobgoblin entry. Put this dog in a safe place. Turn on the television or the radio. Turn it up loudly and let him lay low until the All Hollows invasion has ceased.

Extra Vigilance For Pups and Senior Dogs

Very young puppies and frail, elderly dogs must never be subjected to the evening of constant visitors. While humans may be delighted by the parade of Halloween creatures, dogs who do not understand or do not feel up to the excitement, may find the evening to be one of torture.

This is not the night to socialize the untrained dog to like little children. If you have a dog who is normally well behaved but is nervous in crowds or when over stimulated by noise or high activity, this is not the night to 'help him come out of his shell.'

Respect the dog's natural tendencies. If you have a terrier that believes barking is his calling in life, don't promote the habit by letting him bark to his heart's content. If you have a herding breed, perhaps a Sheltie or Border Collie that likes to herd children from place to place and perhaps nip the clothes of moving humans, this is not the night to let that dog act as greeter.

All dogs are different in their preferences and greeting styles. Make sure your dog is up to the task of door person if he is near the door on Halloween.

Polite Door Sitting Skills

Halloween offers a ripe opportunity to work on "sit–stay" at the door with the trained dog. There are calm dogs who can sit calmly when a doorbell rings and who will remain sitting to be petted or ignored by visitors. If you are blessed

563

with one of these special , well trained creatures, I suggest you stop reading for a moment and go and kiss him on the head and give him a biscuit. The dog that can sit or lie quietly while visitors come and go is a rare treasure.

Squealing And Shouting May Bring Out The Beast In Some Of The Nicest Dogs.

Bear in mind that even the most well behaved dog has a breaking point. Nice , quiet children may cause him no apprehension. A swarm of squealing, jumping, door slamming hobgoblins could try the patience and control of even the most gentle dog. Any time you think your dog has had enough of any activity, don't press him to the breaking (or barking, lunging or running away) point. Anticipate situations that are no fun for your dog and get him out of them right that minute.

If You Eat Too Much, You'll Awake With The Tummy Ache.

The day after Halloween, many dog mothers or dog fathers will be calling the veterinarian describing symptoms of dogs who raid the children's Halloween loot. From the mild discomfort of a tummy ache, the work intensive clean up of diarrhea on your best rug, or the more serious danger of dogs poisoned by chocolate, the day after Halloween can be perilous to dogs. Dogs feel about most foods like I feel about pasta, grits and potato chips: they will eat with delight and abandon and have no little voice in their head to warn them they are in dangerous territory. Think of the times you have over eaten to the point of pain and regret. Realize that dogs have no regret.

Be warned. Put all Halloween candy, treats. and toys in places that are secure from dogs. For many years I had the privilege to be loved by a brilliant, problem solving Springer Spaniel named Bonnie. She loved chocolate. She could open any cabinet door or drawer that her nose could find and her paw could reach. She once climbed onto the back or a wing backed chair and removed a five pound box of chocolate off a mantle over a fireplace. Her desire and her sense of smell were relentless. She spent Christmas that year with her veterinarian and was a very, very sick girl. I felt guilty and she could have died. Make sure your dog cannot indulge in his own Halloween party while you sleep.

Decorations: Dog-friendly Or Dog-dangerous?
Dogs can knock over all kinds of jack-o'-lanterns and decorations. Candles can be dangerous to the curious dog who could be burned investigating with his nose or start a fire.

Dogs often like the smell of party favors and Halloween ornaments and may eat or chew them. Consider your dog's likely interest and reaction to anything you place in his environment. Tell yourself he is as smart and as aware of safety as a two year old human child and treat him that way. Never blame the dog. Think about

565

possible dog problems before he discovers he is in trouble.

Dressing Up The Dog.

Some dogs love to put on clothes and be admired. I once knew a Jack Russell Terrier named Delia, who had so many fancy outfits that she required her own large steamer trunk when she traveled. Admirers sent her hats, velvet dresses and every imaginable finery. On holidays , Delia would come to visit me and when she left , I would feel the need to re think my own wardrobe. What style she had.

She made me want to dress up my own spaniels. They leaned to submit to wearing clothes, but when I turned my back they ripped each others ensembles off and tried to eat them. I regret to admit that in the frenzy of undressing and ingesting each other's fashions, sometimes fights broke out.

Not all dogs are born to wear clothes. If you want your dog to dress up, it is best to begin this activity early. Begin with accessories like hats. Don't rush out and buy an elaborate costume for your dog who has never sported clothes. He will be frightened or insulted and you will be angry or defeated.

EVERYDAY AND HOLIDAYS

If you do have a dog that dresses up for Halloween, make sure he can see clearly around any head gear. Make sure he can answer all calls of nature. A nice outfit is spoiled if one cannot conveniently go to the bathroom.

Don't Forget To Get Out The Camera
Your friends and relatives will be delighted to buy a frame and add your dog to their gallery of loved ones.

Give A Dog Halloween Party
Many well socialized, outgoing, well-behaved dogs are invited to dog parties. My dogs have hosted many dog parties and we have all lived to tell about it. If it is too cold to hold the festivities in a fenced yard, we suggest a tiled or other waterproof floor. Even if the dogs have never had a housebreaking lapse, dogs do not have the same table manners as humans. Food will definitely be served on the floor.

Try not to serve anything so delicious that jealousy or food guarding is likely to break out. Rawhide, juicy bones, pig parts and cow delicacies are best sent home in individual doggy bags. Give out small, quickly eaten treats and have many bowls of water available for guests. Be sure to invite dogs who have met before and who are known to be gentle around other dogs. Dog brothers or sisters who are known to be shy, to need to have the last word (or growl), or who have not had a few obedience lessons are best left resting at home. Send them a token of the festivities .

Prepare This Year For Next Year

If your dog is not ready this year to greet guests or attend a dog party, make a list of commands and tasks you want to teach him right now. Begin your obedience and socialization for your dog this week. Every dog can be trained. No dog is too old. All dogs are smart enough to be the dog of your dreams.

Begin slowly and know that your dog will find more joy in being your constant, well trained companion than in anything else he can do. Try teaching him something new every week. By next Halloween he will behave like an angel.

Wise Dogs Tell
Me Christmas
Photography Secrets

"No matter how long we exist, we have our memories. Points in time which time itself cannot erase."
Anne Rice

Speaking in barks, soulful glances and expressive tail wagging, dogs have revealed secrets for a joyful Christmas portrait.

Dogs expect to star on the family Christmas card. They want to brag to other dogs while out in public cavorting and sniffing. Is your dog not watching when you open your Christmas cards and 'ooh' and 'aaah' over the precious holiday photograph of Aunt Margot's new Poodle?

DEVOTED TO DOGS

Would you make your lovely dog sit and glumly wonder, "Why am I not the star of Christmas cards and internet searches?"

Lights, camera, action are the three necessities to the perfect pet portrait.

Light is the key to spectacular photographs
 Make sure that light, whether from the sun or lots of lamps, is behind you and the camera. Never take the picture with the sun streaming into the camera lens.

Forget taking pictures with the dog posed in front of a window. All that light glaring behind the dog will confuse most cameras. You will not get the great shot you think you saw. Remember, light needs to be shining on the dog's face.

Taking the dog outside for photographs is the best insurance against the dreaded and despised 'red eye'. Early morning or late afternoon will produce most pleasant light to close down the red eye and still light the dog nicely.

The further the flash from the lens opening, the more insurance against the 'red eye'. An auto focus camera, set to automatically choose the best lens opening and shutter speed, will take your attention off technical details. Your efforts will be focused on keeping the dog posed and attentive.

Small point and shoot cameras with the flash on the body of the camera almost always

 570

produce red eye on flash pictures taken indoors. Again, take the dog outside for his Christmas portrait.

Red eye can be reduced by taking the picture from an angle, instead of dead on flashing into the dog's eyes. If you must take the picture indoors with a point and shoot camera , try to take the picture during daylight hours. Turn on every light in the room. Have a high intensity lamp on your desk, by your bed or in your workshop? Focus the high intensity light directly into the dog's face. Not close enough to blind the willing subject. Just close enough to light her eyes brilliantly.

Action. You don't want action

The best behaved dog may not sit still long enough to capture the perfect Christmas pose. Attach a lightweight leash and tie that leash to a solid object. For goodness sake, not the Christmas tree, or disaster may follow.

Since the best pictures may be taken out doors, attach the leash to a nice leafy tree or shrub. Let the dog walk forward to the end of the leash. Position yourself at an angle that hides the leash.

Props, decorations and costumes are needed

Some dog enthusiasts feel it is demeaning to the dog to decorate her with fine clothes and elaborate jewelry. Humbug. My dogs and I believe that is scarcity thinking. We say live life extravagantly. We subscribe to the "too much is not enough" theory in jewels, couture, and worldly goods. Vivien and I are material girls, living in a material world. Sure, we want to be spiritually evolved, high minded intellectuals. But we plan to do that while covered in jewels, dressed to perfection.

Gather every decoration you own that is unbreakable and festive into a large plastic trash bag and haul these treasures out into the yard. Fake Christmas greenery and flowers, sparkling garlands, plastic tree decorations. Festoon a tree and the surrounding ground with these bits of finery and leave a spot to position the dog.

Devise a Christmas costume for the dog

Hats are nicely attached with long pipe cleaners that can be bent securely under the dog's chin. Festive baby bibs will festoon a proud canine chest. child size glittering headbands will crown a dog noggin. Anything you want the dog to wear must be attached to the little dear. Do not expect her to sit like a rock and

have an unattached chapeau remain on her lovely moving head. Dazzling candle rings from the craft or greenery shops make wonderful dog crowns. Attach shining Christmas tree decorations or sparkling garland to the collar.

Round up a photography assistant

Promise this person that they may use all your props and photograph their own handsome dog if they will help you with your holiday photo shoot.

Bring food

Delicious, stinky, dog attention riveting food. High smelling cheeses. Chicken hot dogs. Yum. Have the assistant stand behind you holding a delectable treat over your head. Get down on your knees for eye level pictures. See those canine eyes sparkle in anticipation of the treat that is coming after the picture is snapped. A dab of peanut butter on a panting tongue will close the mouth nicely for a few seconds.

DEVOTED TO DOGS

Make sure the dog is perfectly groomed before the photo session. Clean corners of eyes. Fluff up ears and chests and tails.

Have fun!
Do not even consider a holiday dog photo session if you know your patience is short-fused.

Dogs have asked me to remind you that they are enjoy being preserved on film primarily because it brings them such fun attention and pleases the dog mom or dad to share the Christmas portrait with adoring friends and relatives.

If you think you will be impatient, or loose your calm dog loving demeanor, by all means take the dog for a holiday light viewing drive all over town and county and forget all about dog Christmas photography!

Vivien, Quinnton and Gabriel challenge you and your dog to produce your most spectacular Christmas portrait ever.

Gather your pictures while ye may.... Christmas comes but once a year.

Feels Like A Holiday!
Whole Lot Of
Clicking Goin' On

"Tis sweet to know there is an eye
will mark our coming and look
brighter when we come."
Lord Byron

Dog obedience teachers, who once prided themselves on their ability to teach pet owners to jerk choke chains and sling recalcitrant dogs into heel position, are now teaching timing, clicking, and hot dog rewards.

Dogs are breathing sighs of relief. Yip! Yip! Hooray! Clicker training feels like a holiday!

Dogs who loved us when we did not always train as if we loved them, who suffered decades of "jerk and release" and force training, have owners who now hear advice that any trainer who hurts your dog is a bad trainer.

Hallelujah! Enlightened dog training finally reflects the gentle spirit that dogs have shown humans through eons of training techniques based on all command and little reward.

Trust Your Conscience

If any trainer ever physically or mentally hurts your dog in the name of teaching a better behavior, gently take back your dog's leash, get your car keys in your hand and run away. No organism, dog, human, fish, orangutan, no organism will learn at an optimal level while suffering pain or fear.

Clicker training is based on principles discovered while training large animals like dolphins and whales, which could not be petted or physically punished, into offering or learning a desired behavior. Trainers found that if they made a unique sound that the animal could hear at the precise moment that the animal performed a desired task, trick or movement, that sound could "mark" the behavior.

As soon as the behavior was marked by the click noise, the trainer gave the animal a food reward. Most often the food reward for sea performance animals was a fish. Suddenly a huge and not easily pettable animal could understand that the click noise meant "yes!" The animal learned that a desired food reward was coming.

When most dog trainers hear "clicker training," they credit the work of unsurpassed animal behavior and learning theorist, Karen Pryor. Pryor's book, "Don't Shoot the Dog," would be one of the books I would take to a desert island if stranded with a pack of untrained dogs. Pryor's work teaching clicker training all over the world makes her dog-kind's angel of mercy from force training and painful methods of harassment masquerading as dog training.

Your Dog Would Love To Be Clicker Trained

To clicker train your dog you will need:

- a hungry dog
- an abundance of yummy, perhaps dog appealing-stinky irresistible treats
- a clicker
- 5 to 10 minutes twice a day to train the dog
- your own desire to train the dog
- patience to learn the clicker method yourself
- belief that you can teach it to the dog
- you must be committed to having fun

The equipment you will need: foremost, you need a clicker. A visit to your favorite dog shop or dog goods web site will yield a clicker, usually for less than $5.

Invest in a quality 6' long, 1/2" wide leather leash. The leash should fold completely and comfortably in your right hand while your left hand holds the delicious treats. Get a treat bag or carpenter's apron to hold lots of soft, quickly edible treats. I use very small slices of nitrite-free chicken hot dogs.

One pack of eight hot dogs will slice into hundreds of dog-yummy rewards. Cook the slices on paper towels in your microwave for two minutes to reduce stickiness of the raw hot dogs. Freeze the hot dog pieces and knock off a chuck of morsels for each training session.

More Treats? Feed Smaller Meals
On the days that you know you are going to work on your dog's clicker education, feed him less dinner or breakfast according to the amount of treats you will be using while clicker training. You do not want to make your dog fat during the clicker training process.

You Click? You Praise and Reward
The one unbreakable rule for training your dog with the clicker:

If you click the clicker, you must reward the dog with a treat for performing the task.

The click sound is a marker that says to the dog, "Right! You did the right thing! Yea!"

EVERYDAY AND HOLIDAYS

After the click sound marks the behavior, the trainer must "pay" for the task by giving the brilliant dog a delicious treat. Never click if you do not have your treat ready to give the dog. Treats given immediately following the click sound teach the dog that pay is coming for work done.

Treats, followed by wildly enthusiastic praise, build dog desire to follow your instruction. You will not have to pay him with a food treat every time he performs the task for the rest of his life. Once the dog masters the command, pay him every once in a while just to reassure him that the treat supply has not gone dry. This is called giving a "random reward," and is the best method of reward after the dog has learned the skill. During the teaching phase, however, he needs *payment for every success*.

No: You Are Not Bribing The Dog. You are not bribing the dog. You are paying the dog for learning and performing a new skill. Be generous. You will produce more good behavior when the dog realizes the pay is coming.

The clicker is not a remote control. Do not point the clicker at the dog and give a command.

Pace Yourself! Don't try to teach your dog every step of the training program at the first session. Attention is the most important step in the training program. Work just long enough that you and the dog have had fun. Stop the moment either of you get tired, or feel confused.

Let's Practice: Step By Step Clicker Training
Ready to begin?

Practice holding leash, clicker and treats before you begin actual clicking with your dog. Fold your supple leather leash completely in your right hand. Place the clicker under the thumb of your right hand. Right thumb on clicker, clicker on top of leash. Practice clicking a few times.

Attach your leash to the dog's flat buckle collar. Thumb and clicker are in position, ready to click. Left hand holds several treats.

Step 1: Teach The "Click" Sound
First, you must teach the dog that the click sound is delightful. He must feel that the click is a magical sound that causes a hot dog to land in his mouth. This process is called "charging the clicker." Like charging a battery. You are investing the click sound with the dog's belief that food is coming.

Step 2: Reward All Progress

To "charge" the clicker, place about 30 small hot dog pieces in a bowl on a table that the dog cannot reach. Leash the dog. Hold the clicker on the leash as directed and "click." As soon as you click, deliver a hot dog reward into the dog's mouth. Look at your brilliant dog with delight on your face: smile and praise. At this point, the dog may or may not look at you when you click. Click. Give reward. Praise warmly. Click. Reward. Praise expectantly. Do this about 30 times. Stop. Sit down and rest. Let the dog wander around the room.

Wait 15 minutes and call the dog. Leash him and get ready to click for real.

Step 3: Click Your Dog For Looking At You

Every time the dog looks at you, "click" and give the treat. Praise him as though no dog in the world every did anything quite so brilliant. Repeat this click, praise, reward process for a few minutes or 20 times, whichever comes first. Stop. Unleash the dog and quit for today. You have just taught the dog to look at you. What a fine "attention" foundation for obedience training.

Step 4: His Name Is Music To His Ears

Now, that your dog is looking at you, hoping for the click, treat and praise, practice this attention exercise and add saying his name in a happy, upbeat voice. The moment he looks at you as you say his name, click, reward, praise for 20 repetitions.

Step 5: "Sit!"

Teach him to sit with the clicker. Dog is on leash, clicker is under your thumb. Walk in a little circle in place. Stop. Look expectantly at the dog. Your dog will probably "sit." The moment the dog's bottom lands on the floor in a sit: "click", give treat, praise wildly.

Repeat waiting for and getting the "sit" as many times as the dog continues to participate with enthusiasm. Stop after 20 repetitions or five minutes of work.

Step 6: "Down!"

Teach "down" exactly as you taught "sit". Follow the steps above, only wait for him to offer the down position.

Step 7: "Go To Your Place"

Another favorite clicker trained command is, "Go to your place," or "place!" Lay a rug, or crate mat near the chair that you sit in while you watch television. Place bowl of treats on the table beside you.

Wait for the dog to walk over to you. When he places a foot on the rug, "click" and treat. Every time he returns and places a foot, bottom, or lies down on the rug, "click" and treat.

When the dog places himself on the rug and looks at you as if he knows he is going to the rug on purpose, it is time to add a command to the action. The moment he puts himself on the rug, "click" and say "place" or any other

EVERYDAY AND HOLIDAYS

command you wish to use for this action: "Spot," "Go rest," etc. Give a treat.

Behaviors you can teach your dog with the clicker are endless. The clicker is a perfect tool for teaching tricks. The video, "The How of Bow Wow" (Broitman and Lippman) is exceptional for explaining how to teach with a clicker to dazzle your friends and delight your dog. Procure this delightful video and follow the fun.

Fine points for more advanced use of the clicker can be found in many excellent clicker training books. Suggested clicker training authors include Karen Pryor, Mandy Book, Cheryl Smith and Gary Wilkes. Internet searches for "clicker training" will yield clicker web sites with training techniques, clicker reading and advice.

Make everyday a clicking holiday! Start clicking.

Credits

All photographs in this book were taken by Sarah A. Ferrell, except for those noted here. Grateful acknowledgement is made to the following photographers:

Ashby Photgraphy (pp. 39, 218)

Dr. Sheri Bakerian and Dr. Ilene Terrell (p. 194)

Mary Susan Billingsley (pp. 43, 63, 68, 75, 104, 131, 142, 155, 237, 296, 298, 300, 360, 364, 382, 390, 419, 450, 455, 474, 514, 527, 536)

Dennis Kennedy Black (p. 81)

Marge Brandel (pp. 51, 327)

Courtesy of Phyllis Broderick (p. 440)

Carol Callahan (p. 559)

Crystal Callovitch (pp. 100, 529, 571)

Neal Campbell (pp. 119, 122, 124, 202, 263, 437, 452, 498)

Amber Carpenter (p. 200)

Ann de Matteo (p. 235)

Dr. Pam Fandrick (p. 368)

Robert Lee Ferrell (p. 556)

Sandra Fischer (p. 282)

Marc Gemis and Tina van Hooydank (pp. 172, 186, 229)

Courtesy of Shelby Lynn Goldsmith (p. 508)

Maureen and Steve Greenwood (pp. 136, 261, 287, 370, 496)

Sheri Harding (p. 429)

Sheri Hayden (pp. 143, 174, 331)

Cindy Heuer (p. 333)

Dr. Terri Horton and Jeff Smith (pp. 45, 575)

Tracey Johnston (p. 105)

DEVOTED TO DOGS

INDEX

INDEX

G

H

INDEX

593

INDEX

INDEX

INDEX

Y

About the Author

Sarah Ferrell is a writer, portrait photographer, pet dog manners teacher, and canine behavior consultant. She writes dog columns: "Devoted To Dogs" for The Free Lance-Star newspaper; "The WebHunter", for the English Springer Spaniel Field Trial Association's, "Springer Spotlight" magazine; and, the English Springer breed column for the "AKC Gazette" magazine. "Devoted To Dogs" has won multiple 'Best Newspaper Column' Maxwell Awards from the Dog Writer's Association of America. Ms. Ferrell was the first recipient of the American Kennel Club's "Responsible Dog Ownership Public Service" writing award. Her dog photography has appeared in many dog magazines and pet education publications.

Sarah is a member of the Dog Writer's Association of America (DWAA), the Association of Pet Dog Trainers (APDT), the National Association of Dog Obedience Instructors (NADOI), and is a

 602

ABOUT THE AUTHOR

Governor on the Board of the English Springer Spaniel Field Trial Association (ESSFTA).

Ferrell has taught obedience classes in the United States and Belgium. She has owned Dog Manners Behavior and Obedience for over 20 years.

When not occupied typing dog stories, with three dogs, Quinnton, Vivien and Gabriel, wedged under her desk, Sarah can be found with her husband, Neal Campbell, and their dogs romping deep in the woods of Spotsylvania, Virginia, or supervising dog swimming in the Neuse River, reading dog books and brushing long-haired dogs on the beach in Arapahoe, North Carolina.

Abroham Neal Publishing
Quick Order Form

Please visit our website at www.abrohamneal.com for on-line orders. Website orders may pay with credit card using PayPal. Please visit website for discounts and internet special offers!

Postal orders, send form to:
Abroham Neal Publishing
Attn: Devoted To Dogs
P. O. Box 1111
Locust Grove, VA 22508

Please send ___ copies of:
"Devoted To Dogs:
How To Be Your Dog's Best Owner"
by Sarah A. Ferrell

___ copies at $19.95 each   = _____

Sales tax:
Please add 4.5% for VA orders = _____

Shipping: $3.95 for first book
and $2.50 for each additional
book. *International orders via*
website only.   **= _____**
                        Total = _____

Payment by check or money order.
Please ship to:
Name _____
Address _____
City _____ State __ Zip ____

Thank you for your order!